DAVID
THE
BELOVED

What people are saying about

"*David The Beloved* is a beautiful, touching and uplifting story to read. Though shaped by David's own personal experiences, it speaks to me and every one of us yearning to rediscover and reclaim our original nature, our beloved selves."

—Mani Feniger, author of *Journey from Anxiety to Freedom* and *The Woman in the Photograph*

"With honesty, transparency, and vulnerability, David shares his journey with cancer, as well as his healing from cancer, in a way that has both informed and inspired my own journey. Thank you, David, for so generously offering your realizations, especially the importance of loving your cancer and learning from it, while fully exploring/embracing the best available allopathic and alternative healing approaches - ultimately trusting your own inner guidance."

—Patricia Meadows, MS, RN, RCST, SEP

"David writes as if he were talking with a dear friend, with the vulnerability and innocence and at times lightness that such conversations happen, about events that are so profound, remarkable, yet occurring in everyday human life."

—Chae McClure

David The Beloved

"A beautiful, engaging rendition, David The Beloved is vulnerable, honest, and insightful. With humor and pathos, David plunges us into his life of challenge and triumph, only to coax us towards the light of spiritual wisdom and the realization of love."
—Kamala Allen, Ph.D. author of *A Woman's Guide to Opening a Man's Heart*

"In Hebrew, the name David is often translated as "beloved." And in his deeply touching, highly personal memoir, *David The Beloved*, author David King leads us through his lifelong quest – across three continents, and through near-fatal cancer – to recapture the unconditional love he hadn't known since early childhood, and ultimately, to reaffirm his true belovedness."
—Rosina Tinari Wilson, author of *Food and Wine Pairing – The Easy Way!*

DAVID THE BELOVED

Journey to Find My Lost Heart

David Alan King

Jenny Lake Publishing
Novato, California

Copyright © 2022 by David Alan King

All rights reserved. No part of this publication may be reproduced, distributed, or transmitted in any form or by any means, including photocopying, recording, or other electronic or mechanical methods, without the prior written permission of the publisher, except in the case of brief quotations embodied in critical reviews and certain other noncommercial uses permitted by copyright law. For permission requests, email the publisher, subject line: "Attention: Permissions Coordinator" at the email address below.

Jenny Lake Publishing
Publisher's Website: JennyLakePublishing.com
Publisher's Email Address: Inquiries@JennyLakePublishing.com

The Publisher is not responsible for websites or their content that are not controlled or owned by the publisher. These websites may change or be unavailable from the time of publishing.

Original cover image of train station provided by New Haven Register, New Haven, CT
Front Cover Design by Caroleen "Jett" Green
Book Production by Ruth Schwartz, thewonderlady.com

Born Free
from the Columbia Pictures' Release BORN FREE
Words by Don Black
Music by John Barry
Copyright (c) 1966 Sony Music Publishing LLC
Copyright Renewed
All Rights Administered by Sony Music Publishing LLC, 424 Church Street, Suite 1200, Nashville, TN 37219
International Copyright Secured All Rights Reserved
Reprinted by Permission of Hal Leonard LLC

GREATEST LOVE OF ALL, THE
Words by LINDA CREED Music by MICHAEL MASSER
© 1977 (Renewed) EMI GOLD HORIZON MUSIC CORP. and EMI GOLDEN TORCH MUSIC CORP.
Exclusive Print Rights Administered by ALFRED MUSIC
All Rights Reserved
Used by Permission of ALFRED PUBLISHING LLC
For Our 100% Administrative Share

Publisher's Cataloging-in-Publication data

Names: King, David Alan, author.
Title: David the beloved : journey to find my lost heart / David Alan King.
Description: Novato, CA: Jenny Lake Publishing, 2022.Identifiers: LCCN: 2021919854 | ISBN: 978-1-7379107-0-1 (black and white) | 978-1-7379107-1-8 (color; hardcover) | 978-1-7379107-2-5 (ebook)

Subjects: LCSH King, David Alan. | Abused children--Biography. | Self-actualization (Psychology) | Self-acceptance. | Self-consciousness (Awareness) | Cancer--Patients--Biography. | Spiritual biography. | BIOGRAPHY & AUTOBIOGRAPHY / Personal Memoirs
Classification: LCC BF575.L8 K56 2022 | DDC 158/.1/092--dc23

Dedication

To all those who ever have thought or felt there was something wrong with them

Contents

Introduction 1

1. A BELOVED IS CREATED 7
   The Begin Lives Train Yard 7
   Born Free 11

2. YOU ARE LOVE AND LOVED 15
   The First Moment of Truth 17
   Mother and Father 18
   Grandmother Yetta 21
   The Truth of My Belovedness 24

3. MARRIED TO MY MIND 31
   Step Into Our Office 31
   Flying Plants 36
   The German Shepherd 37
   The "F" Word 38
   Resilience and Courage 39

4. GRANDMA'S STROKE 41
   A Morning's Panic 41
   Grandma Moves In 46

David The Beloved

    Who Are These People?   47
    I Lost My Family   51

5. **EAST TO WEST**   53
    Watching Grandma   57

6. **ALL WILL BE LOST**   59
    We Were On   59
    This Is Not Going To Be Good   60
    The Kid   65

7. **DAVID – THE MAN**   69
    You're No Longer A Kid, Kid   69
    High School and College: Math, Sports, Poker, and T   73
    Not All Fun and Games   78

8. **HEIGH-HO IT'S OFF TO WORK WE GO**   83
    Avoiding the War   85
    World, Ready or Not, Here I Come   86

9. **MARRIAGE, THEN FATHERHOOD – THE JOYS AND DESPAIRS**   89
    T and D Get Married   89
    Fatherhood – The Birth and My Rebirth   93
    Saying the Word "Divorce"   96
    Wanna Get Off?   101
    The Best Moment of My Life   103

10. **MY FATHER'S GIFT**   107
    My Father's Passing   112

Contents

11. **BUD'S THING** *115*
    Settling into Being a Divorcé *116*
    Saying Goodbye to My Beloved Jason *120*
    Head West, Young Man *122*
    The Adventure Continues *126*

12. **ENJOY YOUR TRIP TO INDIA** *131*
    Santa Fe *132*
    To India I Go *134*
    Hong Kong Basketball *136*
    Am I Really in India? *137*

13. **POONA** *141*
    Amitabh *148*
    Sex, Sex, and More Sex *151*
    Returning to Santa Fe *152*

14. **V** *155*
    There's a Naked Woman in the Hot Tub *155*
    I Am Hooked *157*
    Stormy Night and a Knock at the Door *159*
    Thank God for a Big Table *160*
    Wide Open Heart *161*
    Merry Christmas – A Magic Cookie Night *163*
    Sex Is Not Love *166*

15. **DETOUR INTO MADNESS** *169*
    Madness Destination – Las Vegas *172*
    Leaving India – Without V or … *175*

16. **THE MASTER'S COMMUNES** *179*
    Why Am I Driving to San Francisco to Meditate? *179*
    Buddha Bodhi *183*
    The Subtle Takeover *186*
    Oregon Commune – Buy One, Get One Free *189*
    Back to the Future *194*
    Meeting the Master on the Road *196*
    End of the Ranch *198*

17. **FROM THE FIRE A STAR IS BORN** *201*
    The Fire *201*
    A Star Is Born *211*
    "Greatest Love of All" *219*

18. **FROM RUSSIA WITH LOVE** *221*
    The Connection *221*
    The First Letter from Tatiana *224*
    Trip to Visit the Angel *226*
    Meeting Misha and Mamachka *229*
    The Engagement *231*
    Holiday in London – Glimpse of What Would Come *235*
    Tatiana and Misha to America *239*
    The Divorce – Again *241*

19. **C** *245*
    Finding Out *245*

20. **JOURNEY WITH CANCER** *251*
    Cancer – Treatments Begin *252*
    The Defining Moment with Cancer *256*

Contents

    Finding My Way to Stay Alive   *257*
    Einstein's Quantum Physics and Love   *265*
    Loving My Cancer   *267*
    My Mantra   *269*
    The Gift of Cancer – What it Came to Teach Me   *271*

21. MY MOTHER'S PASSING –
      FOUR FLEETING DAYS   *273*
    I Arrive at My Mother's Bedside   *273*
    Second Day   *277*
    Third Day   *278*
    The Last Day   *279*
    Saying Goodbye with All My Love   *281*

22. YOUR HEART IS HERE
      WAITING FOR YOU   *285*
    The Big Reveal   *290*

23. こんにちは – KON'NICHIWA   *293*
    Seeking A Japanese Wife   *293*
    Meeting J – Wow!!!   *297*
    Married Again – Really?   *298*
    Day-to-Day Life   *300*
    Divorce Again? Yes, Really!   *302*
    Did I Learn This Time?   *302*

24. DAVID THE BELOVED   *305*

AFTERWORD   *313*
    Healing My Cancer   *313*

David The Beloved

"Diamond Approach to Self-Realization" *321*
Inquiry *322*

ACKNOWLEDGEMENTS *325*

DEAR READER *329*

Introduction

Thirty-five years ago, I had not given one thought, not even a rumor of a thought, to writing a book - let alone a book about Love and Belovedness - until an unforgettable evening with a psychic at a friend's house. I was reluctant to attend the event, as I had a cast on my leg from knee surgery; but he insisted, and he drove me to his house and plopped me down on the couch. The psychic was a tall, very heavy-set young man with a neatly trimmed beard. Looking at him, I could not believe he possessed any "psychic" abilities. When he sat down on a cushion on the floor, his big belly reminded me of statues of the Buddha. That was as far as the connection went. The others at the event that evening asked him questions about their future - where they would live, their relationships, finances, health, and so on, and he answered them. I thought, there's no way for anyone to know whether there's any truth to those answers.

When everyone was done with their readings, in a "just for the hell of it" moment, I decided to ask him about my idea of teaching computer programming at schools in underserved neighborhoods, as a way of giving back. He looked at me, closed his eyes briefly, then opened his eyes and said "No." I thought,

David The Beloved

What do you mean, No? I just told you what I wanted to do with my life, and in less than two minutes you're telling me I'm wrong? He continued by saying, "You are going to write a book, and then you will go around and share what you have written with others." I had struggled with English in high school and college. How on earth was I going to write a book? Now I *really* had my doubts about this guy. And then he got me! He really got me when he closed his eyes again and said: "The subject of the book will be Love." I was stunned, bewildered, mind blown. In one jaw-dropping moment, he had brought the entire apparatus that I knew as "David" to a halt.

I allowed this man's words to sink into my heart and soul on the drive home with my friend. And as I was falling asleep that night, the title of the book came to me: *David The Beloved*. The title just came to me without my looking for it. That was thirty-five years ago. It was only from the title of the book that I remembered that my name "David," in Hebrew, has meanings that include "beloved one" and "the beloved." I did not make the connection of this meaning of my name with who I thought myself to be, nor did I associate myself with the word "love" – in fact, I didn't even realize at the time that I did not know what that word meant. It was not until my experience with cancer that I realized that cancer came to teach me the most important lesson of my life, and it would bring understanding of all that I lost during my childhood, namely my innocence, my feelings, my connection to my heart, my belovedness – and the knowing of love.

This is a story about a precious young child who was dearly loved by many people early in his life. Yet unexpected and tragic events led

Introduction

this child to experiences inconsistent with his preciousness. From these experiences, he took on heartbreaking beliefs about himself, and he kept these beliefs hidden – and treated them like gospel – losing his true, loving nature. How could this have happened? To truly understand the events of my journey that I share in this memoir, I had to reflect on my life and ask myself some profound questions. And I had to be willing to see the truth.

How could I explain that I was touched by loving beings, without fully realizing it, for years? It was as if a light had illuminated a path in front of me, coaxing me to go that way, even though my experiences in life said, "Don't go." How could I explain why I took so many risks without realizing what I was doing, as if I had no choice in the matter? And even though my mind said there was something wrong with me, that I somehow deserved the childhood abuse and cancer I suffered through, I brought loving human beings into my life. How was that possible? They touched me without my realizing it – and they reminded me who I truly am just by the nature of who they were. And where did I find the will, strength, and perseverance to keep the journey alive to find the truth of who I really am?

While writing my memoir, I came up with a train station metaphor for my journey.

There's a true story behind this. When I was around six years old my Uncle Bernie, to the dismay of my Aunt Roz, kept a big piece of plywood under their bed. On the plywood my uncle had nailed a set of tracks for an American Flyer train set. There were only two train cars – a black locomotive and a red caboose. The power box that ran the train had a dial with a knob that you turned to make the train go faster or slower. I can still remember the creaky sound as I moved the dial. I was captivated not just by the train going around the tracks, but also by the fact that I could control it. The circular tracks gave me the metaphor for my life story, as I will present it to you here.

The tracks of my life started at my birth and will end at my death. Each step of the journey creates the next step that leads me toward future life adventures. My story starts at the station where conception of a precious, innocent, openhearted new human being occurs, followed by many stations where the child's innocence and openheartedness will get lost - yet not totally lost. And there are many more stations, some magical, as the tracks of my life wind around to head back toward the station at the end of the line. Each significant event along the tracks - birth, marriage, divorce, fatherhood, to name a few - will be the stations on these tracks. What I am to encounter at each of these stations will be a mystery, influenced by the many people I meet, and by events impossible to predict.

Cartoonist Sudi Narayanan (Swami Anand Teertha) has created a series of charming cartoons of train stations, used as chapter titles. Several more of his cartoons, scattered throughout the text, are meant for comic relief - as the nature of the subject they are depicting could otherwise be seen in a negative light. For instance, the way that our minds develop in early childhood, which affects the way we live our lives, is in no way negative or bad. It is a natural part of our human imprinting that comes with being birthed into this world.

I invite you on board for a train ride through my life, as I share certain events and experiences that I would not have imagined possible in a million years until I arrived at the train stops along the tracks. This is the Bronx version of the Orient Express - a train ride

Introduction

that is both a love story and a mystery – never knowing what the next station would have in store for me and my heart. Yet with courage and moments of fearlessness, like the Energizer Bunny, I just kept on going – as my quest to reclaim all that was lost unfolded before my eyes.

Let the journey begin . . . .

The Begin Lives Train Yard

I find myself, though only a rumor, on the platform in the Begin Lives Train Yard. This train station is like most any other one, except that the train yard at this station is filled with souls who are only rumors to themselves. The Train Yard Master announces, "The next train out of the yard is for David King." These words have no meaning for me. The Train Master looks over at me and says, "That's you, kiddo. See those people on the train? They've already named you and have created you at this very moment. So, hop on board."

David The Beloved

I would say to him (if a rumor could think and speak): "I don't know these people. What if I don't like them?"

"Sorry, kiddo – you don't have a choice. This is your train. Look, you will have a nine-month ride to the first station called Birth. Not to worry." As if a rumor could worry. "It will be an easy ride until you get to the Birth station, and then it is going to be touch and go. Then you will have a choice whether to get off the train or stick it out. Good luck, kiddo. I'm rooting for you!"

The moment I got onto my parents' train I was no longer a rumor. For better or for worse, I was now David King. The Train Yard Master was right about a few things. The first station would be called "Birth," and it would indeed be touch and go; there would be moments when I could either choose to get off the train or fight to stay on board.

My mother wrote about my traumatic birth in an unpublished manuscript that I rediscovered while writing this memoir. These are my mother's words:

> . . . I labored from Monday night July 9 to Thursday morning, July 12. In the meantime, they gave me injections to force labor, instead of performing a caesarean. The doctor let me suffer. . . . At 7:00 a.m. that morning, I was taken into the delivery room. The baby had the cord around his neck three times. It was a dry birth and a high forceps case. It was a miracle, I was told, that I and my son lived.

Delivery with the use of forceps was basically like putting salad spoons around my head and pulling me out, while the umbilical cord tightened around my neck. While trapped inside my mother's womb and then being forcibly delivered, I must have felt everything she was feeling, as we both were fighting for our lives.

A Beloved Is Created

I invite you to look at this picture of a fetus with the umbilical cord wrapped around its neck. Notice how one hand is reaching for the cord, apparently trying to free itself from being strangled. I imagine that this was my own experience inside the womb, from the time my mother's water broke until I came out into the light. How terrified I must have felt. If I had adrenaline in my body, I was using all of it, as my heart must have been pumping as hard as it could to survive. To say that this experience was beyond anything that had happened in the previous nine months would be an understatement. It was *way* beyond "touch and go," as I was fighting for my life. I was probably trying to free myself from being strangled, as in the picture – but I wouldn't have given up, because I'm so willful.

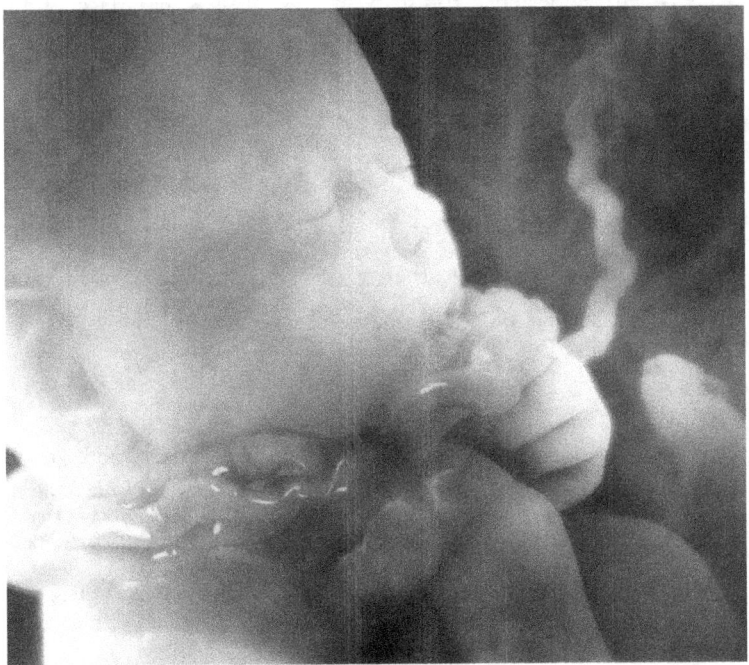

Credit: Medi-Mation Science Photo Library

David The Beloved

It was a miracle that we had both survived, and a testament to certain qualities with which I was born – a strong will, strength, and perseverance – qualities I have in common with my mother. She was a survivor.

As I came out into the light, they would have cut the cord, my lifeline up until this point; smacked me on my soft bottom (they still used that insane practice in 1945), and handed me from person to person, finally handing me to my mother – who was, not surprisingly, in shock. During this two-and-a-half-day ordeal, in the moments when death was imminent, I wonder whether my life force ever abandoned my body. Was the pain or terror of this experience too much for my infant nervous system? Maybe I had a near-death experience to escape it. Seventy-six years later, I am still exploring the answers to these questions with a trauma therapist. Why didn't the family doctor perform a caesarean section? In the 1940s this procedure had already become common in the U.S. Maybe the doctor didn't know how to do it or was afraid to.

I have no idea whether an infant can make conclusions during those moments. I have read that birth trauma can be imprinted on an infant. If that is indeed so, here are a couple of beliefs I have a feeling I would have created:

> The world is a dangerous place. You must always be hypervigilant.
> Death is just around the corner.
> Don't relax. If you relax, something bad will happen to you.
> Change is dangerous and you could die. Become a creature of habit.

A Beloved Is Created

I believe there were lasting effects on my development from my traumatic birth experience. I am convinced, and I have read validations, that my intolerance and anxiousness were due to the birth trauma I experienced. When I asked her about it, my trauma therapist confirmed this belief: "David, from what your mother describes in her journal, your birth was traumatic for both of you. There were multiple layers of trauma for you - the length of the labor from Monday evening to Thursday morning; the medication used to induce labor, which often increases the force of the contractions; having the cord wrapped around your neck three times, as well as the high-forceps birth. This was a very difficult labor and birth, and one that would have made a deep and lasting impression or imprint on your body and your soul." (Patricia Meadows, MS, RN, SEP, Trauma Therapist). *As my life unfolded, this would unquestionably prove to be true.*

Born Free

There was a wonderful, endearing movie released in 1966 called *Born Free*, with its wonderful, heartfelt theme song, also called "Born Free." I was touched each time I listened to it. Its lyrics call out my birthright and my journey. This song accurately describes the state in which I was born, with the words: *"Born free, as free as the wind blows, As free as the grass grows, Born free to follow your heart."* Just as these lyrics describe how the wind and the grass blow and grow naturally and instinctively, at birth, I lived naturally and instinctually and moved where the moment took me. I am now envisioning my son as an infant, when I would put him down on a blanket in

David The Beloved

the park and watch him freely move where his senses and his heart chose. *"Live free and beauty surrounds you, The world still astounds you, Each time you look at a star."* I picture my son as a toddler, freely exploring wherever his curiosity took him. I remember the wonderment on his face when he experienced snow for the first time, falling from the sky and landing on his face, and the way he tried to catch it on his tongue so he could taste it. This was my true nature, my birth gifts, until my mind developed and took control in the months and years to come. Here are the lyrics:

Born free
As free as the wind blows
As free as the grass grows
Born free to follow your heart

Live free
And beauty surrounds you
The world still astounds you
Each time you look at a star

Stay free
Where no walls divide you
You're free as a roaring tide so there's no need to hide

Born free
And life is worth living
But only worth living
'Cause you're born free

A Beloved Is Created

Stay free
Where no walls divide you
You're free as a roaring tide so there's no need to hide

Born free
And life is worth living
But only worth living
'Cause you're born free

The train ride from the birth station to the next station was short. To see the station out of the train car window, I had to stand up on the seat, and the sight filled me with wide-eyed curiosity and open-hearted joy. There at the station, many smiling people were blowing kisses and waving. Quite a welcome! If I could have read words, I would see that the sign said: "You Are Love and Loved."

I have many fond memories of being loved by my mother's mother, my grandmother Yetta, who loved me unconditionally. And I remember how loved, and even adored, I was by many of my aunts and uncles. Looking at pictures from those first years, I can see that my mother and father were loving toward me as well. Although I have no conscious memories of my mother's love, I can intuit this love from early photos. With my father, I have a mixed bag of memories. One moment, I'd be playing with my toys beside my blue wooden toy box near the front door, and my father would walk into our apartment and growl at me because my toys were spread all over the floor in his path. The next moment, he would be "playing horsie" with me on his knee, bouncing me up and down, or he'd sit me on his lap to watch our five-inch-screen television. I feel sad today as I recall these moments. I had no idea as a little child what my future tracks and stations would look like, or what I would encounter when I turned seven years old.

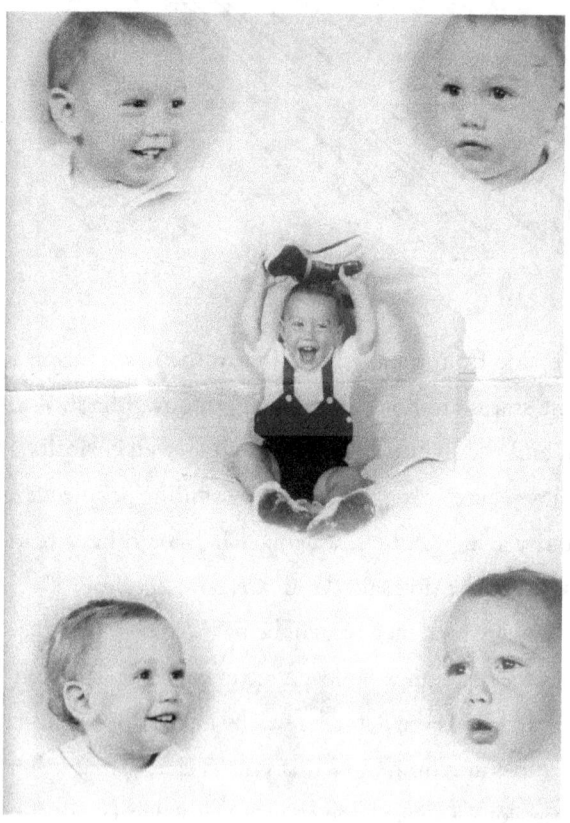

You Are Love and Loved

The First Moment of Truth

From the moment of my birth, the truth is that I was *a beloved* - "love-able," and deserving of love. This picture of me at about one year old tells the story. I see a beautiful child with changing expressions as he experiences the world of having his picture taken. He is a new human being, starting out life with an inherent trust that he will be loved and cared for, have his needs met, and be held lovingly in every possible way. I had everything I would need to evolve into a "wonderous" human being. What gave me this trust, I'd like to think, were the nine months in my mother's womb, cradled close to her heart, feeling secure and nourished with the love she had to give. Being a beloved is made evident whenever I see a mother tenderly breastfeeding her newborn or holding her infant in a caring way, such that the mother and baby appear connected as *one* body - nourished and supported by their love for each other. Later, I would experience this love affair while holding my own son, as I cradled him in my arms in the rocking chair feeding him his evening bottle. And I had the same experience when holding my grandchildren when they were infants.

What I *don't* see in these photos of me is a child who feels there is something wrong with him. I am not talking about what I can see with my eyes, but what I know in my heart and soul about the essence of who I am. I don't see the child who, starting at age seven, would be physically and emotionally abused and yelled at by his parents. His father would hold his neck while whacking his behind - or worse, one day in a rage, he beat his son and threatened to kill him. Certainly, this innocent child did not deserve this abusive experience. Nor looking at this innocent child would I ever envision him having cancer much later in life. Or that he would spend most of his life believing he *deserved* all this – that there was something wrong with him, and that he was unlovable and undeserving of love. I no longer believe that I deserved these unfortunate acts and events, or that I am unworthy of love. I no longer believe that I deserved *anything* of this nature – yet that is exactly what would be in store for me.

Mother and Father

My mother was born in 1916 in Manhattan, the borough of New York City south of the Bronx. My father was born in Poland in 1907 and emigrated with his parents to Manhattan as a young child. Both my parents were brought up in an orthodox Jewish culture, but once they were married, they decided to follow a conservative Jewish practice. My parents had met in a Jewish social club on the Lower East Side of Manhattan near Houston Street. They had grown up during the Great Depression in the U.S., from 1929-1939.

When my father and his family arrived at Ellis Island, the federally owned island between Manhattan and New Jersey, for immigration processing, the family last name was Siroka. The immigration officer kept asking my father for his last name, and my father kept saying his Jewish *first* name, "Shlomo." The immigration officer could not understand him; frustrated, he gave him the *last* name "Solomon." Years later, when my father decided to go

You Are Love and Loved

into show business, he changed the name Solomon to "King." That's how I became a King.

I don't know much about my father and his family, other than a story about his brother that I will share later. I know that my mother disliked my father's mother and sister. I remember visiting his father with my parents at a home for the aged, though I never understood why he was put into an old-age home. My grandfather was a very sweet, shy, warm-hearted man. I have a feeling that is where my father's heart came from, even though he hid it from me from the time I was seven years old.

My mother told me stories about her childhood, how poor the family was, and how difficult life was for the eight children. One of her sisters, the oldest child, died in childhood in the Ukraine, and another sister disowned the family when I was about five years old. My mother's parents had a small tailor shop to support their family. Unfortunately, sometimes my grandfather would gamble away the money they needed to buy food. When he did, my grandmother would cry, as there was no food to feed the children. My mother often told me that she'd had to work at a five and dime store at an early age, and when she got older, as a bookkeeper, to help support the family. Some of her brothers and sisters who were old enough also found jobs, as best they could, to support the family. Their life during the Depression was a life of poverty. Many nights, she said, they would have no more to eat than some watered-down chicken soup. The Depression had a lasting effect on her, as she was always in "survival mode" around money, even though she had more than enough to live on.

My father was a very good singer. As a young man, he had yearned to sing in a Broadway show. In fact, it was a dream he had for his whole adult life. When he was in his nineties, he confided in me about the time he finally landed a role in the chorus of a Broadway show that would pay him fifty dollars a week; in those times, that was a king's ransom. He and my mother were courting at the time. My mother said to him that if he took that job, she would have nothing more to do with him, as she had heard about drugs and sex behind the scenes at the Broadway theatre houses. He reluctantly turned down the job, and eventually found work as a legal typesetter and proofreader. In 1944 they became engaged, then married, with yours truly making himself known fifteen months later in 1945.

What he confided in me next surprised me for a moment, though I wasn't shocked. He said he was sorry he hadn't taken the job in the Broadway show. I totally understood, as this was his dream. Singing was the one thing that brought him joy, and a part of his life over which my mother had no control. I would not have been even a rumor in the Begin Lives Train Yard had my father taken that Broadway job. Seeing and feeling his brokenheartedness, I told him I was sorry he hadn't. I understood how my mother did indeed control everything. For example, my father would bring home his pay (in cash), and she would only give him enough money for the subway and for lunch at the Horn and Hardart automat on workdays. She would pay all the bills and control whatever else the money was spent on. In later years, when his hearing started to go, she would yell at my father the same way she used to yell at me when I was a kid. He did not have a happy or joyful life, except for the times when he was singing. And my mother did not have a joyful or happy life, except when there were celebrations related to the family. This was the home environment I grew up in during my childhood years. My gratitude for my grandmother Yetta is beyond words.

Grandmother Yetta

Grandmother Yetta, taken at the home of my Uncle Max and Aunt Fay in Brooklyn, New York.

I was the first grandchild for my mother's parents. Though I never had much to do with my mother's father or my father's family, I was everything to my grandmother Yetta, and she was everything to me. I have seen pictures of her holding me as a baby, with such joy on her face. My grandmother's apartment was six blocks from our apartment, half a block from there to the family doctor, a long block then to my uncle's store, and another block to the apartment house where two of my aunts and uncles and five cousins lived. Whenever I went

David The Beloved

to visit my grandmother and walked through the door, she would be standing near the kitchen. I would run over to her and wrap my arms around her waist, and she would bend over and kiss the top of my head. My grandmother was a short, stout woman, so when I hugged her I couldn't get my arms anywhere near all around her, but it didn't matter – I was home, I was safe. I was happy to be around her, so full of joy knowing how much I was loved. In the twenty-two years that she was in my life, my grandmother, never once said "no" to me. Always "Yes!"

Until I was about seven, I would occasionally sleep overnight at her place. One time in the middle of the night I wanted some of my grandmother's crispy French fries. I woke her up and said, "Grandma, I want French fries." She got out of bed at three in the morning and made me French fries. If that is not love, what is? She used to play the card game "Casino" with me for pennies. And whenever she went to the kitchen, I would stack the deck so I could win a lot of pennies. I have no idea where I, as a small child, could have learned how to stack a deck of cards. My grandmother must have known I did it, but she never said anything. She just enjoyed playing cards and being with me, and I felt the same way about her. Tears of joy come to me as I recall the love we shared. I could always go to her, knowing that my wide-open heart would be met with her wide-open heart with no barriers between our love for each other. And there was nothing I could do or say that would change that – even stacking the deck! This is my definition of unconditional love. No barrier to our hearts meeting, and no requirement to be anything but our authentic selves. This is how we were each other's beloved. My grandmother taught

You Are Love and Loved

me unconditional love, and I feel I have passed that on to my son Jason. And it's a joy to watch how he shows his love for my beautiful grandchildren, Jacqueline and Joshua.

My grandmother, the love of my life, died a year after I graduated from college. After I moved out of the house to work for IBM in Maryland, she told my mother that she had nothing more to live for. Those words still affect me, and bring up such deep sadness, knowing how heartbroken she must have felt when I left home to go out into the world. It did not occur to me at the time what an impact my move would have on her. If I had known, I would have visited her more often after moving to Maryland. And even more heartbreaking, my mother didn't tell me that my grandmother was dying of leukemia and was wasting away. I only received the news after she had died. My mother said that my grandmother didn't want me to see her in that condition; she wanted me to remember her as she was. When my mother told me this, I yelled at her, holding back tears, "I didn't get to say goodbye." I repeated this line a few times and then removed myself from her presence. Even now, I feel such a deep, sharp hurt for not being able to say that goodbye - to tell my grandmother how much she meant to me and how much I loved her.

Since her passing, I have always had the feeling that my grandmother's spirit is near me, watching out for me. Later I felt a confirmation of this when I tried the alternative healing practice called Reiki, an ancient healing art, to support healing my cancer. Reiki healers put their hands on you and channel energy to your body, and your body figures out where it is needed. It was a bit out of my comfort zone, but as I will explain later, cancer expanded the zone so wide you could drive a truck through it. I went to see two different Reiki healers, and in both cases, without knowing anything about me or my special connection to my grandmother, when they put their hands on my back, they said that she was in the room. And both times, I lost it. Through one of the healers my grandmother said to me, "Do not fear death; there is an afterlife, and I will be waiting for you." She knew I was terrified of dying. There was no way to know whether these healers were indeed connecting to my grandmother's spirit. It was already clear to me that her spirit would be close beside me. But the words they shared from her gave me comfort.

The Truth of My Belovedness

Traveling the tracks from the Begin Lives Train Yard to about age seven, when my developed mind had taken root, there were many moments when this human being called David expressed himself with his birth package of qualities such as kindness, caring, empathy, compassion, innocence, and especially love. I didn't take note of it because my awareness of myself had not yet developed. Even in adulthood there have been and still are such moments. But now they do not go unrecognized. I take note of these moments!

    I want to share a few instances from my childhood that remind me how connected I was to my belovedness as a young child. The first one involves my grandmother Yetta. I described to you how unconditionally loving she was to me. In a later chapter, I will explain how circumstances dictated that she would live with me and my parents for part of the time. While living with us, because she had diabetes, my mother cooked our food bland, with no seasoning whatsoever. Then at the dinner table, my parents would add the seasonings *du*

You Are Love and Loved

jour to their food. To me, it looked as if my grandmother was eating alone. I am sure now that I was projecting my own feelings onto my grandmother, yet to this day, my reaction surprises me. I would lift up my plate filled with my dinner so that my grandmother could see it, and say to her, "Look, Grandma, you are not eating alone, I'm eating the same as you. I didn't put anything on it." My true nature, in this moment, found a way to shine brightly, lovingly, and caringly, by protecting my grandmother from feeling separate and alone.

There was a boy in my neighborhood, a little older than me, who was mentally challenged. The other kids wanted to exclude him from playing with us, and they made fun of him. Without knowing how my heart went out to him, I chose him to be on my team and told anyone who made fun of him to "shut up." Remember, I was only seven years old.

One day his mother called out from their second-story window asking me to come up to their apartment. When I walked in, she offered me a cookie. Normally I would have immediately put the cookie in my mouth, but as my hand was heading for my open mouth, I froze; she was crying, and I had never seen an adult cry before. Through her tears she thanked me for including Robert in the games and being protective of him. At the time I had no idea what she was talking about – but writing this now, I feel touched. When I left the apartment, I finally ate the cookie.

My last story from childhood took place in 1950, when I was five years old. I was walking home from my first day of kindergarten, hand in hand with my mother, feeling a bit lost after a whole day of firsts. That morning I had walked to school with the neighbor's daughters, crossed big streets without my mother, met a teacher

David The Beloved

who acted as if she was my mother, and played with other kids I did not know – and who wanted whatever I was playing with. I had been thrown into the "Kindergarten Twilight Zone." At the end of the day, there was the familiarity of my mother's hand as we walked home. On the way, we saw a blind man on the sidewalk standing next to an iron fence selling pencils, three for a nickel. As we walked past him, I turned my head and body, feeling so drawn to him I couldn't look away. My mother tugged on me to keep walking, but finally stopped when she put two and two together, and without any words being said between us, she gave me a nickel to give to him. In those days, you could get a half a loaf of rye bread for a dime, so a nickel was not "nothing." I walked up to him and without saying anything, I dropped the nickel into his cup, and he put the pencils out for me to take. I am deeply touched as I write these words, the tears flowing. I took the pencils from him and started to walk back to my mother. But just before I took her hand again, I turned around, looked at the blind man, and ran back to him. With a tear running down my cheek, I gave him back the pencils and told to him to "sell them again." And as I ran back to my mother I continued to cry, sad for him that he was blind, and feeling compassion for him. True compassion from a child's innocence and open heart. Was I not still a beloved being? My tears tell me yes, absolutely!

There are three stories from my adulthood, as well, that give credence to my belovedness.

I was in my early thirties. At that time, I was in a therapy group called Transactional Analysis (TA). One day, one of the women in the group announced that she would be leaving. She seemed like a very scared person to me. (Here I am, Mr. Big Shot, saying that *she*

You Are Love and Loved

seemed to be a scared person, when *I* don't have a clue to my *own* feelings!) On the last night she was with the group, the therapist had everyone close their eyes and point to the center of their thought. After everyone was ready, she said to open our eyes, and everyone was pointing to the center of their forehead. Then she asked everyone to point to the center of their feelings. And again, when everyone was ready, she said to open our eyes. Everyone but me was pointing to their belly. I was pointing to my forehead. Looking back, I think the therapist may have done that exercise for my benefit. It was only a seed; I didn't have an *Aha* moment. Yet the seed may have supported what I was about to say to this woman. The woman who was leaving town had a great fear of the windows in her house not opening. The few times in our group when she talked about it, she seemed to have a panic attack. At the end of our group session that night, everyone wished her well in whatever she was doing and wherever she was going. And when it was my turn, I didn't know where it came from, but I said to her, "May all the windows in your life open easily." She fell apart, sobbing uncontrollably. I am touched as I write this.

After my first marriage ended, which will happen at a later station, I started dating a woman who lived nearby. She was from a small Cajun town in Louisiana. We met one night at a local bar and dance place. She and her friend just sat down at my table without asking if it was all right with me, and she introduced herself by saying, "That woman you were dancing with is not for you." Her name was Cindy. When we first started dating, I noticed a lump on the back of her neck and said to her that it didn't look good. I was only in my late twenties, but I had a strong gut feeling that this was serious. I made her go to see my doctor, who did a biopsy.

David The Beloved

When we came back for the results, he looked pale and said the tissue was cancerous. He set up an appointment for her at MD Anderson Cancer Center in Houston, about forty minutes away, for a consultation. Driving there in complete silence, I could barely keep my attention on my driving as my head was swirling with fears of the unknown.

Arriving at the hospital, we were taken into a consultation room where four doctors were discussing her case and her test results. The lead doctor turned to us and began hemming and hawing. I stopped him and asked point blank, "Are you saying she is going to die?" He said, yes, that she had lymphoma. I looked at Cindy, who was now in total shock. I was more concerned about her state than what was going on inside of me. Before we left the room, one of the other doctors said for us to sit in the waiting room for a few minutes, because he wanted to check one more thing. A while later, he came to us and said it was not lymphoma after all: yes, it was cancer, but the disease was treatable. It is hard to imagine two people hearing the news that one of them has cancer and feeling relieved. Yet we were indeed relieved to hear that word still hanging in the air in front of us: *"treatable."* We left the hospital with hope for Cindy's recovery.

This was back in the 1970s. Each weekday morning for some weeks, before going to work, I would drive Cindy to MD Anderson for her radiation and chemotherapy sessions. She was very irritable during this time and I gave her a lot of space. She survived. I remember feeling very close to her, without being conscious of it at the time. I wanted to be with her as a couple. After her recovery I bought a two-bedroom townhouse for us to live in together . . . yet that was not to be. She showed up one day at the front door of the new place to say she could not come and live with me because she was not in love with me. She said she was very grateful to me for all that I had done to save her life. I listened to what she said, but many minutes passed before the loss of my dream to be with her would soak in. When she left, I ran upstairs to the bathroom, fell to the floor, and wept.

Last story. I find myself on the train heading to San Francisco from Berkeley to attend my weekly singing class. I was about fifty-five years old at the time. On the train sitting opposite me was a mentally challenged girl, about fourteen, talking out loud to her grandmother (who was not physically present). As she talked, she motioned with her hands to accentuate what she was saying. I could see and hear her feelings by how her body moved and how the inflection in her voice changed. I am caught up by the fact she had no self-consciousness or judgments in what she was doing. I thought to myself, *Who between the two of us is really the challenged person?* My compassion and empathy went out to her. When I got to class and shared this story in my prep for singing, I fell apart. I was so touched by my heart's caring about her that I wept. There was yet another gift that came from this experience. As the train was moving along, two teenage boys, about fifteen or sixteen, came from another car and passed between the girl and me. They looked at her as she was talking out loud, gesturing with her hands; they paused very briefly, and then moved on, snickering. I knew in the moment they were standing there that I would not let them hurt her in any way. I would protect her even though I did not know her. The caring and protective instincts that I felt for this girl and

David The Beloved

for others I see as innocents, angels of the world, is something I have felt throughout my life.

Each one of the people in these experiences gave me such a tremendous gift by just being themselves. What beautiful human beings. As I write this, I can see that from an early age, I have been a beloved, loving, and compassionate person. I just didn't know it. In all these moments in my life, the true nature of who I am came out, and yet I did not take notice. Certainly not enough to say: *Wait a minute! This is who I really am!* Not the intolerant, judgmental, tantrum-throwing person who thought he was unlovable, who imagined there was something very wrong with him. These experiences may have planted a seed, and they touch me deeply as I write this. They were validations that I have always been – and always will be – "David the Beloved."

There was a natural lovingness, compassion, empathy, and much more that shone out in those unique moments of my life. Yes, it is true that my grandmother taught me about unconditional love. It would be too much to conclude that these qualities – love, compassion, empathy, joy, and more – are learned. They must have been with me as my true nature when I was born. I ask myself what realization do I see from these stories? The answer that comes to me: *I was a beloved child the moment I was born, with "wonderous" and beautiful natural qualities as my birthright, and as such, worthy of being loved thereafter for every moment of my life.*

Sadly, this was not to be my fate, as you will see shortly.

Step Into Our Office

While I was working on this chapter, I watched the movie *The King's Speech*, the story of King George VI of Great Britain and his struggle with stammering. The movie depicts the relationship between King George and his speech therapist, Mr. Lionel Logue, who worked with him in an unconventional manner to cure his stammering. I was touched by the King's struggle to overcome his stammering and admired his resiliency and courage to keep going for over thirty years. Mr. Logue's techniques helped him to establish a relationship with the King, even becoming his "friend," which enabled him to get to the root of the issue. Early on, he pointed out to the King that babies are not born with a defect that causes stammering. In future sessions, Logue discovered that one of the roots of his stammering was caused by his father, King George V, who had forced his son to write with his right hand as a young child, rather than allowing him to use his left hand, his natural writing hand. I had empathy for this suffering that had started in the King's childhood. Just as the King was not born with the defect of stammering but learned this behavior, I was not born with anything wrong with me. I was not born with the dysfunctional behaviors that would show up in later years: intolerance, yelling at people, being hurtful to others. This was behavior learned in childhood from my experiences. I was not born feeling terrified of being late, having a fear of big dogs, believing that if I felt my feelings I would die. These and other patterns resulted from my marriage to my mind.

"Married to My Mind" by Cartoonist Sudi Narayanan
(Swami Anand Teertha)

Married to My Mind

My transition from living with an infant's innocence, openheartedness, curiosity, and the many gifts that come with life, to being angry, intolerant, fearful, and distrustful (my unique equivalent of King George's stammering) was a gradual process. In the view of psychologists, this transition starts in early childhood, between one and two years old and is completed within several years. From my inquiry into my own childhood experience, I feel the transition didn't complete itself until I was seven or eight years old.

I have an image of myself at age two, sitting on the floor of a wedding ceremony. Next to me is a caricature of my undeveloped mind. My parents are standing behind my undeveloped mind, and my grandmother is standing behind me. The significance of this arrangement will be explained shortly.

The presiding official at the wedding says to me, "Do you, David, take your undeveloped mind until death do you part?"

My imprinting leaves me no choice but to say, "Yes, I do."

"And do you, David's undeveloped mind, take David until death do you part?"

My undeveloped mind says, "Yes, but we are going to avoid death at all costs?" And my mind does that by taking control and making sure I get nowhere near the "death do us part" part.

In the 2020 reality TV series called *Married at First Sight*, couples do not meet their spouses until they are at the altar for the wedding ceremony. Well, this is how it started for me with my family. I didn't get to choose my mind, my parents, or my grandmother Yetta - they were all provided at the altar. My grandmother Yetta stood behind me, since she would give no support to the development of my mind, only to my heart and my innocence.

David The Beloved

My parents, however, said to my undeveloped mind: "Step into our office and we will give you everything you need to know, based upon our developed minds: how David can avoid hurt, pain, and death. And it doesn't matter if any of this goes against who he really is or what he wants or feels. We know what's best for him."

"Step Into Our Office" by Cartoonist Sudi Narayanan
(Swami Anand Teertha)

Remember, I didn't get to choose which mind or parents I got. The programming inside my developed mind was also not of my choosing. For the rest of my life, my developed mind's programming would run the show, using the beliefs, judgments, and strategies it created as a child, and it would hold that programming as sacred as the Bible. My child's programming was driving my adult car, though it couldn't see over the steering wheel even sitting on a pillow. It was important for me to understand that my partner, my developed mind, was necessary and imprinted on me for good reason – to protect me when I was young. As an adult, there were times when I would have liked to say to my partner, "Thanks very much, I'll take it from here." But not until I had cancer would I realize that my partner was still driving the car. My partner was not bad; it was just doing what it was designed to do: keep David alive and help him to avoid overwhelming feelings, no matter what it takes to carry out the agenda. "Do what I say, David, and we will be okay." Notice the "we," as if it's a partnership – but it's not. My developed mind has hidden itself very well, and I marched through my life believing I was making all these choices out of free will. *Not so fast, Mr. King.*

My parents and my mind started as a match made in heaven. But for me, it turned out to be more like hell. I will share the details of that story in the next few chapters. My dear friend and psychologist, Amitabh, explained to me that when I was a very young child felt compelled to make my parents right no matter what they did or said. That's because my fragile, still-developing nervous system could not handle the feelings that would arise if I realized that they couldn't see over their steering wheels either – the people responsible for taking care of me in this big world. My parents, being the parents that they were, implicitly or explicitly started the development of my undeveloped mind. They did this by telling me many times a day what I should do and shouldn't do. "Don't do that," "Stop touching that," "Don't go there," "That's bad – you are a bad boy," "You're doing it wrong, do it this way," "Stop crying, boys don't cry," "I'll give you something to cry about" ... SMACK on the backside! and "no," "no," "no," over and over again. I was just being a kid, exploring my new world, being the authentic and curious young person I was born to be. All these no's and shoulds would create the beliefs, strategies, and self-judgments that programmed my new, developing mind. And this gave birth to my foundational belief that *There is something wrong with me.* This belief was reinforced daily, and it was locked into place for many years – until cancer's gifts brought a key to start picking that lock and started to free me from my marriage to my mind. I will share with you some experiences to show what happened when my young mind stepped into my parents' office.

Flying Plants

I was five years old in kindergarten at P.S. 26 in the Bronx. On the windowsills were potted plants. One day, probably in the spring when the windows were open, I walked over to the window, looked down, and saw a gardener below digging trenches in the school garden. I don't remember what prompted me to do what I did next. I pushed a few of the potted plants off the windowsill, watching attentively as they rained down on the gardener, and looking to see where they landed. Thankfully none of them hit him, but he screamed up at me, *"You this, you that . . ."* I don't remember his exact words, but he was pissed. Then the teacher came over to me and started screaming, "*You this, you that.*" Then she called my mother, who came to school to get me, and there was more "*You this*" and "*you that.*" I was just being a kid. Kids do stupid stuff like that.

The German Shepherd

We all have traumas along our life's path. I have learned that traumatic events leave collateral aspects or traces in the mind that can get triggered, and I have developed strategies to avoid repeating the experience for the rest of my life. I avoid even thinking about the experience, because it could bring up the feelings at the time when it happened. There are many examples of this pattern in the chapters to come. Here I want to give you a simple one. I am a four-year-old running around in an empty field, which happens to be a softball field. Either my mother has lost track of me or she felt I was safe playing in this big empty field; in either case, what she cannot see is the steep drop-off at the other end of the field near the backstop for home plate. This adventuresome four-year-old is heading for this steep drop-off, in total innocence, enjoying the freedom to explore. Suddenly, I am on my back, knocked over by a German shepherd, who plants his/her front paws on my chest and starts barking loudly. I was in terror, screaming and crying as my mother ran over with her friend and got the dog off me, as she yells at me, "*you this, you that,*" for innocently exploring my world. I was no doubt traumatized, but instead of coming over and comforting me, she was freaking out and saying it was my fault. As it turned out, the dog was trying to save my life. He had been trained to do what he did, as I was not the first child to explore this end of the softball field. Even though the German shepherd had saved me from bodily injury or worse, I was still traumatized! To this day I will not go near a German shepherd even though I know where the fear comes from. In fact, for many years I avoided all big dogs - until the day my friend's golden retriever licked me up one side of my face and down the other. The trauma built a belief system in my mind that German shepherds were dangerous, and the strategy was to avoid them so I wouldn't have to feel the terror of an event that happened when I was four years old. The mind is a survival machine, and *my* mind keeps the books on everything it thinks may put my survival in jeopardy. And long after any such incident, my developing mind would continue to treat those books as gospel.

The "F" Word

I was playing with my friend Larry, who lived down the block at the end of a series of apartment buildings in the East Bronx. We went up to his apartment for something, and his mother started giving him grief. Suddenly, Larry said "Fuck you" to his mother. Now it was not shocking to hear him use those words, because I had no idea at the time what they meant. It was shocking that he stood up to his mother. And at the same time, it was amazing that he could get such a reaction from her just by uttering two words. I was probably thinking, *Wow - this is pretty good*, and decided that the next time my mother gave me grief I would do the same. And I did! At first, she was shocked, and then she yelled the dreaded words at me that I heard way too often, "Wait till your father comes home."

When my father came home, exhausted from work and riding for an hour in the crowded New York subway rush hour, she unloads what I had said on him, prefaced by the immortal words of a mother throwing her son under the bus: "Guess what your son said?" The key word here was "your," implying it was all my father's fault that I had said it. My father never uttered that word, ever! Yet it seems he was blamed anyway. He grabbed me and took me in the bathroom, then he proceeded to wet a bar of Ivory soap and stuck it in my mouth and held my mouth closed around the soap. It was more shocking and scary than the horrible taste from the soap. My hunch is that he or his brother had said something bad when they were kids and that's what their mother did to punish them. It is interesting that to this day, whenever I taste ginger, it tastes just like that soap. It reminds me of the trauma of sitting on the toilet with a wet bar of Ivory soap in my mouth with my angry father tightly holding my mouth shut. I never eat ginger!

Resilience and Courage

Every day, day after day, children are told in many ways that there is something wrong with them. *Just for being their unique selves.* I was no exception. I am grateful that I was given resiliency and courage as part of my "birth package." No matter how badly I was abused by my parents, causing me to shut down my heart, lose my trust in people, and fear being in the world, I slowly learned the value of an open heart and began putting more and more trust in people. Thankfully, Amitabh taught me that the two basic lies my mind had created were just that - lies. The first lie was that there was something wrong

David The Beloved

with me. The second lie I told myself was: I can do better; I can fix whatever is causing me to get abused. I can be perfect. I have lived most of my life with this second lie. Only in the past few years have I become aware of the basic lie - that there was something wrong with me that needed to be fixed. There is nothing to fix! I am absolutely, perfectly imperfect just as I am, just as I was created. And I completely deserve to receive all the love that surrounds me to fill me each moment. If I am a beloved, then it seems to me that we are all beloveds!

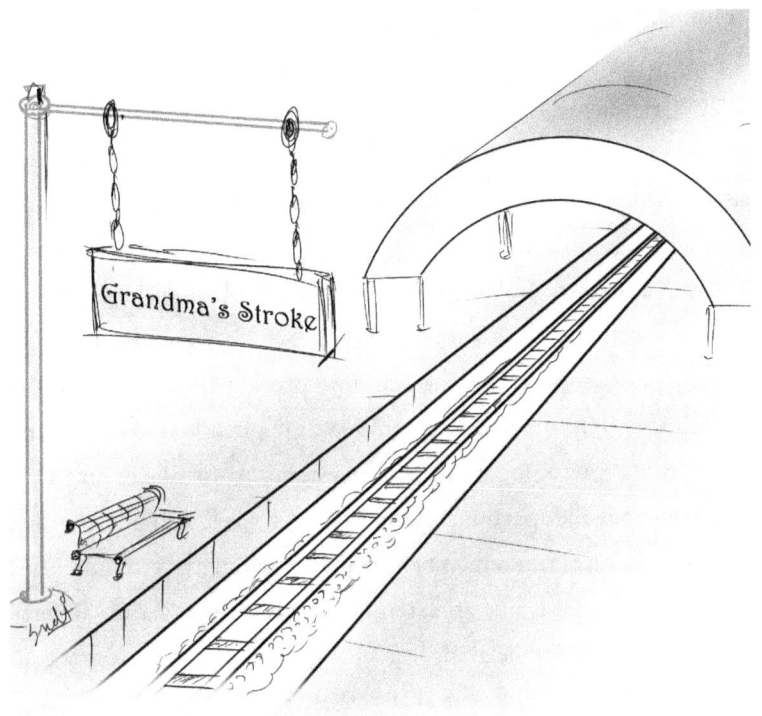

A Morning's Panic

In plays and movies, there are defining moments that suddenly cause the life of the main character to change in some dramatic way. This was certainly the case in my life when, one day, my train headed down the tracks to the next station. As we approached the station, the train started sputtering, and the doors began opening and closing, even though we were not quite at the platform. Clearly something was wrong. What could it be? I had left the last station feeling loved, like a beloved. Suddenly I heard the Train Yard Master announce, "At this station, Mr. King, you will experience great turbulence and upheaval." Yikes! And so, it was! When my train pulled into the station, the sign said: "Grandma's Stroke."

One morning, at age seven, I awoke on a school day feeling tired, as if I hadn't gotten enough sleep. My mother was rushing around doing things, including helping me get dressed, rather roughly. I always got dressed by myself at this point. Still half asleep, I felt it was all a bit of a blur. Before I knew it, we were out the door. No schoolbooks, no teeth brushed, and no breakfast. Now I was really confused and bewildered. Everything was happening so fast it didn't occur to me to ask my mother what was going on. She grabbed my hand, and out the apartment door and down the four flights of stairs we went. I don't even remember my feet touching the ground; in the hurried panic I was like an extension of my mother's arm. My arm ached as she tugged me along, forgetting that one of her steps would take two of mine. Still a bit asleep, I said nothing and tried to keep my arm in its socket by running or skipping every couple of steps. It was as if we flew the six long blocks to my grandparents' apartment.

My grandparents, my mother's parents, were of Russian ancestry. They had been born in neighboring villages in the Ukraine. They were happily married in the Ukraine, but a tragic Romeo and Juliet-type event suddenly separated them. My grandfather was working as a schoolteacher, and once in a moment of frustration, he lost his temper with a student who was disrupting the class and grabbed him by the collar. The boy pulled away, tripped, and banged his head against the corner of a desk as he fell to the floor. Everyone thought the boy was dead as he lay there unconscious. Fearing retribution, my grandfather fled in a panic to America without his beloved wife

Grandma's Stroke

Yetta, who was pregnant. As it turned out, they had rushed the boy to a doctor in a neighboring village, and the boy lived. My grandfather did not hear the news of the boy's survival until he was on the streets of New York. Eventually, he sent for my grandmother and their son, my Uncle Max, to join him in America where in 1913, my grandfather met his son for the first time.

My mother wrote that my grandmother and grandfather had loved each other when they got married and that he was a loving father to all his children, though I never got that impression of him. Whenever I visited my grandparents, he never said a word to me, and was usually absent from the house. Something must have happened to him that was a game changer to have caused such a change in his demeanor.

The best description of what grandmother meant to me is in the lyrics of a song by Jeff Silbar and Larry Henley, "The Wind Beneath My Wings." My grandmother was indeed the wind beneath *my* wings, and so much more. Later in life, I would sing that song in her honor, and I could never make it through to the end without falling apart. In her eyes I could do no wrong, and her heart was always open to me and my heart to her. One of the lines of the song (as I reworded it) says it all: "I've got my grandmother all here in my heart." I had *all* my grandmother in my heart, *all* her love - and I still do. My grandmother was my protector from my parents as a child. They would not so much as say "boo" to me when she was around.

When my mother and I walked through the front door of my grandparents' apartment that morning, I was very surprised that my grandmother wasn't there to greet me, as she never missed being there when I arrived. This time, she wasn't there - and I felt confused! My

David The Beloved

mother took my hand and led me to the spare bedroom, where she put me on the bed and told me to stay there. Then she went into my grandparents' bedroom. I heard a lot of talking going on - a lot of it in Yiddish, which I did not understand. After a few moments, my mother walked out of the bedroom and went into the kitchen. I jumped out of the bed and went to the doorway of my grandparents' bedroom. I saw my grandmother lying in a hospital bed with her left leg raised in a sling. In the room with her was my uncle, the family doctor, and an older man, not my grandfather, who was not at home. I ran to her side and said, "Grandma, it's me!" Her eyes were closed and she didn't respond. I kept saying, "Grandma, it's *me*, it's *ME!*" raising my voice louder with each attempt to get her attention, but with no response. Each attempt brought more fear. My seven-year-old nervous system was on overload, not knowing which of the many feelings to feel - one moment fear; the next moment, panic; then confusion. What the hell was going on? And with all these emotions building up inside, from wanting my grandma to see me, to respond to me, when I said, "Grandma, it's me, it's me!" I was in total panic. I did not understand when my uncle said that she was in a coma, that she could not hear me.

All this intensity lasted for only a few minutes, as my mother returned, took me by the hand, and started pulling me out of the room. I desperately tried to break free from her and run back to my grandmother's bed, tears running down my face, I kept crying out to my grandmother: "Grandma, Grandma, it's me, it's David!" My arm was already aching from the sprint to my grandmother's house with my mother pulling me; now it was being badly strained because, this time, I was not willingly going along for the ride. I desperately wanted to return to my grandmother's side.

Grandma's Stroke

But my mother finally won. She pulled me out of the room and sat me back on the bed in the spare bedroom. This time she yelled at me to stay there. It turned out that my grandfather had come home drunk during the night, got into bed, and forcibly pushed my grandmother away from him, causing her to roll off their high bedframe. She fell onto the floor on her left side and had a stroke. She had been lying on the floor for several hours by the time my uncle came by in the morning to give my grandmother her insulin shot before going to his job. When I was a teenager, I found out about what my grandfather had done, and I hated him for it. I moved him to the top of the list of people I hated, right after my mother and father. Not until recently, while reading my mother's unpublished manuscript, would I learn how much my grandfather adored and loved me when I was a baby. He would walk over to our house every day to see me. That softened my hatred towards him. I now forgive him as a person, but I haven't yet forgiven him for what he did to my grandmother.

My grandmother's stroke was a defining moment in my life. It transformed my life, in what seemed like only a heartbeat, from a life where I felt loved, safe, and confident to one in which I felt unloved, unsafe, and insecure. Before that day I could walk the streets between my grandmother's apartment and ours as if I (to use a "Bronxism") owned the joint. No more! Now, just leaving the house made fear and anxiety take over, as if I were about to relive that fateful march to the frightening scene at my grandmother's house. Now I crossed the streets running, not walking, to get to the other side as safely and quickly as possible. I no longer sneaked under the turnstile to take the train one stop to my uncle's store, because now I was afraid of falling into the gap between the train and the station platform. And

I had lost my grandmother as a protector from my parents. I feared the awful things that might happen to me without her – fears that would soon be realized. I also no longer felt like I owned the joint. All these fears and more would lie buried in my mind undetected – until I got my wakeup call, years later, from cancer.

Grandma Moves In

I am not sure how long it took for my grandmother to "wake up" from her coma, start to notice me and other people, and know who we were. Nor do I recall how long it was before she started the shuttle operation between staying at our house and my aunts' and uncles' homes. Once my grandmother moved into our one-bedroom apartment, the day-to-day routine changed a lot. In our one bedroom, there was a double bed for my parents and a single bed, three feet away, where I slept. My grandmother and I went to bed earlier than my parents. She slept in my bed, and I was put temporarily in my parents' bed until they were ready for sleep. At that point my father would carry me to the couch. Whenever my grandmother stayed with us over the next three years, this was the nightly routine. This was a pain for my father, especially, yet this bedtime ritual was minor compared with what was to come.

My grandmother would spend a week or two at the homes of my uncles and aunts, except for my Aunt Mary, who had disowned the family a few years earlier. I might have been the only grandchild who had ever met her yet I am sure, to this day, that my Aunt Mary loved me. Once my Aunt Mary disappeared, my mother – being the oldest daughter – had taken it upon herself to have my grandmother

Grandma's Stroke

stay longer in our apartment. It was hard for my grandmother to go up and down the four sets of stairs to our third-floor apartment, and it was a long way from the street to the front steps. Yet my grandmother was a strong, tough, persevering woman. She never complained. She would get up at least once or twice a night to go to the bathroom. And with a brace on her foot, she had to use a cane, so it was very noisy. I am sure it woke up my father, as my mother had to get out of bed to walk with her. For me, well, not only had I lost my bed, I felt as though I had lost my grandmother! I don't remember these feelings; yet I am sure that compared with the first seven years of my life with my grandmother, it was hard to comprehend – and even harder to truly let in and feel this reality. Even though, after waking from the coma, she still loved me unconditionally, I had somehow decided that she was lost to me – that I had lost her love. The change in the living situation of my family, now that my grandmother was often staying with us, would set the stage for the next big change in my life.

Who Are These People?

The Train Yard Master had said that my "Birth" station would be "touch and go," and he was right. I had almost died. So, at the "Grandma's Stroke" station, when he used the phrase "great turbulence and upheaval," I knew that this station was not going to be good. But after my grandmother's stroke, my life turned out to be far worse than I could ever have imagined. My mother's and father's behavior changed dramatically after my grandmother moved in with us. Now, whenever I crossed the line or did something that took my mother out of her comfort zone, instead of just saying, "Wait till your father comes home," she would yell things at me. "What's wrong with you?" "What am I going to do with you?" "Won't you ever learn?" These were some of her "greatest hits." When this seven-year-old heard her say those words, he would think: *"There must be something wrong with me."* I was seven years old, doing what a kid that age does - kid stuff!

I want to give you another example of what I had to endure as a kid, from the age of seven until I was thirteen. During those years my life would be filled with such experiences. One day during the winter, I went down to the street outside our apartment building to pitch baseball cards with a couple of friends. We pitched the cards from the sidewalk curb, and the card closest to the building would win the cards. I was really "on" that day, "in the card-pitching zone," and I won all the cards. I was so excited and happy that I ran upstairs to show my mother all the cards I had won. She looked at me holding the cards and said, "Where are your new gloves?" She had bought me a new pair of gloves at my uncle's store. I ran downstairs to where I had put them while pitching the cards, but they were gone. She hit the roof! A chorus of her favorite chants came out: "What's wrong with you?" "What am I going to do with you?" "Won't you ever learn?" Then the one I dreaded most: "Wait until your father comes home!" She would never do the physical punishment herself. She left that job to my father.

The wait for my father to come home was excruciating. The minute he walked through the door, she dumped her anger and frustration on him, after he had just worked eight hours at a job he hated and endured a rush-hour subway ride home.

Grandma's Stroke

My father had listened to my mother's favorite chants about me long enough to have taken them on himself. Before the words could even fill my brain, he would take his left hand and put it on the back of my neck, march me into the hallway of our third-floor apartment, and start hitting me in the tush. It seemed he didn't want my mother to witness the abuse she had instigated, yet somehow it was okay for her and the neighbors to hear it. This hitting and spanking had started after my grandmother moved in with us - though it only happened when she was staying with my aunts and uncles. Up to that time, my father would yell at me and had his own strategies to keep me from provoking my mother. His favorite lines were: "Look what you are doing to your mother!" and "Don't you care about your mother?" Remember, I was just a kid! I say this again for the sake of all of us who were abused as children. As kids, we do kid stuff. Give us kids a break and cut us some slack. We are learning how to *be* in the world. To learn, we kids had to cross lines, make mistakes, lose gloves, break glasses, and God knows what else. There would be no breaks and no slack for me. When the hitting and spankings were about to start, I would get so scared before the first whack that I'd start crying. My father would shout, "I'll give you something to cry about!" Then he would hit me harder and harder. After the first few spankings, I would stop crying and stopped feeling fear. To this day, I still have a resistance to feeling fear, afraid if I feel it I will be hit.

I wondered what the heck was going on. My heart was being broken on almost a daily basis. I did not think, *What did I do to deserve this?* but, instead, *There is something wrong with me.* Writing these words now, I can still feel that heartbreak - and I feel deep sadness that I had to go through all of this as a child.

David The Beloved

The worst part of all this abuse was that no one knew about it. My grandmother was in no position to be able to stop it, had she known. Thankfully, my father never touched me when she was around. No one knew! Almost all my aunts and uncles were very loving toward me. But even if they had known, I am not sure whether they would have done anything to prevent it, or whether my mother would have listened to them. Maybe if my Uncle Bernie had known, he would have stopped it; not only did he love me very much, he was also very close to my mother. I did have a few opportunities to tell people. After she'd had an argument with my mother, one of my aunts would tell me my mother was crazy. What if I had said, "You have no idea!" Or when one of my uncles told me he didn't believe in hitting his children, my cousins, what if I had told him about my father? I didn't have the wherewithal to tell either of them what was being done to me. My mind decided that I was on my own. I would need to do everything for myself, as I could no longer count on anyone to help me, or care about me for that matter, let alone be loving. I started coping with the feeling of being alone in the world, and strategizing how to stay safe.

I wish I could go back in time to those years, to one of those terrible moments, and say to both my parents: "Stop! You cannot do this to me! It is not why you brought me into this world. I am too beautiful, too precious to have my heart broken by your yelling and hitting."

One day, in my forties, I was in a Safeway store in Lafayette, California. I saw a woman screaming at her daughter, who was about six years old. When I saw her raise her hand to strike the child, I ran over and yelled at her to stop. "She is only a child, stop yelling at her! She doesn't deserve this." Then I yelled at other people to call the police. The woman shouted back at me: "Mind your own business, don't tell me how to be a mother!" I just ignored her and followed her as she walked from aisle to aisle until the police came. Then I shared what had happened with the police and left. I was stopping this woman not just for the sake of her little girl, but also for the kid in me who could not say those words to his *own* mother and father. NO MORE!

I Lost My Family

Looking back on my life, I realize there was a deeper loss that I experienced during my childhood years, from the time I was seven. The loss of my grandmother as I had known her, my mother's constantly reading me the riot act, and my father's tirades and beatings had made me come to a decision: "I no longer have a family." My mind decided that to feel safe, I would need to find a new family - and I have been looking for that new family my whole life. Until recent years, I hadn't realized that's what I had been doing. Even today as I write these words, there is still such a desire to plug into a beautiful and loving family who would love me. I wish I could have shared my true feelings with friends and other people: that in order to feel safe, I needed them - I needed their help. As a child, I didn't have the wherewithal to speak these words.

When I was seven years old I started spending a lot of time at my friend Ross's apartment on the first floor. He lived with his mom, Charlette, and his grandfather. I would never have anyone

David The Beloved

over to play at my house; the entire time I lived with my parents, I never invited anyone to my house. When we played at Ross's house his mom would sometimes give me lunch. His mother and grandfather were always sweet and caring toward me. I remember thinking that I wished his mother were my mother. No, it was much more than a wish – it was a *want*, an expressed need to bring me a feeling of safety. This was the first time I tried to make myself a part of another family. It would not be the last.

The sputtering noise and crazy door openings when my train was pulling into the "Grandma's Stroke" station was nothing compared to the ride to the next station. The train car was swerving, shaking, and bobbing up and down on the tracks without a single smooth, peaceful moment. I began to wonder if I would even make it to the next station, and just as I was about to give up all hope, we pulled into a station called "East to West." There was not one person waving at this station, nor did anyone smile at me the way they did when I arrived at the "You Are Love and Loved" station. Am I not still Love or Loved? The answer would come.

David The Beloved

The three years my grandmother Yetta had lived with us part time in our small apartment were stressful and overwhelming for my parents, with my father having to carry me to the couch every night, and my grandmother sleeping three feet away from my parents, disturbing them whenever she got up to go to the bathroom. Not to mention that my mother was in constant uproars when my grandmother wasn't around. So, when I was ten years old, we left the tracks of the East Bronx and crossed over into the West Bronx. We went from a one-bedroom apartment that housed four people, at times, to a two-bedroom, two-story rowhouse attached on both sides.

My East Bronx neighborhood was crowded with five-story apartment buildings, one after another, on both sides of the street. With fifty apartments to a building, maybe a hundred and fifty people lived in each one. And with ten buildings on every block, there were a lot of kids to play with, just on your own block. That one block became the center of my universe. I didn't know any of the kids on the other blocks. My whole life revolved around playing stick ball and slap ball in the street or playing stoop ball off the steps of the walkway to our building entrance. Since we didn't have much money, we would fish the balls out of the sewers, when they got lost down there, with hangers and milk cartons. And for a stick, we would climb up the fire escape and "borrow" someone's mop handle or broomstick. Playing ball in the streets was my distraction from my unhappy life inside the apartment from the age of seven until we moved. Except for meals, school, and sleep, I lived and played in the streets. Most of the time, if my grandmother was not staying with us, my mother would make my dinner early so I could eat and be playing outside before my father came home. This was for her own benefit primarily, as she didn't like it when *he* initiated the yelling. That made her feel as though things were out of her control.

Our new neighborhood in the West Bronx had no apartment buildings in the immediate vicinity, only a long series of attached rowhouses and single-family homes. The street we lived on had about forty of these brick rowhouses, each one complete with a small backyard, a one-car garage, and a small porch. The houses were built narrow and the walls were thin. On one side I could hear the two kids that I shared a bedroom wall with getting beaten by their father, who always sounded drunk. On the other side there was an Italian family. I heard the father yelling a lot of Italian curse words. I learned how to swear in Italian, but I would never say these words to the Italian kids. This new neighborhood was a mix of Jewish and Italian families, and it was not far from the projects, where many African American families lived.

When we moved, I had to leave everything I had known in the East Bronx behind me. I had to say goodbye to my friends on the block who I played ball with, along with my status as a ball player. I also lost my status as a math whiz at P.S. 26. I had to leave the barbershop on the corner where I would take myself for a haircut. There was a bakery around the block where my mother would send me for half a loaf of rye bread; I'd always eat a few slices by the time I got home. I would also go to an underground shop for pickles out of the barrel or fresh-baked bagels. I would no longer be able to walk to my grandmother's apartment or my uncle's store. The familiarity that comes from living in a neighborhood, knowing who I was with people, having connections

David The Beloved

with people – all of that was gone. The biggest adjustment, at least for a while, would be the loss of my sense of independence. I knew how things worked in the old neighborhood. Everything in front of me now was unknown.

The new neighborhood had many surprises and shocks in store for me. Even though there were many Jewish kids, there was an equal number of Italian kids. On one of my first days in the neighborhood, the kids my age on the block told me I had to take the block initiation. That was to lie on a mattress in my neighbor's garage while they gave me a "pink belly." This was a shock. Six kids, with three of them kneeling on either side, pounded on my chest with their open palms until my chest was bright pink; hence "pink belly." Welcome to the neighborhood, David!

My first day in school came as another shock to me. It was the first time I was around black kids. The elementary school was a mix of three cultures – Jewish, Italian, and African American. For me, the doorway to being friends with anybody, no matter their religion, race, or culture, was sports. In the years to come, I played basketball with the black kids; sometimes I was the only white kid on the court. I was a very good baseball player, and when I was high school age, I played on an Italian *men's* softball team at the elementary school playground. Whenever we won, the manager of the team would slip me a five-dollar bill. The manager was an important figure in the neighborhood, and it was known that I was to be "left alone."

I made two new friends, Ira and Arty, who lived on Fish Avenue around the corner from DeWitt Place, the street where I lived. Just like in the old neighborhood, I would never invite my friends over to my house; we would hang out at their houses. Ira and I would play gin rummy with his parents, who were really good players. When we beat them, which was rare, we would gloat over them, and if they won, Ira's dad would have this great smile on his face. With Arty and Ira, we played poker. I remember one time when Arty, Ira, and I committed a sin by playing cards on the Jewish holiday Yom Kippur. We felt guilty about it but played anyway! One night Arty, Ira, and another kid named Phil and I played a night of basketball games together that would lead to the worst night of my life (a story I will relate in the next chapter).

Watching Grandma

At the new house I no longer had to go to sleep in my parents' bed and be carried to the couch. I now had a room that I shared with my grandmother whenever she stayed with us, and my parents slept in the other bedroom. With the benefit of having my own room came the new responsibility of taking care of my grandmother. Every night when she got up to go to the bathroom, I would walk behind her until she sat down safely on the toilet seat. Then I would go and sit on the side of my bed until she was ready to come back. I didn't dare lie down; if I fell asleep, she might fall walking back by herself. When she was ready, I would escort her back to her bed. She got up twice a night. And I did this for twelve years. To this day, I often get up two times a night.

On Saturdays, my mother would sometimes work in my uncle's store in the West Bronx, which was close to where my grandmother had lived before her stroke (and where my grandfather still lived). On those days, I would have to watch my grandmother. I passed the time watching sports on TV. She had learned the word "Yankees," and whenever she saw sports on the screen, she would ask me, "How are the Yankees doing?" "Fine," I would say, as I didn't know how to explain what was really going on with sports. I was basically there to watch her climb up the stairs to the bathroom on the second floor and then back down. Even with a paralyzed left side, she managed to pull herself up the fifteen stairs to the bathroom. She was a tough lady! Years later I realized the amount of resentment and guilt I still carried from that time. I had wanted to be outside playing ball, not stuck indoors watching my grandmother. But I loved her so much that I could not refuse to do it, and not once in all those years did I complain. Only years later would I realize that she had given me the greatest of gifts – all the love in her heart.

We Were On

My life's train is not far from the next station and it is cooking, running on all cylinders, as it pulls into the station where my three friends, Ira, Arty, and Phil, are waiting for me. The doors open and they start singing in harmony, "It was the best of times, it was the worst of times . . ." I ignore their singing and say to them, "Let's go play basketball at the gym." Then I notice the station sign, "All Will Be Lost." I thought, What? Are we going to lose all the games tonight?

Something was not making sense. I got distracted by this chorus of off-key singers.

David The Beloved

I was twelve-and-a-half years old, a student at Junior High School 135 in the Bronx. On certain nights of the week the school gym was open for pickup half-court games of basketball, four on a side. My friends Ira, Arty, Phil, and I headed up to the gym with no special feeling that we were going to kick butt that night - yet that is exactly what happened. A miracle happened that night. To our amazement, we won every game - for us, better than a gold medal. The winners stay on the court and play the next team, and that next team is well rested. Because of that, it was rare, almost impossible, to win every game in a night. Did I mention we won every game? We were on cloud nine, tired puppies, dripping with sweat. We stayed a bit longer, all smiles, joking around, replaying the highlights of the evening as we waited to cool down before going out into the cold evening. On our way home, we danced in the middle of the streets. Traffic was not an issue for us - let them go around us. We were big shots! The stuff legends are made of. Because of our joy, without giving it any thought, we took a different route home than usual. We had not a care in the world, no thought that our parents might wonder where we were or why we were late. Remember this was 1958; cell phones were not even a rumor back then.

This Is Not Going To Be Good

I was the last one to peel off from the group and head home. When I walked in the door, I was at first surprised and then shocked by what I found. Except for the entry light, the house was totally dark. My parents were always home when I got back from basketball. My intuition told me I was in big trouble. Up to this night, I had always

All Will Be Lost

kept a fear present in my mind: *Is this the day I will get hit again?* Like an athlete when preparing for a game, this question would get my mind, body, and soul ready in case I did get hit. Yet even this could not have prepared me for what would happen that night. My mood went from happy, without a care in the world - "Look at me, Mr. Basketball!" - to "Wait till your father comes home" mode. I stood by the storm door and looked outside, and within a few minutes, the car pulled up with my parents. My mother got out of the car, and as she was running up the front steps, she saw me at the storm door and started screaming at the top of her lungs: "Where were you?! You scared me to death!" She shouted this at me again and again, with every breath in her body. By now all the neighbors had heard her. It seems that when I was not home ten minutes past the normal time - that's right, *ten minutes* - she had called Ira's parents. Ira had not yet arrived home either. My parents drove over to the school and found it dark. Then they drove down Allerton Avenue (our usual route home because it was a well-lit main street) but saw no sign of us. Now, my mother was in a panic. And when my mother had a panic attack because of something I had done, I would get hit hard and painfully, in the you know where, by my father. This time it was a *far* bigger deal!

After my father put the car in the garage, I watched him run up the front steps, fuming with anger. The second he came through the storm door he looked at me with rage, his eyes wide open, his nostrils flaring. His face was bright red. In fact, everything about him was red. The words that came flying out of his mouth, "Look what you did to your mother!" didn't register, even though he shouted them several times. I was in too much shock. You know the drill. It was my fault that my mother had gone bananas again, and by now, it was so ingrained in me that I believed it. "Get to your room!" he screamed. This was the most incensed I had ever seen my father, far beyond his anger level during the usual spanking and hitting. This was *pure rage!*

He came storming into my room after me and boxed me between the end of my bed and one corner of the room with my back against the wall; there was no way for me to move to avoid what he was about to do. He hit me in the head, and I fell to the floor, feeling as if I had died. I was in survival mode, struggling for my life and feeling helpless, just as I must have felt in the womb during those two-and-a-half days my mother was in labor. Then he started hitting me in the head again and kicking me in the legs. All the time yelling: "What are you, crazy?" "What's wrong with you?" "I'm going to kill you!" and "Look what you did to your mother!" I absolutely believed that he was going to kill me. I thought for sure I was going to die on that floor that very night. The pummeling went on, the raging went on. I was frozen, in a state of deep shock. In these moments time did not exist. I took every punch, every kick, as if I were watching it on TV. I detached myself from my body, my feelings, my heart, so that he could no longer hurt me – physically or emotionally. If it weren't for my mother suddenly coming upstairs and acting like Florence Nightingale, I am not sure how this beating would have ended. She started yelling the same things at my father that my father was yelling at me: "What are you, crazy?" "What's wrong with you?" She knew that it was her panic attack that had set him off in the first place. But rather than waiting to make sure he would indeed stop the attack she left the room and went downstairs. *She didn't even ask me if I was okay!* Here I was, lying

All Will Be Lost

on the floor in the corner of the room, having just been beaten, and she just walks out without even saying a caring word to me. I came out of her own womb; didn't she care enough to ask me if I was all right? The only thing that mattered to her was that I wouldn't do it again. My father stood over me for a few more seconds, seemingly deciding whether to continue the attack or leave the room. He deferred to her as usual and left the room.

I stayed on the floor for a while and eventually found the strength to pull myself into my bed, fully dressed, and fell asleep. When I awoke the next morning, I looked across the room to my grandmother's bed; it was empty. Then I remembered that she was staying with one of my aunts and uncles. If she had been there, that beating would never had happened. Even with a stroke and a paralyzed left side, she would have hit my father over the head with her cane and screamed at him. I slowly lifted myself out of bed to go to the bathroom; my head ached, and my legs were sore and bruised. When I got to the door of my bedroom, I became aware of two thoughts that I would later realize were vows. The first was: *I will never let him get to me again.* Twenty years later, I would realize that this vow I had made was to no longer feel any of my feelings and to totally close my heart. Fear, terror, hurt, joy, love - all my feelings would be locked away. When I shared this story with a friend, he said that this incident was also the time when I lost my innocence. I feel the truth of that. I feel that the light had gone out of my eyes and my heart, and I know that the experience had closed me to feel being loved.

The second vow I made was this: *If he touches me again, I will get a knife from the kitchen drawer and kill them both.* I had no idea at that age that just because you think something, it doesn't make you bad or insane or unlovable. They are just thoughts – and it's no harm, no foul if you don't act on them. The second vow gave my mind the final evidence to confirm that I was crazy, and the beating from my father gave it the final proof that I was unlovable and didn't deserve love.

The overload on my nervous system from the beating, my father's rage, and the thought of killing my parents solidified my belief that *If I feel my feelings, I will die*. With this belief in my mind, at the first sign of any feeling, I would contract the muscles in my belly so tightly that there were times when I didn't even the feel the tightness. *I just felt nothing!*

That night, the man who I had thought to be my father was no longer my father. The woman who had claimed to be my mother was no longer my mother. *They were both dead to me!!!* My question to the Train Yard Master, *"What if I don't like them?"* came back to haunt me. I not only didn't like them, I *hated* them! The next morning, after making the two vows, my train solemnly pulled out of the station, as if it were a funeral train. It had black curtains hanging in the windows. And it slowly entered a dark tunnel . . . the train was now running underground, and it would be underground for the next fifteen to twenty years. On the night of the beating, my innocence and openheartedness had died! My developed mind finally had the total control it had wanted when it married me.

A few years ago, I shared the story of my two vows with the Shaman I later had sessions with to heal from cancer. He explained to me that making these vows had served to protect me. I feel that the Shaman was right. After that incident, my father never touched me again. Never so much as raised his voice to me. Maybe what he had done scared him as well. And for the next twenty years, we had very little to do with each other. Later, however, I will share the story of our healing together.

This trauma from this beating cemented ways of relating to the world in my mind for most of the rest of my life. That I must be perfect: if I am perfect, I will not be hit again. I lived my life being hypervigilant, trying to say and do the "right" thing in every way possible. I started with not making my mother upset, which would turn into accommodating women's needs and wants and ignoring my own. I learned to use comedy to make people laugh so I could feel safe, and wouldn't have to worry about being hit. I felt that I always had to be in control, and if there was a situation that felt out of control, I must either fix *it* or fix *me*. Tatiana (one of my ex-wives whom I will introduce in a later chapter) used to call me "Mr. Fix-it" and "Mr. Control," and she was right on target. The belief that "if I feel these feelings I will die" is the one that still activates in times of crisis. It's a belief I continue to work on, even today.

The Kid

In the movie *Disney's The Kid* (2000), Bruce Willis's character suddenly finds himself with an eight-year-old boy visiting him, who turns out to be himself at age eight. He tries to get rid of this seeming hallucination, until he realizes that his eight-year-old self has come to remind him of an event that had changed his life – his mother's death. His father became detached from him after his mother was gone, and angry with him for his kid mistakes. The boy started to believe that he was a loser and that there was something wrong with him. And the man he had become as an adult reinforced this belief: No wife, no kids, and no dog. This eight-year-old Buddha had come to him so they could remind each other that all these beliefs and judgments were not true. That as an eight-year-old he was a sweet, beautiful child, and these beliefs and judgments had been created to shield him from the heartbreak of losing his mom.

And I sat watching this movie for the third time, I felt sad to the depths of my heart. What would my eight-year-old self say to me if he landed on my doorstep today? He would say, through a rainforest of tears, that his heart had been broken by his grandmother's stroke and her inability to recognize him; by his mother's yelling, which now filled the household almost every day; and by the spankings that had started from his father. He would say how he had felt scared, confused, and all alone, because no one knew what his parents were doing to him; no one knew how he was being treated. He would say that he had wanted to cry out for help but was afraid no one would hear him - no one who would bring him comfort. If his parents heard him cry out, it would only bring him more pain and brokenheartedness. He would say how he had felt that it was all his own fault. They were punishing him, so they must be right that he was a very bad person. He would tell me that his mother yelled awful things at him like, "What are you, crazy?" and "What's wrong with you?" He would tell me how his father put one hand around the back of his neck to hold him in place, and then hit him hard in the ass with his other hand.

Little did the young David know that it would get much worse. How could he *not* believe that there was something wrong with him? It was next to impossible when day in, day out he was being hit or

All Will Be Lost

screamed at by his parents, and most hurtful of all, his parents withdrew their love from him.

And how would I respond if the eight-year-old version of myself knocked on my front door? First, I would take him into my arms, hold him close to my heart, kiss his head, and tell him how much I loved him – and say how very sorry I was that he had to go through all those years of punishment and cruelty. I would tell him that there was nothing wrong with him. *His mother and father* were the ones who had something wrong with them. I would say over and over what a beautiful, gorgeous, precious, sharp, and loving child he was, with such a big heart. I would tell him the absolute truth: "You were a beloved when you were born, and nothing you ever did or did not do your whole life – nothing you ever said or did not say your whole life – can change the truth of your beloved-ness." And as I was falling apart, with the boy in my arms, I would tell him: "I love you so much!!!"

You're No Longer A Kid, Kid

After leaving the "All Is Lost" station and entering the tunnel underground, the train started a short descent until the tracks leveled off and became a subway line. The train was moving slowly. I was glad for this speed, as I wanted to rest on the train, lick my wounds, and orient myself to the world again. I had lost my compass with that brutal beating. But there would be no such rest for this kid. I saw the sign coming up at the next station: "David - The Man." What?! What was this all about? I was disoriented *before* getting to the station, and

David The Beloved

now it felt as though my life was taking a bizarre turn. Most of the previous stations had been empty, but at this station, lots of people seemed to be celebrating. I was puzzled and I did not want to get off the train! What were they celebrating? When the doors opened, I could hear the crowd singing a song to the tune of the nursery rhyme, "The Farmer in the Dell."

David is a man,
David is a man,
Hi-ho the derry-o,
David is a man . . . .

Oh no! was all that came to me as I stepped onto the station platform amid this jubilation.

In the summer of 1958, at the age of thirteen, I graduated into Jewish manhood with my bar mitzvah ceremony. This ritual requires you to say a passage from the Torah (the basis of all Jewish sacred texts) in Hebrew. I had misbehaved in Hebrew schools throughout the East and West Bronx. I would purposely say the Hebrew words in a comedic way to make the other boys laugh. For example, when saying the Hebrew words "mazel tov" (good fortune) I would hold down one nostril with my finger and say "nasal tov." Silly stuff. Sometimes I would trade stamps in the back row, or I would put my hand out the open window and play catch with the boys waiting for the next class. Because of my misbehavior my mother was called to the schools on several occasions so the teachers could complain about me. Finally, I was expelled.

David - The Man

Since I had been expelled from Hebrew school, my father decided to teach me the Hebrew I would need to say in the synagogue on the occasion of my bar mitzvah. Unfortunately, I never really learned to pronounce the Hebrew words correctly. After all the years of being hit and yelled at, he expected me to learn this Hebrew passage from him. It did not go well. I would repeatedly say the words wrong, not on purpose, but because of all the times saying them wrong to create comedy in Hebrew school. He probably had an expectation for me to "make him proud" when I said these words in front of people. His expectation went against the reality of my performance during our lessons. His frustration would grow as the session went along, and from the redness on his face and neck, I knew he was angry. His impatience came through in his angry tone, which made me start contracting. Finally, he would end the session by just walking away. I coped, coped, and coped . . . .

The big day finally arrived. I did my thing at the synagogue. I stood there in front of all these people, afraid I would accidentally revert to saying the words for comic effect. But I didn't, I was okay, and when I made mistakes no one seemed to care. What a relief I felt when this ritual was over. That evening my parents put on a catered dinner at a big hall attended by a hundred and fifty people - all my aunts, uncles, cousins, cousins of cousins I didn't even know. Grandma Yetta was there, of course, beaming with joy. But not my grandfather, though I didn't even notice his absence at the time. At my mother's direction I walked the room collecting envelopes with money from the guests, like a train conductor collecting tickets for people to spend a few minutes on my train. These envelopes were not long in my possession, as my mother periodically took from them from me. By the way, she never gave me a dime, and that was that. As the saying goes in the Jewish religion, when you are thirteen and you have your bar mitzvah, you go from being a pencil to a fountain pen. *May my ink runneth over.*

That day, I knew it would be the last time I would ever go to the synagogue for a Saturday service. And that's how it was until my grandkids had their bat mitzvah (the equivalent for a girl) and bar mitzvah. I had never liked going to the service as a kid, having to sit still in the chair for over an hour, not knowing what was going on. I wanted to be out playing ball with my friends, but I had to go or else my father would hit me. Some way to teach a kid about religion! I never forced religion on my own son. He did not want a bar mitzvah, and his mother and I didn't force it on him. My mother (his grandmother), tried to get him a bar mitzvah without his or my knowledge. She schemed with the local rabbi to call Jason up in front of everyone during a Saturday service, while he was visiting my parents, and do the ceremony. This smart kid got wind of the scheme and ran out of the synagogue. I was furious with my mother and if there hadn't been three thousand miles between us, I would have killed her. I was proud of my son for his act of defiance at thirteen, and even prouder of him when, as an adult, he chose to investigate Judaism and decided to have a bar mitzvah on his own terms. In that moment when he stood up for himself, he was acting more like a man - more adult - than both of his grandparents. My son had the confidence of a child who knew that both his parents loved him deeply and that there would be no punishment for his actions. I certainly did not have that confidence and knew that the consequences, if I had committed such an act of defiance, would have been just short of the guillotine.

High School and College: Math, Sports, Poker, and T

The stations in the next part of this chapter continue to be underground subway stops and they come up fast, one after another, so hold on to the overhead bars. All of these below-ground stations are well lit, with outdated architecture, as if they had been built many years ago when I first boarded the train in the Begin Lives Train Yard.

David The Beloved

They had been built by my parents, who would guide my train to them – for my own good, of course. Nothing wrong in this, but they could not prepare me for any of the experiences at these stations. The train was now at number 9 on my circular track, running counter-clockwise from number 12, as it pulled into the next station: "High School and College."

Almost all the kids that I went to junior high school with attended a different high school than I did because of school-district boundaries. Whereas my elementary school was racially and culturally mixed, my junior high school was mostly white. The school boundaries were different, once again, as my high school was racially mixed. This never bothered me because I was totally focused on sports, and it did not matter who was on the field or the court. What I did notice, however, was that I was a small fourteen-year-old in a school with "big" guys and girls up to eighteen years old. I was overwhelmed, to say the least, by their body size, and especially by their height. I kept a low profile.

My home-room teacher, Mr. Liberti, happened to be the high school baseball coach. I was a real pain to him. I kept making jokes and disrupting the class, and he kept making me sit in the corner on a stool with a big dunce cap on my head. Yes, Mr. Liberti had a real, three-foot-high, cone-shaped dunce cap and a bar stool in his classroom. It was embarrassing for a while, but that didn't stop me from causing him grief. After a few times in the penalty corner, I figured how to be disruptive silently when his back was to the class. I hated that hat. Mr. Liberti did not let me be on the high school baseball team because of my antics – even after I promised to behave. It was his way of retaliation. Because of this, he missed

David - The Man

out on one hell of a baseball player for the high school team. At twenty-one, I had a tryout with a professional baseball team, the Philadelphia Phillies, who held an open tryout near Yankee Stadium in the Bronx. I was good, yet not big enough or powerful enough for the baseball scouts.

There were some guy friends from school that I hung out with, as well as a girl named Alexis who was like a sister to me. I called her Alex. The movie *Forrest Gump* reminded me of my time with Alex - and just as in the movie, when we were together, we were two peas in a pod. Whenever I gave her grief just for fun, she would hit me in the arm. I loved that! I took it as an expression of love. To this day, whenever a woman hits me in the arm for any reason, it brings me joy. I tried recently to connect on Facebook with Alex, but sadly, she did not respond. What to do?

In high school I was one of the brightest students in math classes. There were five of us that Dr. Wernick, the head of the math department, decided to teach special courses like Calculus and Matrix Algebra. In 1963 this was far from standard in New York City high schools. I started hanging out with these guys from the math class even though they lived a long bus ride away. For the first time, I had found other guys who were not only good at math but also liked to play ball and poker. Most of all, it was a way to be away from home and all the walking on eggshells around my parents. As always, I found other people's homes and families to be with. I feel sad letting this realization in. There was an unexpected bonus to being with these guys in my math pod. One of them would play a major role in my meeting my first wife T, as well as in the birth of my son Jason (more about this moment and my time with T in the next chapter).

David The Beloved

Life in high school was about sports and girls - on cue. Once T and I started seeing each other, it was sports and T. Life was good. For the most part I was never home except to watch my grandmother. I spent my time with T at her house, or with the guys at their houses, only coming home to sleep, or if my grandmother was staying with us, to have a meal with her.

High school days passed by, and with college looming on the horizon, I knew my grades were a bit short to make it into City College of New York (CCNY). And yet I knew at the time I wanted to be an engineer, and CCNY had a highly touted school of engineering. The college was basically free to students who lived in New York so my mother bribed me, that if I went to City College, she would get me a car. I didn't know it would be the cheapest and most dilapidated car she could find. I needed an 85 average for entry into City College and an 85 in English. There were two drawbacks: I was not good in English, with an average of 75 on tests, and I was the class comedian - and Mrs. Greenspan, my English teacher, was not too thrilled with my disruptions. With all the moxie I could muster, I went to her and explained why I needed to get an 85 in English. I promised to keep a new code of silence in class. She said, "We will see." I felt hopeful, as she didn't say no. I was quiet in class for two days. Whenever I felt the urge to crack a joke, I would put my hand over my mouth to keep to my new code. After the second day, I lost my self-control, and resumed my comedy club routine. I couldn't help being a comedian. It was such a big part of my personality to want to hear people laugh at my humor; that's how I knew they liked me and that they would be my friends. I continued to be the class comedian for the entire rest of the school year, and dear Mrs.

David - The Man

Greenspan gave me the 85 anyway, so I could go to City College. I went back to see her after I got my report card, and without thinking, gave her a big hug.

The last big event of my high school years was the senior prom. My friends from the math class and I took our dates to see the off-Broadway show *You're a Good Man, Charlie Brown*. The theatre was in Greenwich Village in lower Manhattan, then known as the home of the New York City hippie population. There were no hippies in my neighborhoods in the Bronx, so their appearance and dress were eye-opening to me. Then we went to the famed Copacabana for dinner and a show. I had never been to a nightclub before or watched a show with women dancers wearing scanty outfits. That evening knocked my socks off! (Actually, the theatre and the Copa only knocked one of my socks off – the first one had flown off when I picked up T in a strapless dress that really showed off her endowment.) I could not believe her parents would let their not-quite-sixteen-year-old daughter out of the house in that dress. T had always been cute, but tonight she looked sexy and beautiful. What a way to pull out of the station, with three toots!

I had that summer to breathe, and celebrate getting out of high school. I had no idea what college was going to be like, and most of that summer I gave it no thought. The first time on campus to register for classes I felt young again, small and insecure, compared to the twenty-plus-year-old students. College classes were difficult, and I did not like to study. I had to find the discipline to meet demands in college that never were necessary in high school. Luckily, I had to take Calculus again, and since I had aced it in high school, the college course was no big deal. I got A's in both semesters and rode those A's to the end of college to balance out some D's (the first of my life) in French and Mechanical Drawing. "Though, your honor, in my defense, two of the D's were because I took the finals with chicken pox and drove to the finals through a snowstorm with a high fever." This detail is not fiction. After the first year, I was burned out from forcing myself to study that much, and spent most of my last three years in college playing sports or cards.

My days in college went by fast because of all the sports, card games, and time with T. Two years after I had started at CCNY, T followed me and enrolled there as well. Now T was on campus and I had connected with two sets of guys in college for the past two years, so I had friends around me all the time when I wasn't in class. No one talked about how grateful and lucky we were for the brotherhood we shared in college. I appreciated being with both sets of guys I spent time with and have dearly missed having them in my life.

Not All Fun and Games

There were two events during my high school and college years that were not in the "fun and games" column and that caused my behavior to change for many years to follow.

After the beating that fateful night at not-quite-thirteen years old, my father never touched me again. My mother, on the other hand, had stopped yelling at me as often, but she resorted to a new strategy for me as a teenager - guilt. Every time she did it, I felt confused and distrustful, as if she were dealing from the bottom of the deck. One night, I was going out with a friend of mine to meet two girls for a double date. This was during a period that T and I were taking a break from dating each other at the direction of T's mother. My mother asked who I was going out with. When I said the name of the girl, who had an Irish last name, she went berserk. "Go ahead, kill me now," she yelled at me. "Do it before you leave, go get a knife from the kitchen and kill your mother so I don't have to feel the shame of the family." I sat there in total shock. Wow! I was blown away and could not think of anything to say to her. I went out with my friend anyway. This was my mother's strategy to keep me from going out with any girl who was not Jewish. Can you imagine? I was just going out on a first date.

When I was in my thirties, this incident came up in therapy and if I hadn't been so stunned by what she said to me I would have said "But we are only going bowling!"

My mother had triggered the guilt I had carried since the night when I told myself that I would kill both my parents if my father hit me again. That guilt from wanting to kill my parents took many years for me to clear up. And by the way, I did start dating Jewish girls and would marry a Jewish woman, T, my first wife. This is another example how the environment and my developed mind came up with a strategy that would determine who I would marry out of fear that my mother would get angry and my father would beat me.

The second was a horrible event during college that caused trauma that I still live with. It amazes me that it didn't affect me as much as I thought it would. One night, in the clubhouse of one of the groups, most of guys were playing poker. I was hanging out with T, with her on my lap, listening to music. There was a knock on the door and since I was the only one not in the card game I went to answer the knock. I asked, "Who is it?" as there was no peephole in

David The Beloved

the door. I thought I heard someone say "Joel." Without it dawning on me that Joel was already inside playing poker, I opened the door. A thirteen- or fourteen-year-old black kid lunged at my chest with a knife that must have been six inches long. Luckily, I was an athlete with great reflexes, and I moved quickly back a step as the knife swooshed past my body. Then, with all the adrenalin I had going, I slammed the door in the kid's face, put my back to the door, and screamed. The guys who were playing poker picked up some baseball bats and ran out of the apartment looking for the kid. I slid down the wall and sat on the floor in shock. The guys couldn't find the kid and they suggested I go to a nearby police station and report what happened. T and I and Joel and his girlfriend drove there in my parents' car (as usual my car from hell was at the repair shop). As we got near the police station, we passed about a dozen black kids walking down the street, and through the side window I saw the kid with the knife, and he saw me. They all jumped out into the street and started chasing the car. It seems I had not used all the adrenalin in my body after all: I slammed on the gas, ran a red light, and finally got to the police station which was only two blocks away. The kids ran the other way when I pulled up in front of the precinct. By now I was a wreck and truly do not remember anything that happened inside the station, how I got my friend and his girlfriend home, got T home and myself home with my parents' car. To this day I am aware that I contract when people hold their knives a certain way when they are eating.

What amazes me is the fact that I did not pick up my parents' prejudices as a child towards anyone not Jewish, black people included. I could easily see how I could have resented black

David – The Man

people for what this one black youth tried to do to me. That is not what happened. Many years later, after starting theatre, when I was around fifty, I auditioned for the lead in the Neil Simon comedy *Rumors* at a theatre that did alternative casting. To prepare for my audition for the lead character, Lenny, I had practiced a few monologues from the play in acting class, and I had a good grasp of both my character and his wife's character. When I read by myself, it was obvious that I had practiced – and that did not go unnoticed by a tall, heavy-set black woman named Sharon, who was auditioning for the role of the wife. As it turned out, they sent Sharon and me to practice a scene between the husband and wife. As we walked out of the theatre, she grabbed my arm, pulled me towards her and said, "Okay, you know what's going on – tell me about the wife." For a moment I was startled, but then I quickly relaxed with her. When Sharon pulled my arm, it reminded me of how Alexis used to hit me in the arm. I immediately trusted her. I told her about the wife's character, we both nailed the scene, and we were both cast in those roles. I never felt anything strange or odd about that pairing.

Why am I telling you this story? After the performances had started, Sharon and I began dating. It was fun with benefits, and it felt like an extension of our roles on stage. We really liked each other. And we played our characters for fun when we were together. One night we drove up into the Oakland Hills, got out of the car, and looking out to the lights of the city we started talking about taking the dating to another level. We talked about the challenges there would be with our families and the public in general. Even in the San Francisco Bay Area, mixed-race couples were still a big deal

David The Beloved

back in the 1990s. She wanted a career in Hollywood, and soon after the show ended, she moved there.

I realized that no matter what race, culture, or religion a person is, if the person treats me lovingly, with kindness and especially as a friend, then I will be their friend. Thankfully, I did not inherit my parents' prejudice against people who were not Jewish. It touches me to acknowledge this, as I never saw this clearly about myself until now.

I had assumed that the next three stations on the tracks would be career, marriage, and fatherhood. While I suspected that these stations would be coming up, I was not prepared for what I would find at any of them. As I pulled into the next station, the décor was very proper, professional, and clean. There was not one worn bench and none of the blue and white tiles were missing from the walls. The station looked perfect, and the sign said: "Heigh-Ho It's Off to Work We Go."

The direction of my career was never in doubt; it would be in the mathematics field, even though my grades were not exemplary in college. Thankfully, the thought of getting drafted or having to

David The Beloved

go to Vietnam never occupied my mind. During the spring semester of my senior year in 1967, I started interviewing for jobs as an actuary for insurance companies. Each interview started with the interviewer telling me what my benefits would be while I was "away," and that I would have a job when I "got back" - meaning back from Vietnam. That's when it hit me: "Oh my god, there is a possibility that I will have to go fight in the war in Vietnam." I was not offered many jobs because my GPA was very low: 2.0 (C average). After thirty interviews, only two government weapons labs offered me a job. At the end of an interview with IBM, they said I would need to take a test that focused on mathematics and logic. There were twenty questions, all of which I answered correctly, which made me wonder, Is this the best IBM could come up with? IBM could not believe that someone with a GPA of 2.0 could get all the questions right, so they sent me to their Manhattan office where they gave me a 100-question exam. This one required more thought and insight, and I now gave IBM credit for a test worthy of their name. Once again, I got all the answers right. These tests were actually *fun* to take.

Weeks went by, and no word on a job offer. Then one day, while I was getting fitted for a suit, my mother called at the tailor's shop to tell me IBM had called to apologize for sending my job offer to a David King in the Midwest. The job offer was to be trained as a computer programmer in IBM's Federal Systems Division in Gaithersburg, Maryland. I immediately accepted the job without hesitation.

Off I went to interview with various managers to see which department I would work in. As I sat in the lobby, before speaking

Heigh-Ho It's Off to Work We Go

with the managers, the personnel manager said to the men waiting there with me: "IBM asked for 935 occupational deferments last year and we received 934." I knew down to my very soul that this was the right place for me, and I thought of the line from the movie *Field of Dreams*: "Is this heaven?" Almost all the managers who interviewed me talked half the time about the job opening and spent the rest of the time questioning me about my athletic skills, as it seems the IBM intramurals were highly competitive. When the personnel manager heard that, at twenty-one, I had gone for a tryout with the Philadelphia Phillies baseball team, he drafted me on his fast-pitch softball team. My college buddies thought I had gone to work at IBM on an athletic scholarship. Deferment, no going to Vietnam, intramurals, working on puzzles as a job - I could not have asked for more!!! Yes, the Field of Dreams.

Avoiding the War

As it turned out, IBM's ability to request and get deferments would save my life. In December 1969, a draft lottery for military service was held - and my birth date, July 12th, was the fifteenth date picked. Those in the first hundred and twenty birthdates on the list would be going to Vietnam for sure. This meant that without a deferment, I would have to go fight in the war. I was shocked that my birthday was picked so soon after numbers started being drawn. Right after my birthday number was picked, in the time it takes for someone to remove your hubcap at a red light in New York, my mother called in panic. I didn't know what to say, as I was at a loss for words.

Luckily, the Lone Ranger rode into town in the form of IBM, and over the next two years IBM requested an occupational deferment for me; the deferments were granted based on my computer programming job on a contract with NASA. When President Johnson ended the occupational deferments, IBM gave me the same letter it had been writing to my draft board, but without using the words, "We request an occupational deferment for David King." I attached a cover letter to their letter saying, "Based upon the attached IBM letter I request an occupational deferment." My draft board wrote back with the occupational deferment and basically said, "Don't send us any more letters asking for a deferment." And that was how I stayed out of the horrible war, and avoided the unimaginable prospect of being killed, or killing people who had never done anything to me. Either the guides from the afterlife had protected me or my mother had bribed the draft board. I leaned towards the idea of my mother's intervention.

World, Ready or Not, Here I Come

On graduating from college, I started working for IBM on June 16th, 1967. Boy, how I looked forward to getting out of my parents' house "for good," away from all the repressed hate, fear, and anguish. One of my good friends from CCNY, Michael, whom I used to pick up and drive to college, also took a job with IBM - starting the same day - and we agreed to share a two-bedroom apartment near the IBM building.

Before leaving town, I proposed to my high school sweetheart T. It was to make sure T would be at the next station, "Marriage." There

Heigh-Ho It's Off to Work We Go

was no discussion between my fiancée and me about taking these steps; we just knew it was in the future itinerary. For various reasons we had to wait a year to get married. I was upset, but in the long run it was for the best. It allowed me to get accustomed to going to work five days a week for eight hours a day.

My eight-hour work schedule only lasted a year until I was promoted and no longer received overtime pay. Then the hours increased to fifty or sixty a week, sometimes seven days a week. I was given the impression that this was expected if you wanted to be promoted and get a high evaluation at IBM. I was also in the full swing of the IBM intramurals and IBM Industrial Softball Team, which was all year round. My days were busy and fulfilling, with work, friends, and IBM sports.

My ten-year career at IBM was rewarding. I learned a lot about writing, communications, working with people, and directing people. It was inherent in my DNA to know how to manage. My style at work was like managing a baseball team. People felt cared for and their opinions were heard and sometimes acted on, and because of this, our group performance excelled. This is not boasting: I managed two projects in my last years with IBM that defined my career. One project, I was told, was for President Nixon, who was conned into selling U.S. wheat to Russia for a discounted price, after which Russia turned around and sold the wheat to their satellite countries at market rate. We had only five months to redesign our data analysis computer system to detect how much wheat was being grown year-round in the Soviet Union. No one at IBM or NASA thought we could pull it off, as it should have taken at least ten months to accomplish it. But boy did we. We delivered 98% of the system on time and NASA and IBM gave me awards and a bonus for managing the project. NASA called it one of the two best systems, up to then, ever delivered to NASA. You can Google "LACIE," the first name for the initial mission, which was renamed "LANDSAT" for future missions.

The second project was to lead a team to program the onboard De-Orbit and Re-Entry computer programs for the first Space Shuttle. These programs would bring the Space Shuttle and its astronauts out of Earth orbit for re-entry, and then down for a landing. It was stressful knowing people's lives were at stake, and I made sure that every possible scenario in those computer programs was tested successfully. Even with this carefulness, we managed to complete the task in nine months, though the project was expected to take a year. This was unheard of at IBM in those days. One of the higher-up IBM managers told me that I was a "star," with respect from management as well as the people I managed. People felt part of our team. They trusted me to lead the project to success and that they would be noted for their contributions. Management knew that I would get the job done no matter what, and that the project would be successful. And despite all that success in my career, after ten years, I decided to retire. Just like that! IBM offered me a leave of absence with most benefits in hopes that I would come back. But I knew I was done. As you will read in later chapters, a subtle energy had started moving into the fabric of my inner and outer life; something was directing my actions that did not seem to be coming from "me." The "me" that I knew would not make these choices. But I am getting a little ahead of the story.

T and D Get Married

When T and D (me) entered in holy matrimony, it had been six years since our first dance together. The very first time she had caught my eye was in junior high school, when she was voted "Queen of Hearts" on Valentine's Day. I thought T was very cute, but I was afraid to talk to her. Later in high school, we were in the same Spanish class, where she sat right in front of the teacher. I sat in the back row. There were no interactions between us, either in class or outside of class, and I never saw her in the halls before our chance meeting. My friend Steve and I needed dates for New Year's Eve, a few weeks away. We had decided to go to the Bronx House on Pelham Parkway, which was having a dance that Saturday night. As I was standing in the back surveying the room for possible dates, up walks this cute girl from my Spanish class, who asked me to dance. This was new for me, having a girl ask me to dance, and pretty "cool" back in those days. I said "Yes!" We danced only with each other the entire time, and at the end of the evening I took her home. After making out in the elevator of her apartment building, dating soon followed. How could it not?

When T and I started dating, she was fifteen and I was seventeen. I felt my life was complete, now that I had a girlfriend to go with playing sports with the guys. Six months later, before I started college, T turned sixteen, and I gave her a 14k gold ankle bracelet, which was the tradition in those days for boys and girls going steady. At her Sweet Sixteen party, she was just that – very sweet, and very beautiful as well. We never had any fights while we were dating and going steady. We spent pretty much every weekend together, and it was wonderful. We were relaxed and affectionate with each other. There was love, though I did not know what love was, as there was so much protection around my heart.

Once again, I had found a family to plug into. T's mother was as down to earth as a human being could be – a wonderful, dear person. If I could see my thoughts back then, I'm sure I wished that she was my mother. T's brothers were both into sports, and we had

Marriage, Then Fatherhood – The Joys and Despairs

a great connection. I have a sweet spot in my heart for them to this day. I appreciate seeing them, T, and their mom at significant events involving my son or grandchildren.

After T and I started going steady, her mother frequently said she thought we were too young for it. A year later her mother insisted that T start dating other guys, as she was too young to decide on just me. We started dating other people, but it was useless, as there was no one else that I felt as comfortable with as T. I perceived that she did not want to date other people either. We (probably mostly me) devised a plot to be together. I recruited some of my friends to pick T up at home and bring her around the corner, where I had the car waiting to take her out. Then T and I would drop my friend at the clubhouse, and later in the evening, reverse the process. I truly don't remember asking T to marry me. It just felt like a given. I do remember T and I meeting my Uncle Max in the "diamond district" in Manhattan, where he had connections with jewelers from his job with a company that transported jewelry. We went to a few jewelers until T found the engagement ring she wanted, and that was that. One year later, there we were, standing under the marriage canopy.

Our wedding ceremony was held in a room used for the "Here Comes the Bride" and wedding vows moments. All my friends who had been in on the dating plot and now served as my groomsmen were standing one side of the aisle. As T's mother walked down the aisle with T and her father, she did a double take looking at these guys - her eyes and mouth couldn't have opened any wider. Later, when T and her mom were walking into the banquet room, her mother said to her, "Does Dave know that you went out with his friends?" T didn't tell her about the secret plot. Later, when T told me what her mother had said, I thought maybe she had been right all along, that we *should* have been dating other people. Maybe it *would* have been better for me to start dating other girls. It had felt good to be with T, though, and I couldn't imagine it getting any better with anyone else. And the depth of my love for my son Jason makes me grateful for all the choices I made that brought T and me together, and for the two of us to create such a sweet, beautiful, loving human being.

Nothing in my life to date would prepare me for my married life to come. There were no chats with parents or anyone else to tell me what to expect. Boy, did marriage change everything! I thought life would be the same as when T and I were in school - school and the guys (playing ball and cards) during the week and T and I on the weekend. That was replaced by work at IBM, playing in the IBM sports leagues, and playing cards with men friends. Then T and I and other couples would spend time together on the weekend. I was young and naive, without understanding or caring about what might be going on inside of T. If she shared that with me, it didn't register. My parents never showed any regard for another person's feelings. I had an assumption that I could go out in the world and not give any thought to the reactions and feelings of others, in response to what I did or said. I had no awareness of how the traumas and events of my early childhood were stressing me in my marriage, driving a behavior with a short fuse, and causing me to treat T uncaringly. I would find out much later in therapy how guilty I had felt about it, and how badly I broke my own heart - maybe even more than hers. Later my father would teach me the truth of that statement.

In 1972, IBM created a new chapter in my marriage. The contract I was working on for NASA in Maryland was ending, and IBM gave me the choice of transferring to work on a contract in Houston at the NASA Johnson Space Center or in Atlantic City at a FAA facility. I would be farther away from my parents in Texas, so it was an easy decision for me. I don't remember whether T wanted the same, because she was close with her family, nor whether there were any big discussions or disagreements about the decision to go. We moved to Clear Lake City, Texas. It was what I had hoped. I think T also felt it would be a new beginning for both of us and our marriage. We bought a beautiful three-bedroom house, with vaulted ceilings, wall-to-wall carpeting, a small backyard with a lanai over a small patio, and enough space to plant fruit trees. It even had a wet bar, as alcohol was part of the culture for IBM folks in the area. Career, marriage, house, and now there was one more piece to the picture - family.

Fatherhood - The Birth and My Rebirth

There was a long ride, five years, from the "Marriage" station to get to the "Fatherhood" station. Looking back, it was one huge shock after the next, without enough time to sit back for a moment and think about what had just happened. It felt like being thrown from one "Indiana Jones" adventure to the next, with only a bathroom break in between. It is a big deal to conceive a child, to create a life with another. I hadn't asked myself, "Do I really want to bring a child into my life with T?" We had never discussed whether we felt ready to be parents. It just happened – and at a place I would not have expected.

During a visit to our parents back in the Bronx, we stayed at my parents' house, where I had lived from age ten until I left for work at IBM. We slept in the same room where I'd had the beating when I was almost thirteen. Without being conscious of all that, there T and I were, in mid-November 1972, sleeping in the same bed I had slept in for most of my life. That very night our son Jason was conceived. And my son left the "Begin Lives Train Yard" with T and me on his *own* life's train. I heard the Train Master say, "Congratulations, Jason – you are a lucky boy. You will love and be loved by your parents."

The doctor said that T was built to have children, and once her water broke, Jason came flying out in just ninety minutes. T barely had to use the Lamaze breathing lessons we'd spent many hours learning and practicing. There I was, in the delivery room of the hospital, watching as the doctor maneuvered my son out of T's body into the world. It was surreal, beyond anything I had ever experienced. After those first cries, the doctor put him in my arms, and he stopped crying. I was holding such a vulnerable human being in my arms, and there was such trust from this being. It felt as though I were walking on a cloud, and I'm not sure my

Marriage, Then Fatherhood – The Joys and Despairs

feet even touched the ground as I made the few steps to gently give our son Jason to his mother. From that moment, his mother knew exactly what to do; it was as natural as if she had done it many times before. It was amazing for me to see this - mind blowing in such a profound way.

Afterwards, I sat on a bench in a little locker room outside the delivery room with my face in my hands. No tears, no joy, just the feeling of being in a timeless state. Later in life I would realize that Jason's birth was the start of my rebirth. This sweet, beautiful child that I helped create gave me moments that all the untrue beliefs I held about myself could not diminish.

So here I was in 1973, a first-line IBM manager, with seventeen people reporting to me - a homeowner, a husband, an intramural groupie - and now I was welcomed into fatherhood. Looking back, I had many fears of being a father, especially because of my own father. And sadly, those fears would be realized. I now had everything I had ever dreamed of - career, marriage, child, my own home - and yet I was not happy. I could not stop thinking: *What is wrong with me? I have the dream, yet I am still not satisfied.* I did not dwell on this thought, but looking back on this time, I can see there was something percolating inside of me, though I had no idea what it was and I didn't dwell on it. Shortly, some external events would launch me from my current life into a life I would never have dreamed of for myself. But, once again, I am getting a bit ahead of myself.

Saying the Word "Divorce"

My tracks started going deeper underground, where it was like diving into the ocean depths in a submarine as gravity accelerated my train's speed. My train was now moving in total darkness. This was not a good sign. As my train slowed and pulled into the next station, I noticed some unusual new features. The station was dimly lit and was divided into two parts, which were separated by a big gap of an indeterminable depth that plunged into blackness. The gap was so wide it would have been impossible to leap over it. There were

Marriage, Then Fatherhood – The Joys and Despairs

two exits and I only had access to the exit on the part of the station where my train had pulled in. This station had a very sad and painful feeling about it, and I was very reluctant to get off the train. I knew what would be at the previous stops: career, marriage, fatherhood, but I had no clue about this one! And from here on, all bets were off. For the rest of my life, I had no idea what would be waiting for me at the next station. As I exited the train, I saw T standing on the part of the station across the gap. She seemed far away and seemed very sad - devastated. I wondered what was causing her to look and feel that way. Then I caught a glimpse of the station sign above the gap. The sign read "Divorce."

Before Jason was born, my marriage with T had been difficult, as I became angry and verbally abusive at times. Even so, I never thought about ending our marriage. I didn't even have the wherewithal to stop and look at my behavior, nor did I have any support system in those days. Despite my struggles, the thought of divorce never entered my mind. Nobody in my family had ever gotten a divorce. So why was I at this station? After Jason's birth I was getting less sleep, taking turns feeding him during the night and getting up early to go to work. It was difficult for me, and yet during the night when I sat in the rocking chair holding Jason in my arms and feeding him his bottle, there was no place else I wanted to be. It was natural that T's energy and time were directed toward Jason - this was appropriate maternal behavior. No one had prepared me for this separation from my wife's attention, in which she focused on our child, not on me. After Jason was about nine months old, I was in bad shape. One of the men at IBM who I was friendly with

David The Beloved

was having marriage problems. He told me about a psychiatrist he was seeing. IBM was willing to pay most of the cost for therapy, so I decided to start sessions. It is amazing how one moment, one set of words out of my mouth, changed my entire life.

I had never been to a psychiatrist, or "shrink," as people referred to them in those days. I was uncomfortable, as he asked me personal questions that in some cases I didn't know how to answer. Not many weeks after starting these sessions, as one of our sessions was drawing to a close, I gave a startling answer. The psychiatrist asked me how I felt about Jason getting most of the attention from T. As I talked about it, I became angrier and angrier. Then he asked me what I could do to fix this situation. I said, "I could kill him." It didn't hit me in that moment that those were my father's words. Some people reading this may think I am a monster. I could never hurt my son. In all the years Jason was a child, there was only one time when I slapped him on his bottom. He was three, and I had told him never to go into the street without holding my hand. But one day, he was stepping off the sidewalk with a car coming down the street. I grabbed him by the back collar of his shirt, pulled him back onto the sidewalk, and gave him that one slap on his tush. He was confused, because he didn't understand what had happened - and then he got scared and started to cry. I picked him up, kissed him, and told him I loved him, and I reminded him not to go out into the street without holding my hand. He never did it again, and I never ever hit my son again for any reason. I love Jason more deeply than anyone else on this planet. Those words to the psychiatrist that flew out of my mouth terrified me. The psychiatrist

Marriage, Then Fatherhood – The Joys and Despairs

said, "Okay, that's it for today." My last words in the session were "I could kill him," and he ended the session and let me walk out of his office. Years later, when I told two psychologists in the San Francisco Bay Area about this experience, they were beside themselves that the psychiatrist would let me leave his office with those words hanging in the air.

I drove home from the psychiatrist in tears, developing a plan in my mind to ensure that no harm would come to my son. My mind concluded that if T and I were not together, it would remove any catalyst for my anger to come out. It was my father's anger toward me raising its angry head. I walked into the house and sat down in the living room, crying. T had never seen me cry before. T sat down across from me, and I told her I needed to get a divorce. It was hard to say this to T and it totally blindsided her; she seemed scared and in shock. I had never used the "D" word before. I am sure that nowhere in T's mind had she ever been contemplating the word "divorce." She sat speechless, yet I perceived what she was thinking and immediately followed the sentence with "divorce" in it by saying "It's not another woman!" Yet in that moment, I could not share the reasons for the words coming out of my mouth. We both started crying and saying Jason's name out loud. In these moments the belief, *There is something wrong with me*, was working overtime.

I have told my son many times that I would take a bullet for him, figuratively and literally. I had just given up the most precious part of my life, the deepest love of my heart, to protect my son. Leaving my marriage with T and leaving my son behind for almost a

David The Beloved

year when he was four years old were the hardest things I have ever chosen to do. I feel I saved my son from learning and experiencing the dysfunction that I endured from my parents. And I recognize and acknowledge the truth of this quite often while talking with my son. He is such a sweet and beautiful person and a wonderful father to my grandchildren.

I don't remember how long it took for me to find an apartment, move out, and finalize the divorce, but I think it all went fast. We agreed to have equal custody. Jason lived with me for three days one week and then four days the next. I found a nice one-bedroom apartment nearby and put a crib in the bedroom beside my bed. By some stroke of luck, right across from my apartment lived a young Vietnamese couple who had a two-year-old. The father was an engineer with NASA and his wife stayed home with their baby. On the days I had Jason and had to work, I paid her to watch Jason. This couple were such sweet people. The woman would sing to both children in Vietnamese, and they were so contented being with her. It came as no surprise to me that Jason would choose to marry a Vietnamese woman, as my neighbor had shown Jason so much love and sweetness.

There was much cruelty and abuse I'd had to suffer in my childhood. But the birth of my son, and who he was and is today, has made up for much of it. His birth was truly the catalyst of my rebirth, as you will see in the later chapters.

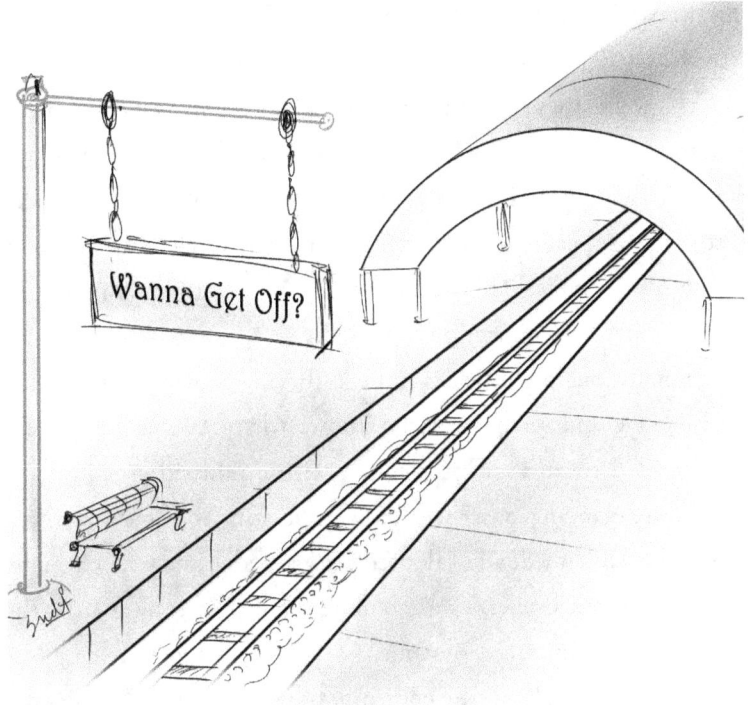

Wanna Get Off?

After I leave the "Divorce" station, to my surprise my train starts to descend even deeper – and still, there's nothing but darkness. I get the feeling, a scary feeling, that I am coming up to the end of the line and I am not even thirty years old. I have reached number "6" on the circle of my life's tracks and the sign at this station says, "Wanna Get Off?"

I was living in an apartment by myself except for the days and nights when I had my son with me. On the days without Jason, I had fewer distractions and started to feel depressed. I was having panic attacks, though I didn't know that's what it was at the time. I had

David The Beloved

an overwhelming feeling of being stuffed down, creating incredible stress and tightness in my belly, stressed from working over fifty hours a week. I was ready to explode from my gut. I felt like a total failure - no marriage, no house, a divorce. The belief that there was something wrong with me was playing like a symphony in my mind, yet I couldn't hear it and was unwilling to feel my feelings. And there was no one I could share all of this with, not even the psychiatrist, as I didn't have any connection to myself.

Finally, one night, I lost it. I was driving angrily down a road, full of rage and screaming who knows what. At that moment, I was headed toward an intersection with a railroad crossing. The bells were clanging, and the gates were starting to come down, but instead of slowing down, I floored the gas pedal, and when I finally slammed on the brakes, I was no more than two feet away from the gates as the train raced past me. I sat there in shock, feeling lost and not able to take in the enormity of what had just happened. I suppressed the whole incident, wiped it from my memory. In that moment death felt like a better option than feeling my feelings. And that belief would stay with me for more years to come.

The Train Yard Master had said that during my birth experience I would get a chance to get off the train. He meant that I would have to fight for my life to stay on the train. And this night, for a few moments, I was ready to get off the train. I could no longer live with the contractions, suffering, and guilt that were playing out inside of me. Yet I chose to stay on the train. You may be wondering why I slammed on the brakes rather than crashing into the train? Why didn't I end my life that night or some other time? I couldn't do it to my son. I loved him so much that I could not place the burden of having a father who committed suicide on him. *There is no one in this world that I love more than my son Jason.* It was my son and the love that we shared that saved my life. This was the beginning of my rebirth. When I slammed on the brakes, my train started heading back upwards, and the lights reappeared on the walls lining the tunnels. And I heard the Train Yard Master's voice: "Hang in there. I'm still rooting for you, kiddo!"

The Best Moment of My Life

My train was now going at a comfortable speed, still heading upwards, but it leveled off as it pulled into the most beautiful station so far. The platform was decorated with many beautiful flowers, especially roses, with butterflies flitting about, and elevator music playing softly. No station up to this point had looked anything like this. Instead of benches on the station platform, there was only a rocking chair. I truly liked being there, and it felt good, but I was also a bit perplexed as to what was going to be presented to me at this place. Then I saw the station sign: "The Best Moment of My Life."

A few months after almost getting off the train for good, I bought a two-bedroom, two-bath, end-unit townhouse near the entrance to the NASA facility. Jason, who was about three years old at this point, now had his own room and his own bathroom. And in his room the absolute best moment of my life occurred. Every night before Jason would go to sleep, I would read him a story, with him in my lap in the rocking chair. When the story was finished, I would carry him and put him into his bed. One night, he kept saying "no" to the books I showed him for that night's story. "No, daddy . . . no, daddy," he would say, shaking his head sideways. I decided to make up a story – and to my surprise, Jason really liked it. He sat mesmerized as I created this story on the fly. From then on, he would not let me read a story from a book; he only wanted to hear made-up stories.

One night I was telling Jason a new made-up story and suddenly out of nowhere, his big brown eyes opened wide and he said to me: "Daddy, I love you." His daddy melted into a puddle of butter. In that moment, my son managed to get through all the protections around my heart, and this touched me so deeply that tears ran down my cheeks. I had only cried a few times in the last few years. This

Marriage, Then Fatherhood – The Joys and Despairs

time it had the flavor of joy to it. *This moment with my son in my lap, looking at me, loving me, was by far the best moment of my life - as good as it gets!* The station sign was right. I will never forget that moment.

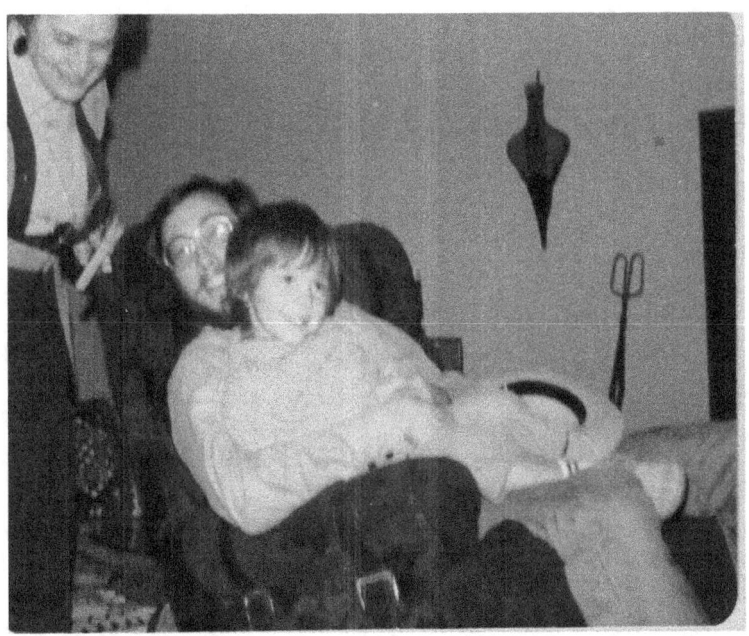

Jason at about three years old, my mother, and yours truly.

As I approach the next station, the train levels off from its upward push, and I truly get the feeling this station will be a respite. I had to wipe my eyes and clean my glasses when I saw the station sign. It said: "My Father's Gift." To me, the phrase "Father's Gift" was an oxymoron. I was very skeptical and wary and moved very slowly, looking all around me, before stepping onto the platform.

In previous chapters I have written how my father acted towards me before I was seven. How sometimes he would be loving, riding me on his knee, and other times annoyed because I and my toys were in his way when he got home from work. All this happened before

David The Beloved

my grandmother suffered her stroke and moved in with us. I also wrote about the abuse and cruelty of the following next six years, the spankings and hitting, and the last beating when I thought he was going to kill me. I wrote about making the two vows. The first was: *I will never let him get to me again*, thereby shutting down my feelings and my heart. And the second vow was: *If he ever hits me again I will get a knife out of the kitchen drawer and kill them both*, meaning my mother as well as my father. By the time my son Jason was three years old, I had shut down my feelings for almost twenty years and hated my father the whole time. Never in my thoughts or even in my imagination did I think anything would change. I didn't even have a conscious thought about the situation. For this entire twenty years I did not talk to my father. If he answered the phone when I called my parents, he would immediately say, "I will get your mother - I know she wants to talk to you - as if to say, *"I don't want to talk to you."* And the disconnect went on and on.

Then one day in 1976, I received a call from my mother saying that my father was going to get on a plane for the first time in his life and fly to Houston to see Jason. And since my mother was terrified of flying, he would be coming alone. I made note that my *mother* was the one who called to tell me my father was coming, not my *father*. Nor did either of my parents ask me if it was okay for him to come. This was my mother's way. I did not make an issue out of it. I let it be, as he had a right to see his grandson and his grandson needed to get to know his grandfather. This would be the first time my father had gone anywhere without my mother. I was a bit in shock, yet it made sense; he was not coming to see me, only his grandson. What else could I think? That he was coming to see me? He didn't love me.

My Father's Gift

I was not *love-able*. If you loved someone, would you hit them, kick them, and yell at them that you are going to kill them? Would you tell them there's something terribly wrong with them and that they are crazy? Of course not! How could I possibly think there was *not* something wrong with me? My mother yelling at me almost daily contributed significantly to this belief. And those years, from ages seven to thirteen, my mind learned how to hide this "something wrong with me" belief. I became a comedian, using humor to make people laugh so they would like me and want to be with me. They would not have a clue about my insecurity and I would not be alone without friends.

It was the day of my father's arrival. I dreaded the moment but somehow avoided freaking out. I wanted everything perfect to avoid any confrontation between us in front of Jason. I truly do not remember how he got from the airport to my townhouse. Nor do I remember anything from the moment he arrived until it was time to put Jason to bed that night. But that moment and the next twenty minutes are etched into my mind.

Jason was playing with his toys on the carpet in the living room, enjoying himself. I told my father I would put Jason to bed. I stayed with Jason for a few minutes until he fell asleep and he made no fuss about not having a story that night. As I went downstairs to the living room, I felt very uncomfortable and awkward about being alone with this man after all that had happened twenty years ago.

When I came into the living room my father was sitting on the love seat and I sat down on the couch, which was placed next to the love seat in an L-shaped pattern. The minute my body hit the couch pillows, my father started talking about his own childhood and his older brother Richard. I was stunned to hear this, to say the least, but I listened attentively. He told me that when he was a boy, his big brother had protected him from his mother, who was always yelling at him. Richard had also protected him from children who picked on him because he was shy and introverted. He told me it had been a difficult childhood, except that his brother cared for him, and he said how much he loved his brother.

This was the first time in my thirty-one years of being his son that my father had talked to me about his childhood. Then he told me the story of how his brother had drowned while swimming in a lake. Even being a good swimmer, his brother could not escape from an undertow that took him down. My father did something I had not seen him do my whole life. He sobbed and sobbed recounting the story of his brother's death. I had not seen him cry when his mother or father died. Now my father was sitting in my living room sobbing. I was in shock and didn't know what to say or do in that moment. And then things got very personal and intimate. He turned to me and told me how sorry he was for all the times he had hit and yelled at me, how much it had hurt him to do that. All the time he was sharing this from the depth of his heart, the tears flowed from his eyes down his cheeks. He said it may have hurt him more than it had hurt me. I started to lose it, slightly, feeling the tears welling up in my throat. Then he *begged* me to forgive him and said how much he truly loved me. That touched me so much that it broke the vow I had made twenty years before. I started sobbing with him. Father and son were sharing the most intimate of moments. I said to my father, through my tears, "All the hate I carried towards you all these years is gone."

My Father's Gift

And since that moment, my father and I would love each other unconditionally for the rest of his life, almost thirty more years. Without realizing it then, my father had given me one of the greatest gifts of my life. My mother's giving me life, my son Jason's love, my grandmother Yetta's unconditional love, and my father's vulnerability and remorse are the greatest gifts of my life. My father and my son gave me the strength, the will, the experience of being touched - all of which contributed to the beginning of my re-birth at the age of thirty-one.

On each of my visits to my parents over the next thirty years, I would have a good visit with my father. I was loving towards him and he would be happy to see me. One day, toward the end of my father's life, my mother called in a panic. She said that she couldn't handle my father anymore. She was now eighty-eight and my father was ninety-seven. My father could no longer walk by himself, which meant he couldn't go to the bathroom himself at night and he had become incontinent. I flew from California, where I was living, to New Jersey, where they now lived. I hired someone to care for him 24/7 and live in the guest bedroom. I rented a hospital bed for him, and put up the rails to ensure he would not wander off during the night. The biggest problem was his incontinence. My father would go berserk when the diapers were put on and immediately tore them off. We could not let him sleep without them because he was soiling the sheets, blankets, and mattress every night. I had to do the unthinkable, the unimaginable - and to this day, I still can't believe I did it. I had to buy restraints for my father's arms and legs so he could not rip or kick off the diapers at night. And he fought to get out of those restraints! He fought to get the diapers off with the ferocity of a young man - certainly not a ninety-seven-year-old man.

I was shocked and brokenhearted watching my father suffer, as he struggled to try to find some dignity. I could not figure out any other way to handle the situation. I whispered to him how sorry I was that I had to do this, and that I loved him.

My Father's Passing

The connection was so solid between my father and me that in 2005, while meditating within a therapy group, I had thoughts and visions. It's not unusual for the mind to have this kind of activity during meditation; it happens all the time. I saw myself dying in a bed, talking to my son and my grandkids. I had never had a "movie" in meditation with words like this in my head. I told them some of the most important life lessons I had learned, and said that after I died, if at all possible, I would be their guide and watch over them. When the meditation was over and there was a break in the program, I went outside and turned on my phone and found I had missed a call from my wife Tatiana, whom you will meet in a later chapter. During the meditation, my father had passed away. Just before he took his final nap, which he did not wake up from, he had asked my mother, "Where is David?" Our connection and our unconditional love for each other were there until his last breath. I feel truly blessed and grateful for our entire lifetime together. I will never forget the lesson he gave me by asking for my forgiveness from the depths of his heart and my lesson of forgiving him for all his cruelty towards me. What a gift my father gave me and my son and my grandchildren! After the funeral I brought his most prized possession, his ukulele, back to California. I took it to a local park that had barbeque pits, and as a

My Father's Gift

sendoff into the afterlife, I burned his uke while shouting out loud, I love you.

I want to share a story about a time I had with my father a couple of years after his visit to Houston. My son Jason was about six at the time. Jason flew from Houston and my father flew from New York to Berkeley (again without my mother) where I was living with a woman named V. (You will also learn more about her in a later chapter.) The four of us drove down to Santa Cruz for the day, had dinner, and then walked through town after nighttime set in. There on the street were two young musicians playing guitars with their guitar cases open for donations from people passing by. They were not having much luck. As we were passing them, my father walked over to them and asked if they knew a particular song; he started teaching them the chords with the hope they would accompany him as he sang it. At this point my father was almost eighty. Now my father was singing in the streets of Santa Cruz. When my father sang, the words and melody came from his heart – and people always felt that. Soon a small crowd gathered to watch this senior singing. The guitar case was filling up with a lot of dollar bills and my father was having the time of his life. He was in his element. Jason and V and I were enjoying being part of the audience, applauding each time he finished a song. I had a hard time getting my father to leave, especially since the musicians begged him to stay; they were setting personal records for earnings in one night. I didn't realize until writing this how proud of my father I was that night. Pop, I hope it is possible for you to sing in the afterlife! I grieved my father's death for a few years, especially around his birthday or the day he passed. The grieving was healing, and it was a good life practice for feeling my feelings once again. One last gift from my father!

After the reconciliation with my father and our time spent together, my train was moving silky smooth up the tracks, as if a crew had been out ahead of my train cleaning the tracks. The train continued upward at a gentle grade and speed, and then once again, when the tracks leveled off, it pulled into the station. The sign said: "Bud's Thing." Who the hell is Bud, and what the hell is his thing? I was not sure this station belonged on *my* life's tracks. When I left the Begin Lives Train Yard, no one could have imagined the stations that would be coming up, starting with this one. Career, Marriage, and Fatherhood were no-brainers. But I could never have seen the next stops coming.

David The Beloved

Settling into Being a Divorcé

Jason was three years old and I was thirty-one, still working at IBM, living in the two-bedroom townhouse, and still seeing the same psychiatrist for reasons I cannot explain. It hadn't occurred to me that he had done anything wrong that fateful session that led me to utter the word "divorce." During the days when there were quiet moments, I realized I was not happy. But by now I had adjusted to being divorced. There were no more episodes of driving toward moving trains to end my life. I had started dating again, but without finding anyone I really wanted to marry or have a long-lasting relationship with. The belief that I needed a woman in my life to survive was simmering on the back burner. This belief went back to childhood. With my grandmother's stroke and the constant disappointment from my mother, which had incited my father's physical abuse, I was devastated and had lost my anchor: those were the two women I had relied on to keep me safe. Thus, I held the belief, "I need a woman to survive" – a woman to replace the two I had lost. My ex-wife T was the "replacement woman" when we were married, and after the divorce I hopped back on the survival raft. What helped me cope was my work at IBM, and thank god! for their intramural sports.

At this time, I was working on the IBM project we had from NASA. Seventeen people were reporting to me and I was feeling the stress that goes with the responsibility of managing such a large group. The psychiatrist said he was going to teach a course at the University of Houston Extension about interpersonal encounters that might help me manage the people in my department. Because of the stress at work, I signed up for the course. The first evening the

Bud's Thing

class met I was surprised not to see my psychiatrist. A Dr. Dinardo was brought in at the last moment as his replacement. He started by throwing out the original class syllabus and turned the focus of the class to self-awareness and spiritual awakening. I dubbed the class, "Bud's Thing," since that was his nickname. I knew nothing about self-awareness or anything spiritual and was venturing into unknown territory. The first evening of class he asked everyone to write down a number from 1 to 10 on how well we knew ourselves. I remember my thoughts being something like, *What is he, nuts?* Mr. Big Shot here wrote down a 10. Of *course* I knew myself. For starters, I was a man, father, athlete, divorcé, and IBMer.

In the weeks that followed, he would play a tape recording of or read from the works of different psychologists or spiritual teachers, and then we'd discuss what we had heard. These included Fritz Perls, Freud, Buddha, Gurdjieff – and then one night he played a tape of Bhagwan Rajneesh (who later changed his name to Osho). I must emphasize that I had never heard of any of these people except for Freud, and the little I knew was that his ideas had something to do with sex. Even more embarrassing was to admit I had never heard of the Buddha. I was truly a kid from the Bronx.

None of these recordings or readings from books had any impact on me until the evening Bud put on the tape of Bhagwan Rajneesh. We were seated on the floor in a big carpeted room used for lectures of forty people, with all the chairs stacked on the side of the room. Bud invited the entire class to lie on our backs. He then put on the tape of Bhagwan, an Enlightened Master who had an Ashram in Poona, India. I knew nothing about Bhagwan, Ashrams, India, meditation, Eastern philosophy, or spirituality. As I listened

David The Beloved

to Bhagwan talk about relationship and marriage, I was struck by the power of the *pauses* between his words. I did not have any *"Ahas,"* but after a few minutes of listening, my head started to feel like a Swiss clock with little men on each side hitting the sides of my head with hammers. Everything he said was simple to understand and didn't sound like Freud's mumbo-jumbo. After a while I got up off the floor, as if in a trance, and walked out of the room and out of the building to the front steps of the entrance. I sprawled out on the steps and spread my arms and legs wide, forming an "X." It must have been quite a scene for the crowd that gathered and watched (I saw them – and didn't see them – at the same time). Then the campus police came. Just then, Bud came out of the building and told the police that he knew what was going on. He helped me up and walked me back to class, holding my arm, and then laid me back on the classroom floor. He sat next to me in a chair, probably to make sure I didn't have any more trance-induced trips to la-la land. He never told me why I had done what I did, and I didn't ask. We would never discuss it.

After the last class, while Jason was with his mom, we had a get-together at my house. Downstairs, people were drinking beer and socializing. Upstairs in Jason's room, Bud was playing another Bhagwan tape. I remember listening awhile and then going downstairs to join the other people, with no repeat of the previous experience, or maybe I got out of the room before anything could happen. Before he left that night, Bud gave me a book by Bhagwan called *When the Shoe Fits*. In the first paragraph of the book, he talks about how when you put on a new pair of shoes you are aware they are on your feet, but after a while that awareness fades completely. That

Bud's Thing

metaphor would be prophetic for the unexpected, unexplainable, unlike-me events that would reset my life from what it had been up to then.

The person I took myself to be was a very good IBM manager, an athlete who played in all the IBM sports, a father, an owner of a nice two-bedroom townhouse; someone who accepted being a divorced man, though not thrilled by it. Being touched by a Master who lived in India was beyond anything I could have conceived happening to me. Here I was, about to make life-changing actions as if I was not the one doing it. I certainly was not connected to my feelings, especially my fear. If I had been, I probably would never have pulled this off. Seemingly out of nowhere, I sold my house and my car, and gave away or sold my furniture and belongings - everything except for what could fit into my new, luxurious, decked-out Ford Econoline cargo van. Then I walked into my IBM manager's office and told her I was planning to retire in a few months, when I reached my ten-year mark with IBM. It was more than remarkable considering how I had lived my life with a non-risk-taking mindset.

Looking back, I truly, truly, truly do not know how I pulled it off without going totally insane. I suppose all the activity involved in closing up my life, job, house, possessions to open up a new life on the road with my new, small, very mobile home, helped me stay out of fear. I created a home inside this cargo van with the help of a small outfit in Houston that customized vans. It had wall-to-wall blue carpet, sliding windows with screens, small fridge, two-burner propane cooktop, sink, couch that opened to a bed when an eating table was removed, drawers under the bed, closet. It had captain chairs and a CB radio. An extended ceiling allowed me to easily stand and walk around in the van. And for the cherry on top of the ice cream soda, the van had an added extended platform in the rear with a generator for power when no other source was available. All in all, quite a machine!

Born in mid-July, I am astrologically a Cancer, the crab; my home has been always important to me. I need a nice home to lie down in to feel safe. Even with this dramatic shift in my day-to-day life situation, I made sure I had the best "mobile home" possible for a journey for which I had no idea where I was going. And inexplicably, I would always keep Bhagwan's book, *When the Shoe Fits*, in the passenger seat. It was not as if I'd been thinking, *Oh, he is the Master and I will take him with me on this journey*. No, I had no idea what I was doing. I did not hear a voice inside my head asking: "David, what the hell are you doing? What, are you crazy? Quit IBM? Sell your house? What are you smoking?" No voice, no questioning what I would be getting myself into. And for sure, I didn't tell my parents until a lot of road to who knows where was behind me.

Saying Goodbye to My Beloved Jason

I remembered reading somewhere that a child takes on all their personality and learning from their parents by age four. This was 1978 psychology. I now know that the undeveloped mind may take longer to form. I waited until after my son's fourth birthday before leaving. I knew we would see each other again, even though I did not know when. In my heart I knew we would not be apart forever. I loved this child as deeply as life itself. I truly felt no one could love their child more - maybe as much, but not more.

Bud's Thing

During the three years after our divorce, Jason's mom and I had split the week with Jason. To go from my half-week with him to not being together at all brought my emotions to new heights. What I was about to do, leaving Jason, was a life-changing event that took an immeasurable toll on me. I would later come to realize the depth of my sadness, regret, and heartbreak over my decision. I would dearly miss holding him in my arms next to my heart, falling asleep with him on my chest, having him in my lap in the rocking chair while telling him a story before bedtime, and all the other moments where we shared our love by playing and just being together.

The day before I left town, I went to the apartment where Jason lived with his mom and stepfather to say goodbye. I took Jason outside the apartment and sat down on the steps that went to the ground floor. Before one word came out of my mouth, I lost it and cried deeply, which made him cry, too. Jason had never seen me cry in sadness, and it scared him. I held him tightly in my arms and told him how much I loved him. I said it would be a while before I saw him again, but that I would call. We hung out together and cried for a while. His mom looked down from the apartment window, and at some point, she came outside to get Jason. He did not want to leave me, and he continued to cry as his mom took him into the house; he reached out his arms to be back in my arms. Then I saw him at the window of the apartment with his hands on the window, as if he wanted to get out, still crying. My heart was breaking into the smallest of pieces watching him desperately try to come back into my arms. I relived my own panic at age seven when my grandmother did not recognize me, and I desperately tried to get back to her side – though this moment with Jason was even more painful. I walked to my van in tears and drove away, missing him terribly already.

Now at 70-plus years old and looking back on my life, this is still the hardest thing I have ever done. It wasn't until I later entered therapy with some very good psychologists that I realized the impact that event had on my heart and soul. I wanted to make sure the generational suffering and dysfunction that I had inherited from my parents, especially from my mother, was not passed on to my son. It broke my heart deeply to sacrifice my time with him to give him a chance at a good life. And years later, seeing the life he has created – and what a beautiful, sweet, loving, independent, and competent man my son has become – I know that my sacrifice supported him in becoming a truly good man.

Head West, Young Man

To this day I cannot imagine how I assimilated the dramatic changes in those months between June and September of 1977 when all the activities of leaving took place. One day in September, after saying my goodbye to my son, I set out, heading west from Houston. My train had left the "Bud's Thing" station and there was light ahead. The light got brighter and bingo! the train was out from underground. I found myself on the upper deck of my train car with big windows all around with an uninterrupted view of the scenery. "This is not the Bronx, Mr. King."

It took me two days just to get out of Texas. Absolutely boring ride for two days! I wanted to see Mexico, or at least set foot into the country. I parked my car on the U.S. side of Juarez and walked across

Bud's Thing

the bridge. As I walked around the streets near the bridge, I started feeling contracted. I had been outside the country twice: in 1967 to go to the World's Fair in Montreal with T, and in 1968 to go on my honeymoon with T to Puerto Rico and St. Thomas. In Montreal I felt contracted when we got lost. One of my friends saw a postal carrier and he started speaking French to ask him for directions. The postal carrier, in a pure Brooklyn accent, said "Go down three blocks and take a left." Hearing that he was from Brooklyn I felt at ease. Now I was in Mexico, feeling contracted very quickly, and after a few minutes I headed back across the bridge to U.S. soil. I got back into my van and headed north, as I had always wanted to visit the Rocky Mountains.

I stopped in Santa Fe, New Mexico, for a meal. Afterwards, I was walking down a side street off the main square when a vacant lot drew my attention. As I passed the vacant lot my hands started vibrating. I looked at my hands in disbelief. Vibrating hands? I was not scared at all, but my curiosity took over. I crossed the street to get away from the vacant lot and my hands stopped vibrating. When I walked back to the edge of the lot they started vibrating once again. And when I walked onto the lot, the vibration increased. Without any idea why, I took it to be a sign that I should stay in Santa Fe. But I didn't - at least not that time.

The vibrating hands reminded me of an experience I'd had with Bud before leaving on my journey. Bud held groups where he conducted awareness exercises. One of the exercises was to put your attention into your hands. When I did that, I became aware of a small vibration in my hands. I started doing this exercise a lot, especially when I took walks. And now in Santa Fe, it was happening

David The Beloved

without my doing anything. I did not realize at the time that I was being introduced to the reality of my body's electrical nature. I found out later that, for many years, a community of Sikh people had had a restaurant on that vacant lot. I could feel their energy even after the restaurant was gone. I was starting to learn about energy, and here again, "This is not the Bronx, David" comes to mind.

I was not quite ready to stay in Santa Fe, so I left the next day and continued heading north for Rocky Mountain National Park. That was the place I was most looking forward to, as I had seen pictures of the beautiful mountain lakes, and I love lakes. As I entered the Rockies through Estes Park, a small parking lot next to Bear Lake presented itself. Bear Lake was visible from the parking area. I decided to walk over to it when I observed several people feeding wild rabbits. Excited as a ten-year-old, I ran back to the van for some bread and then waited for a turn to feed these beautiful creatures. When I got my chance, I kneeled on both knees, and put my hand out to the rabbits. They came within three feet of me but wouldn't come any closer. Gently, I threw some bread to the rabbits and they took it and ate it on the spot. I felt trusted, surrounded by the beauty of nature – and there was still more to come.

I hiked up the paved trails from the parking lot to the upper lakes to eat my lunch. The paved trails ended, becoming dirt trails that overlooked beautiful lakes with no people around. I found a lake with a huge rock jutting over the water and decided to eat my lunch on this big rock. As I approached it, two small chipmunks scurried over to me. I was prepared to do the same thing I had with the rabbits. I put a piece of bread in the palm of my hand expecting to toss it to them, but before I could toss it, the chipmunks

Bud's Thing

came right up to me and put their front paws on my fingers and ate the small pieces of bread right out of the palm of my hand. For a kid from the Bronx, this was really something! I was immediately brought into the moment by the trust these little critters bestowed upon me. It felt as if they were my pets, endearing themselves to me from the moment we met.

There was more to come. In a few moments I climbed up onto this big rock that jutted out into the lake. I was all alone at this lake in the Rockies. Me! I didn't physically pinch myself, yet I had this head shake and thought, *Am I really here? Is this a movie?* Sitting on this rock over a beautiful, peaceful lake with my chipmunk friends at the base of the rock waiting for my return, I became a part of this natural setting. No more, no less. Even though I was totally alone, I was not anxious or scared, not the least contracted. Unusual for me in those days. I took out my sandwich and started to eat it. A bird flew over to me and hovered right in from of me. Once again, I took a small piece of bread, put it in the palm of my hand and held it out. The bird came and sat on my fingers, took a few gulps, getting the bread down, and flew off. "I never want to leave this place," I cried, out of joy. Rabbits, chipmunks, and birds surrounded me, reminding me of "Snow White" in the forest, when she's visited by her animal friends. After finishing my lunch, I sat down on the ground with my back to the rock, and the chipmunks came back with their family and friends. I had nothing to give them, only my gratefulness for wanting to be with me. I did not want to leave this place and for a while I contemplated how I might live there. I have an intention to revisit that park before I venture to the afterlife.

David The Beloved

The Adventure Continues

Leaving Colorado, I headed for Wyoming to visit the Grand Tetons and Yellowstone Park. Throughout this journey, traveling through this natural beauty of the West, the kid in me was wide eyed, like an innocent child seeing a snowflake for the first time. The natural beauty of the Rockies and the intimacy and trust I felt in my encounters with the animals there filled my heart and soul with joy. It was an experience I have cherished ever since.

I had heard many wonderful things about the town of Jackson Hole, and they would prove to be true. I hung out in town for a bit, though all the while itching (a Western term I picked up) to get to the Tetons. In the Rockies all the animals were friendly, social, and trusting. But on my first evening in the Tetons, I would come face to face with the "real" wild. I parked my van near a magical place called Jenny Lake. It was as beautiful as any place on Earth I had ever seen. It felt even more alive than the lake where I'd had lunch that day in the Rockies. I decided to bring my dinner down to the lake. The water was still, and the mountains in the background had a dusting of snow. It was an idyllic setting, peaceful, safe, which allowed me to relax and become part of the scene as I had in the Rockies, no longer an observer. And time seemed to stop. I had the feeling that if I had looked at a watch, the hands would not be moving. I ate my dinner slowly, unlike my usual eating speed, and just sat there for a while in this thoughtless space, then headed back to the van.

As I started my return trip from the lake back to the van, I was walking along, without a care, when suddenly, blocking my path, there was a bear. A REAL LIVE BEAR! A really big, furry, brown

Bud's Thing

BEAR! Not a teddy bear, a real one! I FROZE! The bear stopped in its tracks about thirty feet in front of me; the bear turned its head ever so slowly to look at me. Not one muscle moved in the rest of its body. I stood like a statue. *I was not even blinking!* After what seemed a lifetime, the bear turned its head back away from me and continued the slow walk, probably toward the closed ranger station to look for food. I took a HUGE detour to get back to the van. I am sure I was in shock. This was real life - not a movie. Thankfully, the bear didn't see me as a threat, or maybe I was not on the dinner menu. When I got back to the van, I told two guys who were camping in tents near the van about my bear encounter. They seemed a bit nervous and asked if they could hang out in the van. I said sure, and we listened to the World Series on my radio.

The next day I went hiking with them, as they were experienced hikers. We got to a place where they turned white - and without saying anything, one pointed to scat on the ground and we immediately turned around. When we were safely away, they said it was a mountain lion and the wind was coming from behind us. Not a good place to be. I now had a taste of the Wild West. That was enough for me. Time to "mosey on," as they say in the West.

Off I went to Yellowstone and West Yellowstone. After watching the TV Western series *Lonesome Dove*, I always had a hankering to go to Montana. On the way I passed a herd of bison for the first time, up close and personal. You just don't see too many bison where I have lived my life. I had to stop and marvel at these animals. One of them near the fence let me touch it. Another highlight of my journey with animals. I continued on to visit "Old Faithful" and see the geysers, but after my incredible experiences with the animals, I thought it was no big deal. So, there was water spouting out of the ground. I have seen that in New York when a pipe breaks and shoots water up into the air and all over the street.

I found a local store in the park, with a school nearby, and bought some supplies. When I was leaving the store, I noticed two bucks going at each other with their antlers. I sat on a picnic bench, with light snow falling, watching a real-life male deer match. As awestruck as I was by the bucks, the children coming out of the small school walked within twenty-five feet of the bucks and didn't even take notice of them. Equally surprising was that the bucks took no notice of the kids. The kids and the bucks lived together and trusted one another. What a wonderful way to live with the environment that surrounds you.

I left West Yellowstone and again headed north, this time for Glacier National Park in Montana, and since I was close to Canada, I thought, why not go there as well? By now it was October, the snow was falling hard, and the van didn't have snow tires. My instinct was to head south away from the snow, so I decided to drive back to the airport in Salt Lake City and fly to Las Vegas to gamble for a day. Nothing made sense at this point. I was just moving the way I wanted to go - at least that is how it seems as I look back forty years. When I got back to my van in Salt Lake City after some fun in Vegas, I was very tired of being on the road. I was reminded of the movie *Forrest Gump - the* scene where he had been running and running - and then there was a moment when he got tired and wanted to go home. Me too. I wanted to go home! But where was home? I did not consider Houston my home anymore. If not back to Houston, then

Bud's Thing

where to? I remembered the vibrating hands in Santa Fe, which I had taken to be a sign, and that is where I went next.

Throughout this journey, there were many times when I felt lonely and would lose it and get really scared. When this happened, I would look over at the book in the passenger seat beside me, *When the Shoe Fits*, and I would yell, really yell, in anger or fear or both, at the picture of the Master: "This is all your fault!" *Where the hell did those words come from?* I had no idea who this man was or how my life would revolve around him in the near future. I had no idea who or what was in store for me that would guide my life in the years to come. My life as it was about to unfold was unimaginable. I had not the foggiest idea what the next stop on my life's tracks could possibly be.

I had assumed the next station sign would say "Santa Fe," as that was where I was headed. I expected to see a New Mexico motif at the station and that was exactly what was there as the train slowed into the station. The train doors opened, and just as I was about to walk through them, they closed again. The train pulled slowly out of the "Santa Fe" station and went right into a station with walls decorated with multicolored garlands of sweet-smelling flowers in red, yellow, white, and orange. There was also a strange smell, like a combination of incense and cow dung, and on cue, in came the cows. The aroma of the garlands, incense, and cow manure was as foreign to my senses as the thought of milking one of these cows. I was confused. The line that Dorothy says in the *Wizard of Oz* came to me: "Toto, I've a feeling we're not in Kansas anymore." Well, "This is not the Bronx, David." The station sign said, "Enjoy Your Trip to India." I now assume my life's tracks are going to India. I am quite puzzled about the events about to happen that will get me to India. I am thinking, *There is no way I am going to India, NO WAY!* But there was indeed a way - and it would present itself shortly.

Santa Fe

In Santa Fe I found a beautiful adobe cottage to rent on the Old Pecos Trail. A cute place with a galley kitchen, then down a few steps to a big living room with a fireplace. Two adobe walls about five feet high created a private area for a bed. A beautiful blue-tiled bathroom was a few steps down from the living room. I now had a lovely place to live.

I started exploring the town to find places to shop for food and other needs. Other than the owners of the cottage, a nice couple whom I rarely saw, there was no one to talk to or hang out with, so I spent most of my time in the cottage. I felt lonely spending so much time alone, and I was starting to worry about my savings. For those reasons I went job hunting and found an ad for a computer programmer at a local bank. The manager of the computer operations at the bank told me I was overqualified but said she would make an exception as she was originally from Long Island, near New York City, and would like to have someone around who talked with a

Enjoy Your Trip to India

New York accent. She was right, I was overqualified, and I'd be paid about thirty per cent of what I had earned at IBM. I didn't care and took the job anyway, because I wanted to be around friendly people. I thought this new job would alleviate my constant loneliness; unfortunately, that was not the case. Though it helped a bit, I was still spending nights and most meals alone. Where could I find relief from this lonely feeling?

I have a belief that to feel okay I need the place where I live to feel safe and comfortable, which this cottage was; I need to have a job earning a living, which I now had; and I need to have a woman in my life; this was not the case. I still carried the belief from childhood, after my grandmother's stroke and my mother's yelling episodes that I needed to have a woman in my life or else I would die. It sounds dramatic, but a seven-year-old mind created this belief and it was still active without my awareness of it.

One of the tellers at the bank where I worked was a beautiful Hispanic woman whose ancestors had come from Spain centuries ago. After schmoozing with her a bit, we started dating and I soon fell in love with her and her young daughter, who was a joy to be with. Once more, I had secured my survival needs: safe employment, a cozy cottage to go home to, and an exciting new relationship that included a family - all the pieces of life that would tell me, "I'm okay." But once again, that was not to be.

Behind the scenes there was a longing and heartache stirring in me, the same stirring that caused me to uproot my life in Texas and leave IBM and my son behind. One night, in the depth of this anguish, I lost it while sitting at the dinner table in the living room of my cottage. I wept from the depth of my heart, forlorn and

David The Beloved

brokenhearted. In front of me was the book Bud had given me: *When the Shoe Fits* by Bhagwan Shree Rajneesh. Without a clue why, I put my hand down on the book and at that moment a wave of calm came over me. I felt fine; better than fine. It was instantaneous. I just sat there for a while, taking in this new way of feeling. After accepting this state of being, without thinking, I looked inside the book to see where this man could be found. He lived in the city of Poona (now known as Pune), India. I now know I had a connection with him, that I had experienced his love and grace from halfway around the world. And I know I could send and receive love to and from people not right next to me. This realization would later become very evident when I had my journey with cancer.

To India I Go

Without considering my job, my rental cottage, or my budding relationship, I called a travel agent the next morning and booked a flight to India. This repeated my pattern of leaving Texas, only this time my rent was paid three months in advance, I did not sell any of my possessions, and I had to let go of my relationship. She was such a sweetheart and I loved her, but "the calling" was too strong - I had to go! I did not stop to think about the consequences. I was going!

Just as when I left Texas, there were no thoughts about possible dangers of embarking on such an adventure. *Me?* I'd never been very far outside of the U.S. and now I was flying to India where I knew no one. Only later I would mutter these exact words: "What the hell did you get me into this time, David?" I called Bud and told him

Enjoy Your Trip to India

I was going to India. He wrote to three sisters he had befriended when he was in Poona, who managed the Amir Hotel, and arranged my hotel reservation. They really liked Bud, as he would bring them their favorite chocolates from the United States. He told them to "take good care of him," and they did.

Before leaving for India, I bought a box of their favorite chocolates and would guard them with my life on the long journey, as they were almost as important as my passport. My only previous flight outside of the U.S. was for my honeymoon with T in Puerto Rico. First, I took a flight from Albuquerque to San Francisco to visit the meditation center run by disciples of Bhagwan. It was a stopover before leaving for India in a few days. At the time I did not have a true understanding of "disciple" and "meditation." Disciple, I would learn, meant someone who follows the teachings of a leader of a spiritual sect or an Enlightened Master. I would find out specifically, years later, what it meant to me personally to be a disciple of Bhagwan. It didn't occur to me at the time that "meditations" happened at meditation centers. I had never been to such a place or even tried to meditate. Once I had watched a segment about Transcendental Meditation (TM) on TV and thought the people sitting cross-legged on the floor looked weird.

This day at the meditation center introduced me to meditation in a taken-aback moment. Entering the meditation room, I found people dressed for a workout, not how I had conceived of meditation. I was wearing jeans and felt out of place. This meditation was active (we were not just sitting on a mat on the floor); instead, it included shaking the body, dancing, sitting, and then lying still – all with our eyes closed. I followed along half-heartedly, wary of the experience, periodically sneaking peeks at others to make sure I was safe. Years later, I would be leading these same meditations myself, and guiding new meditators through their fears and hesitations assuring them that "no one has ever died" during this meditation. Most of the time they would laugh, which helped to release stress.

Two days before leaving for India, I flew my girlfriend to San Francisco from Santa Fe. The farewell in Santa Fe had not been enough, and we spent a beautiful weekend together. Two days later she took a flight back to Santa Fe and I was off to Poona, India, with a day-long stopover in Hong Kong (then still a British colony). I would be in the air for twenty-four hours, as we needed to fly around Viet Nam and not over it, even though the war had ended a couple of years earlier. I was on a Pan Am flight that was relatively empty, which gave me the luxury to stretch out and sleep. My meals were cooked to order on a big grill in the middle of the plane. Every moment was a new experience for me; I felt bewildered, in awe, and I questioned myself for doing it. And even though these new experiences were coming one after another without much time to assimilate the experience, this kid - who used to walk the streets of the Bronx like he owned the joint - was hanging in there, humbled by all the newness.

Hong Kong Basketball

Arriving in Hong Kong with a layover till the next night gave me the opportunity to explore. Near the hotel was a park where people were doing Tai Chi. I also noticed a group of men playing full-court basketball. Instinctively, I ran back to the hotel, grabbed and

Enjoy Your Trip to India

laced up my sneakers, and quickly returned to the basketball court at the park. I stood beside the court watching the men playing the game, hoping they would notice my body saying, "Please, please, I want to play, pretty please." My wish granted, they waved me onto the court - I was so happy! Sports had always been the barrier breaker for me with other people - a place where I felt safe. I ran onto the court without feeling my feet touch the asphalt. There was a moment in the game when I realized that I was the tallest player, at 5 feet, 10 inches. I held my own, throwing only one bad pass (not that bad), which prompted a player to say to me, "You are a rousey rasser!" This is not a typo and not meant to be disrespectful of the Asian culture, which I feel deeply connected to. Those were his exact words and the only words spoken to me during the game. After the game a few of the men came over and shook my hand with big smiles on their faces. I felt proud that I allowed myself to be vulnerable and stand on the side of the court as I did. The men's smiles meant so much to me.

Am I really in India?

That night I flew from Hong Kong to Bombay (now called Mumbai), India. Bud told me to take a rickshaw from the airport to the main train station, and take the Deccan Queen train, as it had a nice first-class compartment. As the rickshaw traveled to the train station, we passed the slums of Bombay. The stench was horrible, the poverty was horrible, and it was the beginning of the culture shock of being in India and it's a wonder I didn't throw up. Arriving at the train station, I was mobbed by children wanting to walk me to the station in

David The Beloved

front of me. I had changed money at the airport before leaving and I picked one of the little kids and gave him a few rupees (in those days one rupee was worth less than fifteen cents), hoping he would be happy and the others would leave me alone. The kid wanted to carry my backpack, but I thought it would be too heavy and I was not letting it out of my possession (remember the chocolates for the sisters). Standing on the station platform I realized I was the only American and the only Westerner. That fact made me a bit nervous.

As I bought my ticket, I asked how soon the Deccan Queen would arrive and was told five hours. Now I graduated from nervousness to scared, really scared. If I'd been religious, that might have inspired a conversation with God. Instead I saw two soldiers with rifles, and I went over and sat on the ground next to them. They spoke English fluently and one of them asked me where I was going. I said Poona, on the Deccan Queen. He said the Deccan Queen would not arrive for many hours and pointed to a train a few tracks away that would be going to Poona in twenty minutes. I immediately boarded the train without thinking that the Deccan Queen's first-class compartment might be worth waiting for. The first-class compartment on this train was in worse shape than the oldest New York City subway car. It was all metal, cold feeling, more like a big steel mousetrap. My belly was tight and there would be no relief for a couple of hours – I was in survival mode.

At each stop, people would shove their hands into the windows for *"baksheesh baba,"* wanting me to give them money, but I was too afraid to start. After about two hours, a gentleman in a suit came up to me. He said he worked for the railroad and asked if I would like to join him in his private compartment. His private compartment was like a prison cell. It had metal walls and windows with metal bars to keep people from putting their hands through the windows, and two metal benches facing each other. I thought, *This is an upgrade from first class?* Now I knew why Bud had advised me to take the Deccan Queen. This man was curious about the United States and for an hour we had a nice conversation. After he got off the train and I was alone in the compartment, the enormity of what I had done by leaving Santa Fe finally hit me. That's when I said those infamous words out loud: "What the hell did you get me into this time, David?" I was overtired, overwhelmed, in a state of disbelief and total culture shock. The Bronx kid in me who owned the joint as a small child was exhausted. But I had to find the energy to stay alert, as I had no idea what was coming up next.

I knew I had arrived in Poona, as the real train station sign had Poona in English and Hindi. I was so grateful that the station was only a short walk to Hotel Amir. By Indian standards, it was a three-star hotel. The woman at the front desk (one of the sisters) was expecting me. From the time I boarded the train in Bombay until I got to the front desk at the Amir, I had forgotten all about the chocolates. Now I feared whether the chocolates were going to be good enough, since the quality of my room depended on that. I walked up to the front desk and introduced myself by saying "I'm Bud's friend" while handing her the chocolates. When the woman opened the chocolates, the joy on her face allowed me to relax. I

David The Beloved

was indeed given a good room over the kitchen, on the side of the hotel in the shade in the afternoon. This was important because in a couple of months the temperature in India would become unbearably hot. Thanks to high ceilings and a big ceiling fan, the temperature in my hotel room was delightful. The room had plush old furniture and a private bathroom. When I walked into the room, I collapsed on the bed fully clothed. My words before passing out were, "Thank you, Bud." After sleeping for a while, I checked out the hotel. There was a dining room in a white and blue motif, with big columns along two of the walls. The tables and chairs were simple, and the tablecloths looked meticulously ironed. Outside in the back, there were manicured grounds with chairs to sit in the shade or under umbrellas. The room, the hotel, and its surroundings gave me a sense of being settled after such a long and arduous journey. The expensive chocolates I had brought the sisters felt more and more like a great investment.

Bud had told me to check in at the office at the ashram after I arrived and ask for a Darshan with Bhagwan. I was unfamiliar with the words "ashram" and "darshan," but I didn't ask Bud to explain them to me. I did what Bud told me to do since I trusted him. So, as instructed, I took a rickshaw from the hotel to the ashram. Bud did not tell me that these rickshaw drivers were obviously trained by retired New York City cab drivers. They drove as if they were in a race for their life. I got used to it, but it still was an unnerving adventure every time. On the ride to the Ashram we passed large, old, run-down mansions in need of repair. Because of these mansions, Poona was called "The Beverly Hills of India," though I had a hard time understanding the comparison.

Poona

When I walked through the gates of the ashram, I was hit with another culture shock. Before me were crowds of people of all ages and from all over the world wearing red or orange clothing and dark-brown, wood-beaded necklaces with a picture of Bhagwan hanging from them. This necklace was called a "mala," which means "meditation garland" in Sanskrit. As I walked through the crowds, my blue jeans and blue shirt stuck out like a sore thumb, and that made me contract. I did not enjoy feeling like the new kid on the block. There was nothing to do about it, though. Everyone could see I was a newbie, and some people even smiled at me, knowing what would happen when I met Bhagwan.

I went directly to the office to inquire about receiving a Darshan and was greeted by a short, extremely thin woman – she could not have weighed more than eighty pounds soaking wet. I immediately put aside her fragile stature when I heard her speak with such softness, grace, and clarity. She told me to come back in a couple of days. When I returned, the same woman told me I could go to darshan that very night. I found out much later that darshan in the Hindi language means "a meeting with the Master." In India, this seemed to be the equivalent of a meeting with the Pope if you were Catholic. I spent the rest of the day preparing for the Darshan as instructed. Bhagwan had allergies and I was told to wear clean clothes, be freshly bathed, with hair shampooed, but with no scents of any kind.

That night I lined up with others as we made our way to the entrance, where we were sniffed by two people to make sure there were no lingering scents on our body. We then entered a small outdoor patio, beautifully paved in marble. In the middle of the room was an empty chair, placed there for Bhagwan, with the attendees seated

David The Beloved

on the floor in a semi-circle in front of the chair. To the right side of the chair, "mediums" – all beautiful women – sat on the floor in a cross-legged position. I was told that they channeled the energy in the room through them, which Bhagwan would then direct. I now understand why they looked so blissed out during the darshan, but at the time I thought they were just out of it. Off to one side of Bhagwan's chair, a redheaded bodyguard sat cross-legged on the floor. The bodyguard had an imposing presence, and even though he didn't appear to carry any weapons, there was no doubt that he would and could protect Bhagwan. All these people by Bhagwan's chair wore red robes and the mala – this was a sign that they had become disciples. Many of the attendees already wore the clothes and mala of a disciple, and others, like me, wore Western garb in all colors. And now, as the last moments passed before Bhagwan would enter, I realized this would be the first time I would finally see this man whose energy had touched me so powerfully that I would uproot my entire life in Texas, journey through the Western states and uproot myself again – this time from Santa Fe – and then travel halfway around the world. The Mr. Bigshot in me thought, *This had better be good!*

A door opened in the house at the back of the patio, and Bhagwan walked into the patio wearing a beautiful white robe. He walked gracefully, without a single muscle moving out of place, while holding his hands in the *"namaste"* position (which means "I see the divine in you," in Hindi), with his palms together and his fingers pointing up and at his nose level. At the time I had no idea what it meant. New words and new experiences were piling up by the moment. His walking was more like shuffling, as the steps were small, and he moved from the doorway to his chair with an authentic smile that lit up the room. During this short path to the chair, he would *namaste* in the direction of everyone in attendance. When he arrived at the chair, he removed a clipboard and pen from the chair and then slowly sat down with such grace and lightness, like a feather falling and landing without disturbing the seat.

At some point, new people to the ashram were called up one by one and asked by Bhagwan if they were ready to take Sannyas and become a Sannyasin (become a disciple). If they answered "yes," then Bhagwan gave them a new name that was representative of "who they really were," and if they were a Westerner, he would recommend a few therapy groups. I had no idea what being a Sannyasin or disciple meant; as I mentioned earlier, it would be years before I really understood disciple-hood. When my name was called, I got up and sat cross-legged on the floor in front of Bhagwan. He asked me if I wanted to take Sannyas and I said "yes." I am not sure who was saying "yes," but "yes" it was. Some might think this was brainwashing, but it was not, not in the least.

"David Becomes a Disciple" by Cartoonist Sudi Narayanan
(Swami Anand Teertha)

David The Beloved

Sitting there, I felt a mixture of being very lost and very present without knowing what was really happening. He then told me to close my eyes, put my arms out to the side, and listen to the birds, which were bountiful in this area. This was the same pose, with my arms extended, that I had taken on the steps of the university after hearing Bhagwan's voice for the first time on the cassette tape in Bud's class. A few seconds went by that felt timeless. All the while during this timeless state he had his finger on my third eye. I felt the awareness that I was empty; I was *aware of* my body, yet it was *not* my body. This "emptiness" gave way to the feeling of knocking on death's door that I may have experienced at my birth. Then he removed his finger from my forehead, and said, "Very good" with a smile. He then wrote on a piece of paper for a few moments, looking at me once. I had no idea what was going on and what was coming next. I was not confused; I was alert and present - just in a "not knowing" place - and fixated on watching his every move. When he finished writing, he looked at me and told me the new name he had given me: "Shunyam Arihanta," which means *Emptiness and Nothingness* - which gave me the image of the double zero on the roulette table. At that moment, I was in the state of being of emptiness, not much life inside of me after the extreme contractions I had lived with. I hadn't known anything else was possible. A few years later I would have moments where I felt an emptiness that felt like being filled with all that life has to offer. I now see in that moment that I was like a caterpillar just starting the process of shedding my outer body, my old ways of being. And I felt the process to my freedom beginning, so that in time, the butterfly - as David the Beloved - would emerge.

Poona

Next, he wrote down three therapy groups, but before handing me the paper, he looked at me once again and then crossed out the third group and wrote down a different group. All new arrivals participated in the first two therapy groups, which focused on connecting with and grounding into the energy of the ashram and ourselves. The group crossed out by Bhagwan was the "Encounter Group," and in its place, he wrote "Tao Group." The Encounter Group was led by Bhagwan's chief disciple. In this group, there would at times be bodily fights between participants, in which people actually broke bones. Based on my history of physical abuse as a child, if he had given me the Encounter group, I would have been on the next flight back to the States. Instead, he gave me the Tao group, led by a man named Amitabh, from Berkeley, California. At that moment and for days to come I would not know anything about these groups or the people who led them. But I would soon find out!

After giving me my Sannyasin name and the three group assignments, Bhagwan put a mala over my head and around my neck. He also gave me a small, beautifully carved teakwood box that would later cause me much grief upon my return to the US. With the gifts of a new name, mala, and teakwood box I went back and sat down feeling even more lost, not knowing the me who had entered the room just thirty minutes earlier. After the darshan was over, Bhagwan slowly rose from the chair, raised his hands in *namaste* to everyone, and then walked back into his house exactly as he entered, with shuffled steps.

I took a rickshaw back to the hotel and collapsed on the bed, fully clothed, without enough energy to even floss my teeth. The next day I went out and bought all new clothes in shades of red and sold my Western clothes to Indian people on the street near the ashram for peanuts compared to their cost in the U.S., without caring. Buying new wardrobes, new furniture, and new cars had become a pattern that would continue, as you will see later in my story. Within a few days, I realized I had only taken Sannyas so as not to stand out, to feel more comfortable being there among all these red- and orange-clothed disciples. I still had no real idea what the hell I was doing there in India. I also still didn't know what Sannyas, meditation, the new clothes, the mala, the groups – and for that matter what *anything* was!

Amitabh

A petite woman from New Zealand, who had already become a disciple, befriended me at a coffee shop the day after I became a Sannyasin. During our chat she asked what groups Bhagwan had suggested for me. That was the moment when I found out I had dodged a bullet by not getting put into the Encounter group. She had done the Encounter Group with her boyfriend and while in the group he cheated on her with another woman. They had a physical confrontation and this petite woman beat the crap out of this six-foot guy. She was *total* in her anger. I decided to add New Zealand to Philadelphia as women not to mess with. I learned that Amitabh was known to be a loving, dear man. Amitabh would become a loving father figure, my therapist, and eventually one of my dearest friends, a buddy. I would love him more than I could ever know, and he would become my support for over thirty-five years of my life.

Poona

Amitabh was fourteen years older than me, but as it turned out we were both born in the Bronx, to Jewish parents, and our birth places were less than half a mile apart. This commonality of culture allowed me to put so much trust in him, even before knowing him very well. Because of all the roles he filled for me, he was the most important person in my life for keeping me from "getting off the train." After I participated in his group in Poona, our years together had me attending his therapy groups and having individual therapy sessions with him. Part of it was needing professional help from all the suffering caused by my mind's judgmental thoughts that seemed to be running non-stop. But I also just wanted to be around him, and felt safe being in his presence.

Years went by, and one day out of the blue, Amitabh asked me to organize his groups. That brought me more into Amitabh's life and unknowingly made my desire to be around him easy to achieve. Years passed, many therapy groups and private sessions passed – like the lyrics in the song, "Sunrise, Sunset" from *Fiddler on the Roof*: "One season following another, Laden with happiness and tears." So was my life throughout the years around Amitabh. He was a constant, an anchor for me. Later in the thirty-five years in each other's lives we became friends. I would find ways to drop the fact that he was my psychologist and just be with him as a friend and buddy. I remember one night we were watching a very exciting University of California, Berkeley basketball game that went into multiple overtimes. I was really getting worked up and yelling at the TV and he said to me, "What would you do if I shut off the game right now?" I turned to him and said in a high pitch in my best Bronx style: "I would kill you." He just laughed. In that moment we were just buddies.

David The Beloved

Thirty-five years after we first met, Amitabh was diagnosed with pancreatic cancer and called me to tell me the news. He said to me, "I'm worried about you." Here was a man who was told he was going to die, and he was worried about *me*. He had so much love for me, more than I allowed myself to let in while he was alive; sadness arises in me as I write these words. He knew the darkest places in me and yet he still chose to spend time with me. I want to share the last two times I spent with Amitabh before his passing.

The first was a week before his spirit left the body. I was there with Amitabh with our friend Narayana. Narayana and I had both known Amitabh for many years through Amitabh's therapy groups. Now in this moment, with Amitabh sleeping, Narayana and I sat there meditating - one on each side of the bed, in line with Amitabh's head. Being with this dear man, whom we loved, and were grateful to - we felt deeply honored to spend this time with him before his journey into the afterlife.

The second time was the night before Amitabh's passing. I was waiting to say goodnight and goodbye as I was told it was getting close to his final moments. Amitabh was sitting on the portable commode with his wife, Mradu, by his side. I kept peeking into the bedroom to see if he was off the commode, but it didn't appear imminent. I finally walked to the doorway of the bedroom, bowed with a *namaste* gesture to him, and said, "I love you, I love you, and I love you," and he gestured *namaste* back to me. And that was our goodbye. He passed the next day. I feel goosebumps as I write this, as I have the feeling that he is in this room with me. Few people can say goodbye to their loved ones in such a simple, heartfelt way. It was a profound experience. It has been several years since his spirit left the body and I still miss him from the depth of my heart.

Sex, Sex, and More Sex

I joined the groups the Master told me to, without really getting anything from them. They called Bhagwan Rajneesh the sex guru, because he wrote a book called *From Sex to Super Consciousness*. I never read the book. At the ashram, everyone was living out their fantasies concerning sex. As I understood it, sex allowed the basic primal energy to move from the sex center in the genitals to the heart. Here was an enlightened master telling us to use sex to open our hearts. I feel many people only heard it as permission to have as much sex as possible. I certainly did. In one group I had sex with a woman in front of a dozen people without even being conscious that they were there. At that time, I believed that sex was love, and to become loved, I had to have sex. It was all about having as much sex as possible. Then one day, it happened - not that I was looking for sex. I had sex with three different women at three different times of the day. And the kicker was that one of the women turned out to be the wife of a man I played basketball with down the street from the ashram. He was furious when he found out. I did not know it was his wife - but that ended our basketball games. By the way, he was having sex with another woman.

The experience of having so much sex took an unexpected turn. Instead of feeling loved after sex, I had a horribly empty feeling in my belly. And on the day that I had sex three times, I swore I would never have sex again. That black hole in my gut had no end to it. This was my first awareness that *sex is not love*. It was not until I met V, whom you will meet in the next chapter, that the realization that sex was not love truly hit home. I would discover that making love with V gave sex a different quality.

Returning to Santa Fe

I stayed in Poona for three months until the weather turned unbearably hot and I decided to fly back to Santa Fe. It was a long trip back with no overnight layover in Hong Kong, just a connecting flight from there to Albuquerque. It felt great to be back in the U.S., except I did not know if I would ever get out of the airport. Right after I picked up my backpack from the luggage area, I was taken by two men in suits and ties into a small room. They flashed badges but I was in shock and too tired from such a long flight to read what the badges said. They searched my backpack and patted me down looking for illegal drugs, which of course they didn't find. Even though this was 1978, I'm sure that seeing a guy with a beard in red clothes, with a picture of a bearded Indian Santa Claus dangling from his neck, looked suspicious. What they did find was the small teakwood box, sealed with glue, that Bhagwan gave me when I took Sannyas. We were told that it contained a hair from Bhagwan's head. I have no idea if this was true, but I loved the box as it was beautiful and skillfully made. They wanted to break open the box to make sure there was no drugs in it. Even though I was tired and intimidated by these men, I protested and refused. Pretty gutsy! I am proud of myself for standing up for myself and saying to them, "Get the dogs to sniff it." The dogs were fifteen minutes away. I pointed out that only a very

Poona

small amount of drugs could fit in this little box. Instead of calling for the dogs, they let me go with the box unopened.

This ordeal made me forget that I was being picked up by the woman I had been dating in Santa Fe and her girlfriend. I was so relieved and happy to see her and I gave her a big hug. When we got to the parking lot, she turned to me and said that while I was away in India she had married the guy she had been dating before we hooked up. I guess when she saw me in the red clothes and the mala it must have removed any doubt about the choice she made to marry the other man. She did make the right choice, and I hope she has had a good life - she was a sweetheart. It was very awkward ride from Albuquerque to Santa Fe. What a "welcome home"! Taken for a drug smuggler and hearing my ex-girlfriend's announcement. My life was now one surprise after another.

I had written to Bhagwan to tell him that I was leaving the ashram to go back to Santa Fe, but that I would be back. He wrote back and told me to start a meditation center in Santa Fe and he named it the "Tao Rajneesh Meditation Center." This was the same name as Amitabh's group in India, and it would lead me later in my life to investigate the philosophy of Taoism. Bhagwan went on to write that, when a few people came to live at the center and take over running the center, I could come back to Poona.

During this time, Amitabh returned to Berkeley and started holding groups there. I would fly there every few months to do the groups. At the third group I had traveled from Santa Fe for, he said to me, "Arihanta (my Sannyas name), why don't you just move here?" And I could not think of any reason why not. There were other Sannyasins now living at the house that was the Tao center in

David The Beloved

Santa Fe, and they could take over. So off I went to Berkeley, where I got a job as a computer programmer at UC Berkeley. As it turned out the timing was interesting. Just as I arrived in Berkeley, Amitabh was heading back to India for a while. He talked to the owner of the place he was renting, and the owner allowed me to move into this wonderful tree house. I called it a "tree house" because looking out of the windows gave me the feeling of being in the trees. And this house, in the lower Berkeley hills, was only a fifteen-minute walk to where I would be working at the university. He also left me his furniture to use. It was quite a transition – beloved Amitabh took care of me. I wouldn't have met this man if the Master had not had a change of heart and crossed out the Encounter Group and given me Amitabh's group. I think maybe my grandmother may have enlightened the enlightened master from the afterlife.

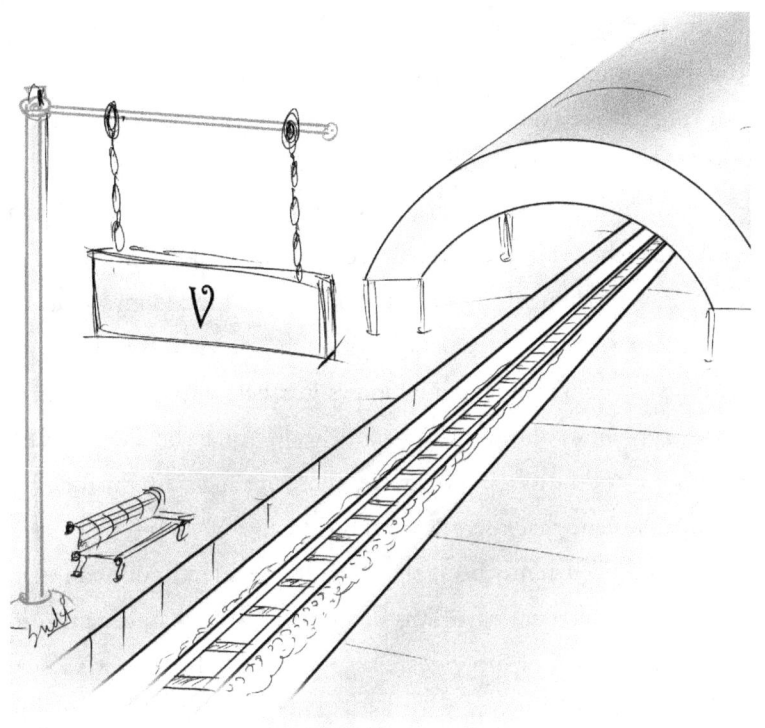

There's a Naked Woman in the Hot Tub

After leaving the Santa Fe station, it was clear to me that the next station would read "Berkeley." How could it not? That is was where my new job was, where Amitabh lived, and where his groups were held. It was a short ride from Santa Fe to the Berkeley station. But when I arrived the station sign said: "V." Uh oh, what's happening? And what or who was V? I would soon find out.

Once in the Bay Area, I started attending meditations at the Rajneesh Meditation Center in San Francisco, doing the same

David The Beloved

meditation as I had whenever I visited before going to India. After the meditation, I went downstairs to the garage, where there was a hot tub, for a soak. I noticed a woman already in the hot tub and I assumed she was naked. Before India, I would have been hesitant to go naked into a hot tub with a person I didn't know. At the ashram in Poona, when doing Amitabh's group, I had to use the communal bathroom. Opening the door to the bathroom, I found myself at the top of a long set of wide cement steps looking down into a huge room with a very high ceiling and windows just below the ceiling. There were many shower heads on two of the walls, toilets on another wall, and in the middle of the room were a host of sinks with mirrors. No big deal, except that there were about twenty men and women in the bathroom currently using these facilities, and most of them were naked. There were no partitions for privacy. And no one seemed to take it as unusual or a big deal except for me. I had never seen so many naked bodies in one place. I stood there frozen on the top step, fully clothed, while people walked past without noticing me.

I finally got my motors going and slowly walked down the steps with my mouth and eyes still wide open, waiting to wake up from this dream. I picked a toilet that had no one on either side of me and started taking care of my business when a naked woman sat down on the toilet next to me and started talking to me in German. Did I look German? I could not say anything in German, so I just motioned with one hand (the other was covering my genitals) to convey to her that I did not speak the language. I finished my business and left as quickly as possible, not even bothering to wash my hands. Over the course of Amitabh's group, I would visit the bathroom many times and after a while it became no big deal.

V

When I first entered the hot tub, I tensed up when I saw V's beautiful naked body. This was different from the group bathroom at the ashram, as only V and I were in the hot tub. My mind began generating sexual fantasies. V and I started talking, and the smile on her face and the sparkle in her eyes made me relax; I assumed she liked me. I also perceived she had a lot of joy and love in her nature, and time would prove my perception right. We moved closer as we talked, touching hands first, and then drawing our bodies closer together until we embraced and kissed each other. I was now really attracted to V and felt she was attracted to me as well. The attraction was so strong that I am not sure how we restrained from having sex right there in the hot tub. This attraction would keep V in my brain cells until the next time we met.

I Am Hooked

V was often in my thoughts until our second meeting a couple of months later at a party in Oakland, mainly for disciples of the Master. I walked into the party feeling insecure, since I lived on the fringe of the disciple community and was afraid I wouldn't know many people. After coming through the door, I scanned the room for a familiar face so I could go talk to someone and not look awkward. To my delight and surprise, who did I see across the room? V. Memories of our time kissing and embracing in the hot tub instantly flooded my mind. I crossed the room towards her, praying that she would remember me, and as I got close she saw me and a warm smile radiated from her face, which put me at ease. We said hi to each other with a hug and I felt instantly attracted to her again, though

David The Beloved

not saying anything about it in the little chit-chat that followed. After a couple of minutes, she found something to say to make her exit from me and went off to mingle and schmooze with others. I kept checking to see where V was in the room so I could gather the courage to walk over to her and ask her out. Before I had a chance to do that, she was leaving the party. I hurriedly got my coat and ran out the door and called out to her to wait a minute. I fumbled a bit with the asking her out question, but when I did ask her, she disappointed me by saying that she wasn't ready to go out with me. I stood there like a sad sack as she walked away. I went back inside and got her phone number from the host and over the next few weeks would call her and chit-chat until she felt comfortable about going on a date with me.

Dating V was wonderful. I now had a playmate to do things with, someone who really seemed to love me, and a friend I could talk to about anything and everything that was going on with us. I felt so comfortable with V, as if we had known each other much longer than we had. This station was getting better by the moment, as I saw that my hope and desire to be in a relationship and live with a woman might be fulfilled. *Not so fast, Mr. King.*

Not long after we started dating, I was hooked and wanted V in my life 24/7. Once again, this was in keeping with my "gotta have a woman in my life" mentality, so I wouldn't feel so contracted and would feel some space and ease in my belly. When I sensed that a woman had loving feelings for me, as I sensed from V, I went to "all in" very fast. V was now the woman I had to have in my life, so I asked her to move in with me. V's reaction and the intensity of her answer surprised me. Standing defiantly in front

V

of me, she said "Absolutely not. Not a chance!" I stood there with my hands in my jean pockets, feeling rejected and dejected, not knowing what to do. I left her apartment feeling lost. For weeks I had fantasized about us living together. After that, we didn't see each other for many weeks. Once the disappointment and rejection were in the past, with a new sense of hope and courage, I asked her out again, and this time she said yes. Once again, we enjoyed our time together. I was especially careful, however, not to bring up the subject of moving in together. This guy was not going to "rock the boat" again.

Stormy Night and a Knock at the Door

I was still living in the tree house that Amitabh had arranged for me before he went to India, a wonderful old house in excellent condition for its age. One day, in the middle of a rainstorm, there was a knock on the door. It was V, soaked from head to toe, with suitcases filled with her belongings. Wow! I could not believe my eyes. It took me a few seconds to tell her to come in and get out of the rain. She had taken two buses from San Francisco, where she was living, to come to the tree house. I wondered what had happened to her "absolutely not" mindset that I'd been confronted with not long ago. Not wanting to look a gift horse in the mouth, I didn't ask her why she had changed her mind. But I guessed it was that she loved me and enjoyed being with me, because she would now have a long bus ride to San Francisco every weekday to her job. I am reminded of the line in the song "Do You Love Me?" from *Fiddler on The Roof*: "If that's not love, what is?" Looking back, I can truly say that, once again, I had no idea what I had gotten myself into. *And I say that in the most grateful of ways.*

Thank God for a Big Table

I am not going to describe all our five years together, only some of the more profound experiences we shared. Even with all the ups and downs, V gave me the feeling of being loved and cared about in the way I wanted. Our relationship felt real, alive, and never boring - but playful. It never felt as if we were just going through the motions, as in my previous relationships. And even when V and I had relationship issues, we worked them out, in a Philadelphia-Bronx way. Our time together was often filled with talking, laughing, playing, being affectionate, and making love, and pressing each other's buttons - saying or doing things that provoked strong reactions in the other person. I have to say that V was the presser for probably 95% of the button pressing, just by being who she was - and I was the landscape with all the buttons. I had a limited comfort zone and was very sensitive, and I easily got hurt feelings, but without feeling the feelings. I used anger to cover up any vulnerability. She could start a sentence with "Arihanta, you are such a..." and I was off to the races.

V and I were participating in Amitabh's therapy groups in Berkeley during the late seventies. If a relationship issue escalated between two people during the group, you could express your anger by hitting your partner below the waist with a bataka (padded bat). We could get into it: Bronx guy, Philadelphia woman. You do the math. We were so into it that we were probably the first couple in our neighborhood in Kensington (near Berkeley) to have our own

V

pair of batakas in the house. I truly do not remember what I did or said to provoke her, but there was a day when the bataka was not going to be enough for V. She went what I called "Philadelphia wild." Think of the image of a bull, with a look of disdain, steam coming out of its snout and ears, kicking dirt back with its front hooves; all the while her eyes fixated on the matador waving the red cape - and wanting to tear the guy apart from limb to limb. Okay, maybe that's a bit over the top, but not much. V picked up the biggest kitchen knife we had and started chasing me around the big table in the kitchen. She held the knife at shoulder height with the blade facing down so that if she could get close enough to me, she would make a downward swipe. First, she would run one way around the table and then switch directions, never getting close enough to even feign a swipe at me. Thank god it was a big table and I still had quick reflexes. All the while the chase was going on I was laughing. I don't know why I was laughing, as she did not look like she was kidding and my laughter only enraged her more. This scene reminded me of a skit out of the "Keystone Cops" silent movies. Finally, she got tired of the chase and put down the knife, and walked over to me and hit me in the arm with her fist. Then I took her in my arms, and we hugged. I had survived the chase! Thank you, V, for sparing my life. Yet this scene would come back into my life in an unexpected way later in our time together.

Wide Open Heart

There was one night in our Kensington house when I pressed V's buttons. (This was during the 5% of the time when I was the button presser.) In that moment, whatever I'd done, I had acted from a place of innocence. But V unloaded on me. I felt stunned and retreated to the bedroom and closed the door. I lay down on the bed and tried to avoid feeling the deep sadness and hurt that hid just under the surface. It was unusual for me to have that reaction. Usually, I would start attacking her (I would go Bronx) and before long, out came the batakas; only this time, it was different. In a few minutes, V came into the bedroom and stood just inside the door. She seemed very different, more vulnerable than at any previous time. She looked so sad, and her look matched how she truly felt – as she looked at me and said how truly sorry she was, that I had done nothing wrong. She kept repeating how very sorry she was that she had hurt me. In that moment, I knew that what she said and felt was the truth. V's remorse allowed me to let go, feel my sadness, and let the episode go.

As we lay in bed cuddled up together, she kept kissing me, as if her kisses would bring healing to the hurt she believed she had caused. Then we took our clothes off and lay naked together, just feeling our bodies together. We did not make love, yet it felt like lovingness was happening; the sweet innocence of two young spirits was there between us. And then for just a few moments, I felt my entire chest open, like opening the doors of an armoire, and I could feel my heart dangling on the heartstrings, so delicate and precious. I felt doubt, initially, that it was my chest and my heart. My heart felt like a piece of Jell-O jiggling as I moved my body a little this way and a little that way. Oh, so vulnerable in that moment, I trusted and loved V as much as any human being can trust and love another human being. It must be the experience a child has of their heart when they are born, though unaware of the experience. This was

V

the only time in my 75+ years of life that I have had that experience, except possibly when I was a newborn baby.

Merry Christmas - A Magic Cookie Night

There was one Christmas party that was very eventful, to say the least. It was at the house of one of V's friends, who also was from Philadelphia. I have concluded, based on my experience with these two women, that if you are around Philadelphia women for an extended period of time you had better give your life insurance agent a heads-up. While the two of them chit-chatted in the living room, I walked into the kitchen. There on the table was a plate of chocolate chip cookies. I am addicted to all types of cookies - especially if they have chocolate in them - and the aroma wafting from these cookies was seductive. I looked around to make sure no one was on their way into the kitchen, found the coast clear, and started eating one cookie after another. They were amazingly good!

By the time the women came into the kitchen, I don't know how many I had eaten. They both looked at me as if I had done something bad, as if maybe the cookies were for other people. They caught me in the act; the cookie in my hand had a bite's worth missing. *Uh-oh, I am in trouble*, I thought, and then V's friend asked, "How many did you eat?" I thought about lying, but to lie to a Philadelphia woman could be worse than fessing up to the truth. I said, "Five or six, but they were really small," immediately starting my defense. She said the cookies had a very pure form of Colombian marijuana in them - that they were *magic cookies*. She went on to say that even for someone who has done drugs, just *one* would be a lot. I told her I had never done drugs before, and as she let my words in, I watched V's friend's face turn pale. Her friend took me downstairs to the bathroom to make me throw up - I didn't or couldn't. While I was in the bathroom, V decided to have one cookie just for the hell of it. The two Philadelphia women decided that it would be best to get me home.

V and I drove home, laughing hysterically. I have no idea how I managed to drive that car, since I was not paying any attention to the road or the other cars. We got home, still laughing as we walked through the door. But a few moments later, when I entered the bathroom, an intense experience suddenly started happening. It felt as if there were wires in my head and they were detaching from one another. I sensed the taste of mercury in my mouth and when it shot through my heart I started freaking out. I ran out to the living room in a panic and told V to call 911. She was on the floor of the living room and started laughing. I went back into the bathroom. I didn't know what to do as in this state it didn't occur to me that I could call 911 myself. I yelled to V that I was going to die. More laughter, she was not going to be of any help to me. I took a crap and it looked like my brain was in the toilet. People used to use the expression "I have to get rid of my shit," meaning those aspects of their personalities that they did not approve of. I thought maybe I had found a quick and dirty way to do that. Then suddenly the voice of the Master whose disciple I had become in India spoke in my head: "Trust Arihanta" (the Sanskrit name he had given me). Three or four times his voice spoke just those two words, "Trust Arihanta." Before that time, I had never heard his voice in my head, and I have not heard it again since.

V

Suddenly a calm peacefulness came over me, like the calm I had felt when I put my hand on the master's book in Santa Fe for the first time. I stopped freaking out and walked back into the living room and sat down in a rocking chair that Amitabh had left me, which was in the center of the room. I didn't sit so much as flop down, since I didn't know how to sit anymore. V was still lying on the living room floor enjoying herself, and really enjoying my flop into the chair. I remember watching the clock and reporting to V everything that was going on, as if I were conducting a science project. I could not move anything below the neck; I could turn my head to see the clock behind me, but I couldn't move my arms or legs. I felt paralyzed, but I did not freak out - and within a few minutes, I realized that I was *not* paralyzed, *I just did not know how to move my body!* It seemed that the computer programs that had moved my arms and legs had been erased, so I decided I would need to reprogram them. I slowly got up out of the rocking chair, like a ninety-seven-year-old man, leaning on the chair arms for support so I could push myself up. I looked at the route in front of me to the couch, no more than ten feet away, but my feet would not cooperate. I had to focus hard on one foot to get it to shuffle a few inches without lifting off the floor, and then focus on getting the other foot to do the same. I could not walk normally, but the shuffling technique finally got me across the room to the couch. Then there was an "oops" moment; I did not know how to tell my body to sit down. What to do? I plopped face first into the couch cushions, my face pancaking into the couch. Now I could roll over and have some sense of being "on" the couch. Time passed, and by the grace of God or V, I got into bed. Time had no meaning, and I had no idea how long it had been between thinking I was going to die and being in bed. And my profound experience was just getting started!

Sex Is Not Love

Lying in bed, I could not go to sleep. It felt as if an aerobics class was going on inside my body; thankfully, though, this brought back the use of my arms and legs. At some point after that I looked at V. I noticed that she was still awake and we moved closer, embraced, kissed, and then made love. I can truly say that was the first time I had ever made love with a woman with this depth of intimacy. We'd had sex many times in the past, but what was still left of those magic cookies in our bodies allowed me the intimacy of feeling no boundaries between my body and V's. It was like the scene in the *Matrix* movie where Neo puts his hand into Trinity's body to try to get her heart pumping again. I knew it was profound, and I was totally there. There really are no words to describe the experience that could begin to give anyone a sense of it. After we finished making love, we just held each other and fell asleep in each other's arms - which brought me the most restful night's sleep I'd had in my entire life to date.

The next morning, I went to work at the university, with a residue of the cookies still in me. I sat at my desk laughing loudly as I looked at my work. People looked at me as if I was nuts, probably asking themselves, "What was he smoking?" If they only knew! I couldn't work in this state of being, so I walked the six blocks home.

When I got home and entered the house, V was standing in the living room. I walked into the room and stood about six feet away from V, facing her. The first thing she said was: "I feel so much love

V

coming from you." My experience in that moment was the feeling of soft energy, mini sensations, moving through me from my feet up my body and out my chest. I said to V that it was her love coming through me, and going back to her. I don't know if that was true, but those were the words that came out of my mouth. This was the only time in my life I had that experience. These two experiences with V taught me that sex was not the same as love. All this time I had believed that if I had sex with a woman, it equated to being loved. And I strategized how to have sex with women, not believing I was bad or doing a bad thing, since I was loving them during the sex. Now I knew the truth. There is sex involved in lovemaking, but the sex is not the love! V *was the woman who taught me for the first time what real love felt like. I guess they really* were *magic cookies!*

I wrote to Amitabh in India about my experience with the magic cookies, and he said the cookies had altered my psyche. I saw that he was right, given the way things unfolded in the coming year. During this period, while V and I were getting ready to go to the Master's ashram in Poona, the second trip there for me, I started doing a meditation that Amitabh had taught me before he left for India. He said to focus my attention on the perineum (the area between my anus and scrotum). This would not create energy, but it could bring back energy that was created previously. I don't know if this was true, but I trusted him and just did it. After doing this a few times, I became aware of

David The Beloved

energy seemingly rising up my spinal cord. This was cool; it was like a magic trick where a kid would say, "Look what I can do!"

I started doing this meditation many times a day, noticing each time that with my attention I could make the energy go up, and then bring it down – I could *control* it. Then one day the energy shot right through the top of my head, and it startled me. For the first time, there were no thoughts. In the past, whenever I was quiet, my thoughts would scare me or bring suffering to me. Now the computer room of my brain was quiet, and there felt like an open space at the top of my head – and the top of my head was missing. I was not prepared for what was about to happen next, and Amitabh (my therapist as well as my friend) was not there to help me. All of sudden, thoughts came rushing back into my head. I raced out of the house and started running up the Berkeley Hills until the mindlessness returned. This went on for days. Then one day, while I was running, I sensed that a knife was chasing me, which made me run faster and faster. It wasn't that someone with a knife was chasing me – a *knife* was chasing me. This would be the beginning of about two weeks of madness. I wondered if the chase around the kitchen table with V had anything to do with this, or the kid that swiped at me with a knife when I was in college. No way for me to know.

When he left for India, Amitabh left all his furniture for me to use when I moved into his treehouse in Berkeley. At the beginning of my two weeks of madness, due to the periods of mindlessness, I decided I was enlightened. I no longer saw the need for furniture, so I gave all of it to Amitabh's sister and niece. I was mad, and I was bringing my dear friends into my madness. My energy was high, like someone in a mental hospital where people have no inhibitions. V

Detour Into Madness

and the other people in my life just flowed with it and didn't commit me or tell me I was mad.

While this experience was going on, V and I were supposed to go to India. The night before V and I were set to leave, I decided that we needed to stay in a hotel in Emeryville (near Berkeley) but that I needed her to stay two or more floors below me. It seems that in the days of running, I came to believe that her love was killing me. I now know that her love was supporting the experience of having my mind disappear, and my mind decided to stay away from V. These days of madness were about to get even stranger.

In the morning I called V in her hotel room below mine and told her to take all our luggage, which were big trunks, and go to the airport without me. I couldn't be in the same car with V and told her I'd meet her at the airport. While V was on the way to the airport, I took a taxi to the airport and rented a car. I started driving south on Highway 101 towards Los Angeles. No cell phones back then, and I didn't stop to call V on a pay phone. There she was at the airport with our trunks not knowing what to do. Go to India or not go to India? She decided to go back to Amitabh's sister Nura's house and stayed with her, not knowing what the hell was going on with me, where I was, or if I was even still alive. Meanwhile, I was traveling down 101 in a state of paranoia. I still thought someone was chasing me and trying to kill me. I pulled off into a shopping mall and went into a department store to get "regular" clothes in blue or white to disguise myself from the ones chasing me so they wouldn't find me. I got into the car and continued south heading for LA, stopping under a highway underpass to change into the "regular" clothes, and then ditched my red ashram clothes on the side of the road. Interestingly, I didn't throw away the beaded necklace with the mala that the Master had given me.

I was in this experience totally acting out whatever my mind came up with, not knowing that it was my mind telling me what to do. I thought I was acting with such clarity, but I was in a state of madness. Amitabh would later tell me that there is a thin line between madness and enlightenment. I now feel it was not even close - I was totally mad and I could have been committed. There was no difference between me and the fellow in the asylum walking around totally believing himself to be Napoleon. There was never a moment where I was a danger to myself or others; in fact, wherever I went, people around me would start up a conversation with me. That just reinforced the idea in my mind that I was doing exactly the right thing. The enlightened Master would say, "Never trust your mind, especially when it's right." Well, I was not listening to that. Mr. Bigshot was in charge!

As I was driving south toward LA, I pulled off the highway to rest for a bit. Suddenly in this area, the wind kicked up strong. I was watching the trees swaying in the wind when suddenly the energy of my body began to sway with the trees. That really scared me. My mind concluded that the trees were trying to kill me. Just as I'd decided to put V several floors below me in in the hotel, I decided I needed to be where there were no trees. *Aha*, the desert! I decided to go to Las Vegas, and off I went.

Madness Destination - Las Vegas

Arriving in Vegas, I found a hill overlooking the bright lights of the casinos on the Vegas strip, and I sat and watched the light show.

Detour Into Madness

Even in this quiet moment, the madness was working. I started to experience the chakras (the seven energy centers) moving in my body from the bottom of the feet to the top of my head. The energy centers were turning counterclockwise, boosting and refining the energy from the ground. I don't know if this is true or not, but that's how it seemed to work at the time. I was in a state of madness, yet there could be some truth to this. Looking back, it was as if I was still feeling the effects of the magic cookies.

After the chakra experience, I headed for the strip and sat myself down on a chair outside the main entrance of one of casinos as if I owned the joint. As people walked up to the entrance of the casino, I started greeting them and had short conversations with a few of them before they went inside. A while later, I went into the casino to gamble with the money V and I had for India, with the expectation I was going to win, and win big, because my mind thought I was hot stuff. I lost a lot, and quickly, and this was the first moment when I knew something was wrong. I knew I needed to call V. I was coming back to myself, but there would be one more adventure to come. I told V I was all right. (I didn't tell her how much money I had lost - remember, she was from Philadelphia!) I asked her to come to Vegas to bring me back. She had reservations about coming - wouldn't anybody, after what I had put her through? Yet she loved me so much that she came.

When she arrived in Vegas, I convinced her that we were going to win $250,000 and she just needed to come to the casino with me and I would show her how. She reluctantly agreed and off we went for this one last adventure of madness; but this time, I had a sidekick.

David The Beloved

When we got to the casino, I took her to a huge slot machine. It was twice as big as V, with a three-foot-long handle to pull after you put in five one-dollar tokens. There were five slots where you could get a picture of a fruit or the number 7. If five 7s came up you would win $250,000. So here was this woman, dressed in a red robe and a necklace with a mala, putting in five tokens and pulling this huge lever. A crowd gathered, and I started telling people to come watch, as if I were V's agent. Then I realized I had to go to the bathroom, so I left V with the crowd and her slot machine friend, and went downstairs to the restroom. I had an epiphany that the restroom was right underneath the floor where V was playing the slot machine, and I started meditating hard on the toilet's door: "7-7-7-7-7." I just kept doing it, as I really believed we were going to win the $250,000. I rushed upstairs just in time to see V's last pull and she got "7-7-7-7-lemon." She only won $100 – that was it. I really thought I just hadn't meditated on the restroom door hard enough. Yet even that thought could not sway me to take it any farther, I was done. My madness was burnt away and I was feeling lost, totally lost. I had come back to Earth, and it was a crash landing. I was lucky, very lucky to have V to help bring me back to Earth. If not, I cannot imagine where I would have ended up. We headed to the airport, returned the rental car, and flew back to Berkeley. V seemed relieved that the ordeal was over. We stayed at my friend Nura's house for a bit, and then V and I went to India together as planned. We were going to stay "forever." Once again, "Not so fast, Mr. King!"

Detour Into Madness

Leaving India – Without V or ...

I don't remember many of the details of our time together at the ashram, though for the most part, there was a lot of love between us. After a few months when the weather turned hot and I could no longer cope with everything else in Poona that was not Western, it was time to go. I told V I needed to leave, and she said she wanted to stay. I was not surprised, as I had a feeling she was not bothered by the heat, or by life in India in general. But the biggest reason was how her heart had connected to the grace and love of the Master. I was in conflict about leaving, as I wanted to be with V; yet I knew I could not stay on in India. I did not want to "talk her into leaving," since I was sure she would resent it later. We agreed on a date to let go of the room we shared in the hotel next to the ashram. On the appointed date, before getting the rickshaws to take me to the airport and V to a hostel, we sat on the front steps of our room in tears, feeling very sad. It didn't occur to me in that moment how much I loved V and how much she loved me. Yet that was the reality – we loved each other dearly. The many environmental issues in India that were outside of my comfort zone would cause me to contract and go into survival mode. By telling myself I was leaving, I could open my heart and be vulnerable to say goodbye to V.

    I got the rickshaws and we loaded V's belongings in one rickshaw and mine in the other. One last hug and more heartache and tears, and we were off. There was a point on the road where V's rickshaw needed to go left and mine right. I didn't look back, but the driver of my rickshaw looked in his mirror and saw they were still behind us and flashing their lights. Both rickshaws pulled over

David The Beloved

and V and I got out and walked up to each other. V said she couldn't leave me and would leave India with me. We hugged and didn't want to let go of each other. We jumped into one rickshaw and loaded all our trunks into the other. We held each other, and I kissed her up one side of her cheeks and down the other. And my cheeks? Tears of joy, not of sadness. I loved this woman so very much, more than I was able to know then. I have apologized to V for what she had to go through because of her love for me with these words: *From the depth of my heart, I am truly sorry, V, for all the hurt and anguish I've put you through.*

I remember that our time together after that was much calmer and more loving. Fortunately, we were able to get our treehouse rental back. And then one day, V got a call from the leader of the organization of the Master to go to Laguna Beach, in Southern California, to do legal-support work there. (V was a legal secretary and could type over 100 words a minute.) It was hard to say no when the person on the phone was saying, "Your Master wants you in Laguna Beach." And with that, she left.

It was very hard to be without her. I was a mess - a total wreck. I missed her very much. Twice I drove down there to see her, and the second time I told her how much I missed her and loved her, and I asked her to come back. I was vulnerable, which was rare for me, and once again she came back with me - and our time together was truly wonderful, the most loving of all our time together, with almost no arguments. The bataka days were long gone.

Then after a few months, another call came from the organizational leader: "Your Master wants you in the new commune in Oregon." Once again, she had to go. I could see that her connection

Detour Into Madness

with the Master was one of pure love, and in my heart, I knew that this time she would not come back. Even though V and I got together a few times when we were both living in the commune in Oregon, I was in in such survival mode over money, food, living space, weather – and so disconnected from myself – that I could never really be with V, even though I sensed she wanted it. For many years afterward, I regretted not being able to be with her the way we had been in Berkeley before she left. I felt much heartbreak each time I experienced this regret. When V left for the Oregon commune it took me two years to process her loss and to realize the depth of the connection we had. Two years to feel open to being in another relationship. I "got" for the first time that if I could not be with myself, then how could I be with V? To this day, I have not had a woman in my life who I feel loved me as much as V did or whom I loved and liked as much as V. I am so grateful to V for being with me for all those years, and sharing all our incredible experiences together!

Why Am I Driving to San Francisco to Meditate?

Throughout my time with V, our trains were coupled, and we were traveling down the same tracks. Sometimes our trains would zip along, dancing on the tracks; at other times, the tracks would be so bumpy that I needed Dramamine. (Of course, what did I expect? When I am in a relationship, sometimes the ride is smooth, and sometimes bumpy - and other times it's *very* bumpy!) After a long ride we reached the next station, which was decorated with red and orange tiles on the wall and pictures of cartoon figures of women and

David The Beloved

men jumping up and down with their arms reaching out to the sky. "Are we back in India?" I asked V. The station sign read "The Master's Communes."

When I returned from India with V, we were lucky to get our rented tree house in Berkeley back. I remember saying to a friend that I would never go back to India again. I hated the environment in India, the pollution, the poverty . . . with beggars using emaciated children as props to beg for money. And the heat. God, I hated the heat. I said to someone, "If the Master wants to see me again, he'll have to come *here*." (Mr. Big Shot once again!) And shortly after I set down how it was going to be, the disciples who ran the ashram in India purchased a ranch, called "The Big Muddy Ranch," in central Oregon near the city of Bend, with the purpose of building a commune. The Master would arrive about a year later. For a moment I had delusions of grandeur, thinking that *I* had created this event, though it was a fleeting illusion.

While the commune in Oregon was being born, I was still doing a fifty-mile roundtrip drive over the Bay Bridge from Berkeley to the nearest Rajneesh Meditation Center in San Francisco. After making this drive multiple times, through rush hour traffic, to attend an early-evening meditation, I asked myself, "Why not have a meditation center in Berkeley?" I let the idea simmer for a while, without talking to anyone about it but V. Then I took the first step and wrote a letter to the ashram in India asking permission to start a new center in Berkeley. I did this despite knowing my mind was generating thoughts like, "Who are *you* to start a center?" "You're not in the mainstream of the disciple community in Berkeley." The best one was: "Who is going to come to this place?"

The Master's Communes

Many doubts and judgments later, I mailed the letter and received a response from the Ashram authorizing me to start a center – and naming it the "Pragit Rajneesh Meditation Center." My initial reaction was WOW! followed by my familiar refrain after jumping into the frying pan: "What did you get me into this time, David?" I had not even thought about all the steps necessary from getting permission to start a center to creating one. So, I started a list (I am good at making lists). At the top of the list was to recruit help; next, to raise funds; then, to find a place like a storefront. That's as far as the list got, as everything else would depend on the funds and the place. I recruited V and another friend to form the leadership of the new center, as I was afraid it was a bit more than I could chew on my own. But I still planned to be the engine, as it was my vision.

The next step was to raise funds for the rent, to make alterations to a yet-to-be-found building, and operate the center until it would be financially viable. I remember being told that my friend Mradu's partner, Asimo, had some significant money. I contacted Asimo and asked whether V and I could come to see him at his home in the Tahoe area, not telling him on the phone about our intention to hit him up for funds for the center. Thankfully, he said yes. Off we went the very next day, as I was afraid I would lose my nerve if we didn't go right away.

Asimo was a big guy who had served in the Marines. He looked scary, as he had a scar on his cheek and didn't smile much, which made it hard for people to approach him. Whenever I was around him, I used my humor to get a grudging smile from him, and I had the feeling that he liked me. I think this was the reason I was able to call him and make the long drive to his home. As V and I were driving to Tahoe, we joked about what Asimo's reaction would be and how many times we would bounce if he threw us out of his home. I was joking, but it was to cover up my fear of this big guy. As we neared the state line from California to Nevada, where we would be turning off before crossing it, I had the idea to continue driving for another few miles and stop at a Nevada casino near the highway. When I told V, her eyes opened wide and she looked at me as if she was ready for the batakas. I had to promise on my son's life she would not have to play any slot machines, and I would only gamble $100. She took a moment and then said okay. At that moment I had forgotten about our adventure in Vegas when I went mad.

We parked in the casino lot, and I told V to wait in the car and I would be back in fifteen minutes. Any money I won, plus the $100 I had in my hand, would go toward creating the new meditation center. I didn't occur to me that I could lose, so off I went. And indeed, I came back in fifteen minutes with an extra $100 that I'd won playing blackjack. We now had $200. So far so good!

We arrived at our host Asimo's home and he immediately insisted that we go out for pizza. I was nervous, as I was about to ask someone I didn't know well for $5,000 (that's 1980 dollars; it would be over $15,000 today). Because of this, I would have agreed to anything he wanted to do. We sat down in the pizza place and ordered our pizza. Without any chit chat, or a drum roll from an imaginary band in my head, I looked at him and said: "I want you to give us $5,000 for a new meditation center in Berkeley that we are starting." Where I got the chutzpah to say this, I have no idea, and it came straight out, without my beating around the bush. Sitting across from me at this table for four, he did not flinch or change the expression on his face, which was not a smile. Then, after a pause that seemed like an hour, he started laughing. (He laughed a lot.) Before he had started laughing, I was sweating bullets as though sweat was going out of style. This big sweetheart just laughed. Then he looked at me and said, "I am not going to give you $5,000. I don't give a shit about creating a meditation center." He paused, and then with a devilish grin, went on to say: "I will give you $500, not because of the meditation center, but because of *you*."

He was a tough cookie, though I saw and felt the mush ball of a man that he really was. I was still grateful and told him so. What I didn't say or realize was that I was touched that he was doing it for *me*. Now I could eat the pizza without any threat of throwing it back up. We went back to his place, talked a bit, and went to bed exhausted from the buildup and fears of asking this one question. In the morning Asimo made us breakfast and as we were leaving, I hugged him and whispered into his ear, "Thank you, man." With that, V and I headed back to Berkeley with $700 to start the center.

Buddha Bodhi

The Berkeley area disciples of Bhagwan were either doing their own thing or participating at events at a psychic center run by two followers of the Master. It was the closest thing to a Rajneesh meditation center at the time, and many people would say it was the center of the disciple community in Berkeley and the East Bay of San Francisco. It was not my intention to step on the toes of the leaders of this center, to appear as if I might be hijacking their leadership. I wanted to start the meditation center in Berkeley so that I wouldn't

David The Beloved

have to drive to San Francisco through traffic. I was just doing my thing: I get an idea, see it clearly, and go for it. Understandably, the leaders of the psychic center were offended that I did not talk to them first. I do understand that talking to them first would have honored what they had created in the community, and it would have saved me from getting grief from many in the community. It did not occur to me, since in those days, I was not taking others into account.

There was so much chatter and openly expressed emotions among the disciples in the East Bay that finally, a meeting of the community disciples was arranged. I went to the meeting knowing this was not going to be easy. Entering the house, I felt very contracted, feeling something like a Benedict Arnold. People sat around in a circle in a large living room with many pillows on the floor and no furniture. It was a room where people would do active meditations, which reminded me of my first meditation in San Francisco before I went to India the first time. The meeting organizer said a few words summarizing why we were there, which I assumed was to give me grief! But as it turned out, that would not be the only reason. After the initial comments, one of leaders of the psychic center spoke, followed by others who took a turn expressing their feelings, some more passionately than others. I am sure I took most of what was said personally, and defended myself quite well. I probably spoke more than anyone else. A lot of what was said was implicitly or explicitly directed towards me. My unexpressed thought was *The hell with them.* People needed to get their resentment, hurt, and other feelings expressed before they could share their support for having a meditation center in Berkeley. Finally, when everyone had had their

The Master's Communes

say, the consensus in the room was to start the center. It was a weird feeling that I was being given permission by the community to do something I was already doing, but I let it go and decided not to say this to them.

By meeting's end, V and I were no longer doing it alone. We now had most of the community behind us - and that would be important to get the center up and running and keep it running. At that moment, a sweet guy named Bodhi suggested we meditate on finding a place. After meditating for a few minutes, this unassuming guy said he saw a place in Berkeley that looked like it was available. He had found the space! It was a carousel animal repair shop run by two beautiful, sweet seniors who were retiring.

The space had a lobby as you entered, a small office off to the left side, and a big doorway leading to the huge room where the carousel animals were repaired; beyond that were other spaces, including a restroom. These two craftspeople had already created a meditative energy in this space by who they were and their love of their work. Within a few minutes, V and I knew this was the right place. The kicker was that the building was owned by Mradu's real estate broker. The owner gave us a few months rent-free to fix up the place and money for the paint, and we provided the labor. I felt as if we had won the lottery! The community donated funds to purchase other materials. The final act of generosity was by Mradu, who donated $3,000 to put in wall-to-wall carpeting. With the help of Bodhi, who was a skilled painter, and a skilled young carpenter named Narayana, as well as many others pitching in, the group transformed the space. We converted the big room where the former owners had repaired the carousel animals into a meditation room; we created a separate room with a full kitchen, sinks, big fridge, stove, plenty of cabinet space and drawers, and on-demand water heaters. We added a small caretaker's bedroom that was disguised as a storage room during inspections, and a shower room with a washer and dryer. Because the meditation room had no windows, it would heat up, so the last upgrade was for Narayana to install windows and exhaust fans on one of the walls. Presto! This space was now ready for meditations. It took many hours for those in the disciple community who had volunteered their time and energy to create the vision I'd had while driving across the bridge six months earlier. Even though I didn't talk to anyone before starting down the road to its creation, I felt that everyone forgave me when they came to behold the beautiful space we had worked together to create.

The Subtle Takeover

The center was flourishing – holding meditations daily, with therapy groups weekly and on some weekends. The daily meditations were active, with shaking, dancing, chaotic breathing, and humming – or silent, quiet sitting. We would usually draw anywhere from ten to fifteen people, with a slightly larger group attending weekly therapy groups where Amitabh would explore their individual or relationship issues with them. There was a charge for the meditations, or monthly passes that would allow the holder unlimited meditation sessions. To augment the finances, we converted the room to the left of the front door into a bookstore that sold books and cassette tapes of Bhagwan.

Word spread to the commune in Oregon that we were doing well financially, and apparently a plan was put into motion to take

The Master's Communes

over control of the center from the three of us – mainly from me – as I was known for "doing my own thing." Think of a large stockholder who installs their people on the board of directors of a corporation, hoping for a takeover of the board. The commune sent their "Closer," a woman who reminded me of my mother – a master manipulator – who would ensure that she (the commune) would be calling the shots. My mother and the Closer could fight for the gold medal if manipulation were an Olympic event.

At this time, V and I were still living in our tree house in Berkeley. Our relationship was sometimes running on smooth, sometimes on bumpy tracks – but it was intensified by the energy of the Center, which was the focus of our lives. The first thing the Closer did when she hit town was to send four beautiful, young, blonde, female disciples to my house to cook and clean, but without asking V or me. This was because V and I were two of the center's leaders, and we deserved some perks, since we dedicated all our time outside of our jobs to the center. Later, it seemed to me that it was a subtle way of controlling me to control the center's positive cash flow for the benefit of the commune in Oregon. If that were the case, why not just ask? How could I say no? Certainly, V and the other center leader would have said yes. What was all the big deal about?

You can imagine the look on my face when I got home from work at the university and saw these beautiful women all over our tree house. V just started laughing when she saw the look on my face. I sat down at the dining table feeling stunned, and within seconds, I was handed a glass of orange juice in a wine glass and the woman asked seductively whether there was anything else she could do for me. I stared at her with a blank look on my face, and did not answer

David The Beloved

the woman. I turned to catch V laughing at me. V did not seem jealous, since I was not showing any interest, sexual or otherwise, towards these beautiful women. It seems everyone was having a great time except me. My mind was blown away, and it could not and would not give up control of my life, which included my house. It seemed the Closer's strategy was to give me all these "goodie gumbos" so I would become a puppet to her direction. She was wrong - although it did have an effect that worked toward her goal.

I walked out of the house without drinking the juice and went to the guest room adjacent to the side of the house to use the telephone. I wanted to call - who else? Amitabh. I told Amitabh that I couldn't do this - I wanted these women out of my house. He called back after talking to the Closer and said that if I would step down from being the center leader, all of this would go away. I needed and wanted control, control of my life, control of running the Center, and I certainly did not want to be under the control of someone who reminded me of my mother. It was as if someone else wanted to link their train car to V's and my trains and we would be going down their tracks. I was not prepared to get off our train cars and onto theirs - no way!

V, my friend, and I stepped down as center leaders. Sometime after that, V left for Laguna Beach at the request of the leader of the Oregon commune. V was not just my partner and my lover, she was my best friend. And even with all the chaos at times, I trusted her more than I could possibly know. I now found myself on the outside looking in to the center I had created, no longer in the role of Center leader, the captain of the ship, no longer the center of attention at the Center, and, with V gone, no longer a relationship partner or a woman's lover. My life as I knew it had evaporated in a matter of weeks and left me feeling very lost, hurt, and resentful.

Oregon Commune - Buy One, Get One Free

A year after I stepped down from the Center leadership, I was invited to the Oregon commune. I didn't have the foggiest idea why I had been invited. I was living on the fringe of the meditation center's activities after stepping down as Center leader, so the invitation came as a surprise. This would be the first of two invitations. Some supermarkets offer deals - if you buy one of something, then you get one free. This is the one I had bought by foolishly donating all my savings to the commune. I was pretty sure this was the reason for the invitation.

The night I left Berkeley I was very contracted. Once again, I had given up everything - the tree house, my furnishings, my job, and my car, and I was going on this new adventure with a woman I had just met while attending a meeting of the disciple community. At this meeting the new Center leaders were talking about the changes to the Center administration, and then acknowledged me, seated in the back of the room, as having created the Center. I did not accept their acknowledgement because I felt I had been deposed from my role. A woman came up to me after the meeting and seemed to think I was still a big shot in the Center. After a brief conversation, we spent that night and the next few nights together before we left for Oregon together.

We left late in the evening for a ten-hour drive, with two people who would be doing the driving sitting up front. The van did not have back seats for us, so for the ten hours, the two of us sat or lay down on a foam mattress pad that covered the floor area behind the front seats. We slept some of the time, but it was a wearing drive being thrown around as the van navigated curves and turns on its way north. As we drove down the final road to the commune ranch, an interesting sign caught our attention. It said, "Warning – sharp curves, steep grade, narrow lanes, big trucks, Good Luck." Once again, the words that I have said to myself on numerous occasions filled my thoughts: "What the hell did you get me into this time, David?" "Good Luck!" This was what people were being warned about coming in? *Oy Veh!*

The morning light greeted us, as did a welcoming committee of two women who went over logistics and rules. I was only half listening as I was observing so much activity wherever I looked. Big trucks, pickup trucks, vans, school buses, people moving all over the place and only stopping for hugs with others. Even though I was a disciple I was feeling insecure and contracted from being the new kid on the block, just as I had when I walked into the ashram in India for the first time. One of the members of the welcoming committee guided us to a tent where we would be sleeping and living. I was exhausted, contracted, and lost. I did not know where anything was. Would I get the food I needed? What if I needed a doctor? One question led to three more, and the stack of questions made me feel overwhelmed. I could not connect to myself, let alone connect with the dear, beautiful woman I was with. *I was gone to la-la land. Totally gone in every way possible.* And within two days, the beautiful woman I had spent ten hours on a mattress with in the van was gone as well.

Netflix released a three-part documentary series called *Wild Country* in 2018, about the Rajneesh commune in Oregon. It was

The Master's Communes

mostly about the woman who ran the commune and her inner circle, and how they planned or carried out illegal and cruel acts against people who they perceived were enemies of the commune. Even though these people were against the commune's existence in what they saw as their backyard, I couldn't come to grips with some of the actions taken by the commune leadership - such as doctoring local restaurants' salad bars with salmonella so diners would get sick and not be able to vote in a county election. There have also been recent reports of more disturbing, unconscionable acts by a few disciples in the commune. I felt heartbroken to hear of them. And I will not share them in this memoir as I had no knowledge of them, nor was I affected by them. My belief is that most of the people living and working in the commune had no knowledge of what these few people were doing. I certainly did not, except for one strategy a few years later that ultimately caused me to leave the commune for good. I will share this in a bit.

The guide showed us the location of the cafeteria and as I made my way there for dinner, I became anxious, as I didn't know if there would be anything I could eat. The cafeteria was a short walk from the tent, with a big mudroom for taking off your foot coverings. During the big rains, the ranch would get very muddy. It was called the "Big Muddy Ranch" before the commune purchased it. The mudroom led into a huge space with a big kitchen separated from a dining hall, which had buffet tables and many large tables for eating. I got a plate and started walking along the buffet table hoping for a miracle. No miracle to be found. All I could eat was the white rice and salad without dressing. I asked someone in the kitchen if I could get my food bland, and they told me that the kitchen couldn't handle special requests. I did not have the wherewithal to be assertive or manipulative to get what I needed. Once again, I had given no thought to what was I getting myself into or how my needs would be met. I calmed myself hoping the breakfast and lunch would be different.

I was pleasantly surprised the next morning to find food that I normally ate for breakfast, such as orange juice, fruit, cereal, eggs, and pancakes. The main breakfast fare was rotated every other day. This would be my favorite meal of the day. After breakfast, and with much fear and contraction, I took a school bus to my assigned job. The commune had a fleet of school buses forming the transportation system, with bus stops spread throughout the 65,000-acre commune. The job I was assigned was at the wood yard, cutting wood and building outhouses. I had excellent skills with computer programming and in management, but even though the commune had a computer department, there I was building places for people to do their business. The Master's whole strategy was to chip away at the disciple's ego, and he started working on mine from the get-go. My mother would love to have heard that her son's new job was building outhouses, but I didn't tell her, as I didn't want or need the aggravation of her response to the news.

At the wood yard, I was under the supervision of a disciple from Switzerland who was a renowned plastic surgeon in Europe before coming to the commune. When I heard what he had given up to supervise the wood yard, I let go, accepting my new job as a builder of shithouses. I became so skilled at building outhouses that I graduated to installing them – quite a promotion! I am not being sarcastic, as I now was able to ride around in a pickup truck to deliver these magnificent

The Master's Communes

structures to their new sites for installation. I felt like a teenager who'd just gotten their driver's license and their first car. Three weeks after my talent for the entire outhouse operation became widely known, I was promoted to managing the building and the installation of the tent platforms used for the many visitors that came for the yearly festivals. I figured that at this rate, I would be running the place within a year - more delusions of grandeur.

For the first few months my daily life was consumed by work, meals, and sleep, with a little time at night for social life if I wasn't exhausted. And the common thread that ran through all these activities was being contracted by my narrow comfort zone. I didn't feel safe or comfortable in this environment, living in a tent where rattlesnakes roamed the area, and the food for lunch and dinner was too spicy to eat. I had no money because I had donated all my savings to the commune, so I was unable to call my son or purchase soy burgers from the ranch restaurant. I ate a big breakfast, as lunch and dinner became boring very quickly!

What never was boring was watching the children, who lived on the commune, while they played - as that reminded me how much I missed my son. I was reminded of our times together, when I would read to him or make up stories before he went to bed, kissing and blowing into his belly button and watching him laugh uncontrollably. I remembered our time playing with a little nerf football in the park. These memories would take me away from the reality of the housing and food issues, and working every day, sometimes long hours, all of which kept me stressed.

The days of the week no longer had any meaning. There were no work-free "weekends." If someone asked me what day of the week it was, I would say "pancakes" or "eggs" to distinguish one day from another. Even though the day-to-day life at the commune was hitting me over the head, there were couple of perks. There were hugs with people all day, and I was never alone. Most of the time, though, I did not feel in the flow like the others, because I was contracted and would not let go - I was wound tight. Finally, after a year, I'd had it and decided to leave. I had no money and was walking around dejected and depressed, afraid I would not find the money to get back to Berkeley. Then one day, this sweet guy, another beloved of my friend Mradu, came over to me, put his arm around my shoulders and gave me $100. I wept in front of him. His name was Arpito, and if you are reading this, Arpito, please know I have not forgotten your act of kindness towards me - even as I write this, I still feel touched. It is amazing that four beautiful men that Mradu was in a relationship with or married to were dear to me in different ways. And Mradu married Amitabh, who was one of the most precious gifts given to me in this lifetime.

Back to the Future

After I left leadership of the meditation center in Berkeley, the center formed an urban commune with several houses, each housing about ten people, and it was still going when I returned to Berkeley. Before getting my job at UC Berkeley back, I stayed in the commune houses and finally became a member. This was not the "get one free" the station sign had advertised. There would be one more commune to come. Living in the urban commune was not as difficult for me as the Oregon commune had been. For the most part, all the people I shared rooms

The Master's Communes

with were wonderful, heartful people. I gave up having my own space, my own house, and found out how wonderful it was to live with other people, though at times, my buttons did get pushed. I now had money from my job at UC Berkeley, food I liked to eat (the commune was vegetarian so I bought Chinese food and ate with the other folks), and I had a nice room. Life was good, and then suddenly the meaning of the "get one free" sign came to light.

The leaders of the commune in Oregon told the urban commune to close the Berkeley meditation center and bring all the members to the Oregon commune. I was going; I felt no resistance to going back. Once again, I was packing up my life to head into the unknown. I was in a cocoon within the energy of all the people who were getting ready to pack up our lives and head for Oregon, which allowed me to *not* think about why I left the Oregon commune the first time. This time I went without giving anything to the commune, keeping what I had saved during my time back in Berkeley in case I would need it - and I would. Finally, I got the "one free" as the station sign had advertised.

The night before we were to leave for the commune in Oregon, I received a call from my mother. My father had become seriously ill and the doctors said he might not make it through the night. I did not know what to do. Fly East to be with my father? Or worse, be with my mother after my father died? Or go to Oregon with the rest of the urban commune folks? I did not sleep well that night, as my mind was obsessing on trying to figure it out.

In the morning, the folks going to Oregon sat and meditated together, and I used this meditation to help me decide what to do. I asked them to send energy to my father as it seemed he might die. Indeed, without trying, the answer came to me: Go to Oregon.

David The Beloved

I realized that I could not do anything to help my father by being around my mother, but what I could and would do was to send my love to my father. That was the best I could do. That night I called my mother from a restaurant, on the way to Oregon. I found out that my father was out of intensive care and was going to make it. I was so relieved, as I loved my father now so deeply. I felt strongly that it was a miracle – and also *not* a miracle. It was focused love!

Once I settled into the commune ranch life again, the same experiences replayed. I still did not have food I enjoyed or a place where I felt comfortable sleeping. I would get into short relationships with women and then because I was disconnected from myself, I could not maintain them. There were several women with whom I wished I could have a do-over, someplace else in the world. They were all such beautiful women who truly loved me. The only one I have ever deeply regretted not being with, though, is V.

Meeting the Master on the Road

Despite the intense experience of everyday life on the ranch, there was one experience that made it all worthwhile. I had a few moments alone on the road with the Master. Bhagwan was driving one of his Rolls-Royces to see a new building that his disciples had built for producing and distributing the many books he had written. When people saw his car heading to the new building, they stopped whatever they were doing and rushed to line up on the path between the road where he parked his Rolls and the building entrance – everyone except for this kid from the Bronx. I was a tough cookie. I remember my thoughts, *So what? Big deal!*

The Master's Communes

After about twenty minutes, I decided to walk up the road to see what was cooking, but now I was going on my terms. As I approached the back of his Rolls, there was Bhagwan, walking slowly in his shuffling style on the road towards his car, with a smile on his face and his woman companion trailing behind him. There was no one standing between him and me, and no one else was on the road. No one! I stopped near the back fender of his car. I was not thinking now; everything that was happening was beyond my control. I was in the moment, and the moment was dictating my actions. Bhagwan did not get into the driver's door of the car but continued past the door and came over to me. *He had come to me!* Remember Mr. Big Shot vowing never to go back to India? And saying that if the master wanted to see me again, he would have to come *here?* Houston, we have h-e-r-e! As he approached me, I was overtaken by his grace, his love . . . I became rolling clouds of light. That's the only way I can describe the experience of those moments. I went down on one knee and bowed my head, not out of respect – but that is what the energy of this moment dictated. That is what this field of love and grace dictated. There was no David, no Shunyam Arihanta, only these waves of clouds of light. He stood right in front of me and put his finger or fingers on my forehead, on the area known as the "third eye" for a few seconds and then said his patent, "Very good." He turned and got into his car and sped off with his companion. I stayed on my knee for another minute or two, shaken and blown away by the experience. Even before the car pulled away the light had disappeared and my human form reappeared. In that moment, five years after first meeting the master, I understood why I had traveled halfway around the world to meet him and endured all the contractions and the difficulties of day-to-day life in this commune. In that one moment, he showed me why he had named me Shunyam Arihanta – Shunyam meaning "emptiness," and Arihanta meaning "nothingness." In that moment alone on the road with the Master, there was indeed an empty nothingness, only a being in light.

End of the Ranch

The commune's previous name was the "Big Muddy Ranch" and it was near the small town of Antelope, Oregon. The state, county, and town officials made it very difficult for the commune leaders to create a commune because the land was zoned for agriculture and the last thing the local or county folks wanted was an Indian guru, also known as the sex guru, and his disciples in their backyard running around in red and orange clothes with wooden necklaces hanging around their necks. There were many confrontations between these politicians and the commune leaders, and the county refused to give the commune the permits to do whatever they wanted to do on the ranch. I can understand both sides, and I am not sure anything could have been handled any better to get a different result. Finally, the commune leaders hatched a scheme to send busses to major cities to pick up homeless people and bring them to the commune, and then ask them to register to vote, so they could vote in the county elections in favor of the commune. The homeless folks were asked to remember where their bread was buttered. They were given tents to live in, three meals a day, and one beer at night, which I was told had a "downer" added to it to keep them from getting too excited.

The Master's Communes

The commune had a weird vibe now that sent me even further out of my comfort zone, as many of these formerly homeless people, mostly men, had been on drugs or alcohol before coming. It sent my contractions off the charts. One night, while out dancing, I heard about one homeless man stabbing another homeless man. That was it, I had had enough and I was gone in two days! The commune ended not too long after that. The deeds of leadership, as described in the Netflix series *Wild Country*, were starting to surface. When I got back to the San Francisco Bay Area, I settled in a town on the other side of the hills from Berkeley and got a job programming for a trucking company. It was a reverse culture shock for a while, because I was still wearing the orange and red clothes and the mala. Once the commune fell apart and Bhagwan went back to India, I was back in blue jeans and started feeling reconnected to the life I knew before all these adventures with communes. I threw away all the red and orange clothes, but I kept the mala for a few more years. A couple of years after Bhagwan returned to India (by then he had changed his name to Osho), his spirit left his body. With his passing, this part of my life was over. Yet I still have many connections and dear friends in my day-to-day life or monthly meditation events – even after thirty-five or forty years – who were also disciples of Osho. When I stopped wearing shades of red clothes, I was asked by people: "Did you get brainwashed while you were on the ranch in Oregon or in the Ashram in India?" I would give each of them the same answer: "Osho showed me the truth of my belovedness and the extent of my mind's lies that I had been married to all the years up to then." This marriage to my developed mind was heading for a slow divorce.

The Fire

Leaving the last station with only my train car, no longer coupled with V's, and no longer part of a commune, the ride felt quiet, reflective. It was a long, lonely ride to the next station. I think it was good that the ride was long so I could assimilate what had happened after I left Texas to go to Santa Fe, India, Berkeley, and Oregon. Without my giving the next train station any thought, my train car pulled into a station. The sign said: "From The Fire A Star Is Born." I immediately thought of a star out in the cosmos, but what it referred to would be more down to earth than that.

David The Beloved

For many years after leaving the commune in Oregon for good, I lived alone in several East Bay communities of the San Francisco Bay Area. My dear friends Amitabh and Satyam lived nearby, and I would occasionally join the community of former disciples that lived in the North Bay (Marin County) to attend meditations or dances. But I was not in the flow of this community. I had regressed to my old pattern of being a hermit, a loner, believing that people could see the old beliefs I had of myself. I only ventured out when my longing for contact with other people was greater than my fear of being with them.

In 1990 I rented a beautiful one-bedroom cottage in the Berkeley-Oakland Hills that was attached to the main house where two sweet senior owners lived. The husband had built most of the inside of the cottage himself with materials imported from Europe, which included beautiful light wood cabinets from Scandinavia, and deep rose floor tiles from Italy. As you walked in, there was a small foyer and then an entry to a small bedroom and bath with windows looking out to what I would discover was a favorite spot for hungry deer to have dinner. When I first came to see the place, the owner observed the look on my face as I walked down the stairs from the foyer to the big room comprising the living room and kitchen and said, "You look like you like the place." To which I replied, "I left 'like' at the top step. I *love* the place." I signed a lease on the spot.

Using my existing furniture, I converted the big area into a living room, where I had an L-shaped white couch with an ottoman, TV, and some plants; an office area for my desk, printer, and my pet goldfish Harry; a breakfast nook and kitchen. This large room

From The Fire A Star Is Born

had huge panoramic windows that covered all the walls except the kitchen area. The views out these windows were spectacular. At night I could see the bright lights of San Francisco glistening, and the lights of Bay Area bridges thirty miles to the north and south lighting up the San Francisco Bay. Instead of still-life pictures hanging on the walls, I had living pictures in front of me to view each moment. Below the cottage deck was a popular viewing area for people on July 4th where they could watch the fireworks displays of many cities all at once. For the first time since the tree house in Berkeley, I had a place to live that I *loved*.

In 1991, an event occurred that would change the course of my life and uproot me again, sending me into uncharted waters. On Saturday, October 19th in the late morning, I left the house to attend a UC Berkeley (Cal) football game, which was not far from the cottage. I had to park my car about a twenty-minute walk from the stadium. It was a great game, but unfortunately, Cal lost. I felt a bit bummed out while walking back to my car, as I was a passionate Cal fan. When I drove up to our driveway entrance, I found firetrucks on the streets all around the house. I parked on the street, and in a total panic ran up the driveway, trying to find out what was going on. A temporary relief came over me as I could see the main house and my cottage still standing. Then I caught sight of the firefighters fifty feet from my door just finishing up extinguishing a grass fire, putting out hot spots. I went over to them and shared my heartfelt gratitude for putting out the fire; I could have hugged them. I had gone from panic to relief, seemingly in seconds. Interestingly, many weeks before this fire I had the idea of getting a new wardrobe that would make me look prophetic.

David The Beloved

The next morning, Sunday October 20th, I awoke to go to a meditation event in Marin County. I left the house at about ten, and as I was walking down the driveway to where my car was parked, I had a very eerie feeling: the wind, the temperature, and even the air seemed surreal. I saw a fire truck at the bottom of the driveway and walked down to talk to the firefighter in charge, who was standing next to the fire truck. I said to him, "Maybe I shouldn't leave. I have this weird feeling." He assured me that they would be patrolling for hot spots all day and convinced me it would be okay. That same firefighter, I was later told, had tried to save a woman and her daughter who lived down the hill from my place, but tragically, all three of them died.

So off I went to Marin County, still uneasy, but feeling somewhat reassured, and I put the whole situation out of my mind. As it turned out, Saturday's fire had re-ignited in one of the hotspots and the strong winds spread the flames rapidly. My landlords, those sweet seniors, somehow realized the fire had re-ignited and were frantically loading up a pickup truck in front of the main house with their belongings when the fire picked up speed and headed for our houses. They ran for their lives down the driveway, leaving the truck behind, to a VW Beetle parked at the bottom of the driveway, as the husband had anticipated this possibility and had wisely parked away from the house. The husband ran faster than his wife down the driveway and the heat from the fire caught her on her back and the back of the legs. He managed to get her into the back seat of the VW and drove straight to Alta Bates Hospital. She survived, though she had to stay in the hospital for a few months to recover from severe burns. I realized that if I had not gone to the meditation that

From The Fire A Star Is Born

morning I might have been in the cottage when the fire came and died or been badly burned like my neighbor. That firefighter had no idea his encouragement for me to leave the cottage had probably saved my life or saved me from serious injury. *Thank you, Sir!*

Without being aware of any of these events - the fire re-igniting, my cottage owners fleeing and getting injured, and the death of the firefighter and two neighbors down the hill - I was returning from the Marin meditation, going over the San Rafael Bridge when I saw a plume of smoke in the air coming from the hills. My heart sank and I said out loud, "Oh no!" multiple times, my voice escalating with each pang of fear. I raced to get home but every route I tried was blocked. I found a pay phone and called my home phone, neighbors' home phones - no answer and no answering machines. I knew the worst had happened, and now I was in total shock. All I had was my car and the clothes on my back - shorts, tank top, and Birkenstock sandals - that's it! The shock and panic felt overwhelming and I was trying to keep it together to be able to think straight and know what to do next. I was in uncharted territory trying to think straight while in a panic. I was sitting in my car at a roadblock, feeling helpless. If I were a religious person, I would have asked God for a sign. But I am not, so I got out of the car, looked in all directions, and then I had a moment of clarity.

I drove to my dear friend Nura's house, who lived down below the Rose Garden in Berkeley. I knew she was in L.A., and I got her key from a neighbor. I watched TV for any news of my place and whether the fire would start to spread toward her house, and I reported to Nura in L.A. to ease her fears. The next thing I did surprised me. I took off on foot to the Chinese restaurant and bought

David The Beloved

$100 of Chinese food. Who would have thought that in the middle of a disaster, the first thing I would think of was to buy Chinese food? I was not thinking straight and was having a hard time connecting to my new reality. My entire life as I had known it at ten o'clock that morning was lost. I monitored the fire all day on the TV, calling Nura every half hour from the balcony of her house to give her an update, like a TV news reporter. I had no idea at this point who or what I was. I was obsessed with whether the fire would consume the part of Berkeley that lies between Nura's house and what was currently burning. I ate some dinner and then went back out to the balcony to continue my watch, only taking breaks to see what was on TV.

When it was clear that the fire would not burn through Berkeley, I crashed in her guest bed, totally exhausted. As I hit the pillow, I remember thinking that I would wake up in my own bed the next morning and realize that this was all a dream. But I woke up in the morning with no such outcome; instead, I was confronted with a harsh reality. I had lost everything I owned. Without thinking, I went to the bathroom, as usual, to brush my teeth. Oops! I did not have a toothbrush, toothpaste, comb, or a hairbrush. And no breakfast food. My normal morning routine had been disrupted, and everything from that day on for years - yes, years - became a new normal.

I made a to-do list for the day: toiletries, breakfast, sneakers, pants, shirts, underwear, socks, and a jacket. I thought that was enough for the first day. Writing the list reminded me that I had almost nothing to my name. The one item I did have no longer had any meaning - the key to the cottage. I walked to the drugstore

From The Fire A Star Is Born

and bought all the toiletries that I used on a daily basis, and then went to Peet's coffee shop for coffee, croissant, and a banana. My tank top, shorts, and Birkenstocks would not work as my complete wardrobe, between the weather and all the walking, so off to the shoe store to get a pair of sneakers and on to Macy's for clothing. At the shoe store I met people who had also lost everything. When we connected and told our stories, I found myself hugging and crying with total strangers. The people at Macy's were so caring and compassionate that they gave each of the fire victims a personal shopper. I sat in a space they created next to a fitting room, the personal shopper took my sizes, wants, and preferences, and brought all the clothes to me. I was one of about six people sitting in this area. Naturally, the scene at the shoe store repeated this experience, with more hugs and tears. I fell apart the first time the personal shopper brought clothes to me; by now the faucet of tears was almost locked in an open position. Making multiple trips out to the various men's clothing departments, the personal shopper had fulfilled my clothing list. As if that were not enough, this dear woman helped me carry the four big bags of clothing I had chosen from her selections to my car. As I thanked her, I wept and she put her hand on my arm and said, "It will take a little time, but you will get through this." As they say in the Bronx, "What a jewel!" That she was, and I hope I thanked her from the bottom of my heart. Over the next few days this experience repeated itself in every store I went to, and I felt cared about by total strangers. Truly a humbling experience to be so vulnerable!

Five days after the fire, I still didn't know for sure that the house had burned. I needed to see it with my own eyes to get closure.

David The Beloved

I went to a Berkeley Police Post setup at Ashby and Claremont Avenues at 4 a.m. in the hope that they would let me drive up there. The police officer told me that only official vehicles were allowed in the area. He sensed how I was holding back my grief and felt sympathy for me, and said that when it was light, *he* would drive me there. I waited a few hours and then he drove me to the cottage in his police car.

There was no cottage, no main house - only ashes and rubble. When I got out of the police car and approached the rubble of the cottage, the first thing I observed was the burned fridge down the hill. Walking toward the rubble, I had no feeling of my feet touching the ground, no sense of myself; I moved toward where the cottage used to be as if I were in a trance. And then a primal force took me over as I went to where my bed used to be and I lay down in the ashes and just kept screaming, "No! No! No!" over and over again, as loud as I could. I had lost a home I truly loved living in and now it was gone forever. I felt hopeless and helpless at this reality. The officer who was standing by the police car heard me crying out and came and got me and put me back into the police car and drove me back down the hill to my car. All the way back, I wept, and this sweet, understanding, and sympathetic police officer tried to comfort me the best he could. I wish I remembered his name to thank him again. Stranger after stranger, I would fall apart in front of. My self-consciousness had no power to stop my grieving. Before departing I apologized to him for getting ashes all over his car, and he said, "Don't worry about it - not a biggie." As I walked back to my car, I held the two items I had found in the rubble that had survived - a ceramic candleholder and a ceramic pen and pencil holder, with "Desk Things" printed on it. I still have the "Desk Things" thirty years later.

Fire Survivor

After confirming that the fire destroyed the cottage, I called my insurance agent concerning my renter's policy and was told to go from Berkeley to a temporary insurance company office that was set up in a motel about ten miles away. I hung up the phone and immediately drove through traffic to the temporary insurance office. When I arrived, I complained quite emotionally about how far away it was. My emotional outburst had nothing to do with where this

David The Beloved

temporary office was located and only had to do with having no coping energy available, plus being overwhelmed and very scared. The agent was very sympathetic, listening earnestly to what I said, and then offered me a seat and a cold drink. After a few minutes in an adjacent room, he came out and gave me a check for $5,000, just to get me going. When he gave me the check, once again, I fell apart in front of a stranger. The insurance agent was a kind man. I had heard a lot about how some people had trouble getting their fire claims settled, but mine showed up for me when I needed them most. Within weeks the insurance company gave me every cent that I was insured for.

Over the next two years, my landlord rebuilt the house for his wife to give her some comfort, as it had taken her a long time to heal from her burns. The sad and tragic end to their life together occurred on the very day they moved into the rebuilt house. The husband suddenly died. I was sad to learn that news, as they were very sweet people who truly cared about me. I asked their family if I could move back into the rebuilt cottage, but sadly they informed me, apologetically, they were keeping it for the family. This dashed a high hope I had in the back of my head that someday I could go back there. I appreciated, valued, and felt very safe living in such a beautiful cottage. When I researched the full effects of the fire, I was shocked to learn that 3,500 homes had been lost; about 10,000 people were displaced and needed new shelters; and twenty-five people had died, three of whom died just down the hill from me. There were 450 fire engines involved, with 1,500 firefighters. With all the trials and tribulations I had

From The Fire A Star Is Born

gone through, I was by far not the only one in shock, lost, and having to slowly start rebuilding a life.

It took years to recover emotionally and find a new place to live that felt like home. The trauma caused me anguish every time I left the house, and it still does today, thirty years later. I was homeless, and for the most part, possession-less, and now, along with 3,500 other households, I needed to find a place to live. I was spoiled by living in the cottage and it took a long time to find a place to truly call home, living temporarily in six places in less than eighteen months. You do the math. I was a vagabond, and it did not serve my nervous system. Then miraculously, I found a one-bedroom apartment in Orinda over a garage with wonderful owners living next door. During the time I lived there, two other miracles were bestowed upon me. I could not conceive of either of them happening to me at any time in my life, especially then. These miracles will be unveiled in this chapter and the next.

A Star Is Born

One day, after moving into my new Orinda space, I realized that I could have been killed in the fire had I not left that Sunday morning. Which led me to ask myself, "What do I *really* want to do with my life?" I was still a computer programmer and supervising other programmers and not happy, with no real joy in my life. I asked myself, "What is it that will bring *joy* to my life?" The answer - I wanted to become a *theatre actor*. My friend Jett suggested I meet her acting teacher, Shari Carlson, who had a studio in San

David The Beloved

Francisco near Union Square. I booked an appointment to meet Shari and when the appointment day arrived I started getting cold feet. Yet cold feet and all I went, not knowing what to expect. I walked into Shari's office and sat down awaiting her appearance. When she entered the room, I was struck by her outward beauty, her relaxed demeanor, and how she smiled so authentically and warmly at me - and she didn't even know me. I was now sitting in front of this very beautiful woman, with constant eye-to-eye contact. As if she could read the depth of my experience, she said to me, very simply, "You don't look so good." I immediately fell apart and wept, finding it difficult to stop the sobbing. I don't remember any of the rest of the conversation, but I knew I wanted to be around her, just like I knew I wanted to be around Amitabh - and that is what I did.

With Shari's help in acting class, I decided to audition for a show in a local community theatre called The Moraga Playhouse. The theatre director was a joyous, passionate, and very dear man named Cliff, who was truly a joy to work with and who gave me private lessons on how to audition. I did two shows at the Playhouse and did well, even being nominated for a local-area "Best Supporting Actor" award for the portrayal of a very scary New England farmer. I performed in many shows during the years between 1992 and 2009.

One of my favorite roles was playing the lead - the character Lenny - in the Neil Simon comedy *Rumors*. (I've mentioned this earlier, in the context of my relationship with the actress

From The Fire A Star Is Born

who played the role of my wife.) Being born in the Bronx, playing Lenny was right up my alley. He was a very outspoken, foul-mouthed, and sarcastic lawyer with great punchlines to deliver. Hearing the laughter from the audience to the punch lines brought me much joy; that was the reason I wanted to become a theatre actor.

My second favorite role was playing Woody Allen, in *Play it Again Sam*. I could play him effortlessly as I felt it was in my DNA; fearing everything and always thinking the worst possible outcome would manifest itself. If the character had a cold, then he was going to die from pneumonia. I was on stage for the entire show except for three minutes for one costume change. The show was performed in the round, with stage pieces put between sections of the audience. I had so many lines to deliver and was scared I would forget some, so at all the stage pieces, such as tables, etc., I had an index card buried under props with some of the lines that I would say in that area of the stage. I only had to use them twice during the entire run - not too shabby. Performing on the stage was such a joy to me - even the rehearsals were fun, as I could ad-lib when I couldn't remember a line. I was finally using the natural comedian in me that got me into such trouble in Mrs. Greenspan's high school English class. With Shari's support and experience with theatre roles and industrial videos, I was able to get my union cards in AEA (Actors Equity Association) and AFTRA (American Federation of Television and Radio Artists).

David Alan King

Acting Headshots

Theatre was a joy beyond my wildest dreams. Out of the blue, after a few years in acting class, Shari suggested I also come to her singing class. I resisted at first, and said to her on more than one occasion, "I

From The Fire A Star Is Born

can't sing." It was difficult to keep saying no to her, so I finally said a reluctant, very reluctant, okay.

On my first night in singing class, I walked into the same room we used for the acting class, and people were warming up with the accompanist. There was a former Miss America contestant and three people who would eventually go on to Broadway. Their voices were amazing. I listened to these folks and my mind and body were in total agreement when I turned around and headed for the elevator. I said to myself, "There's no way I'm going to embarrass myself in front of these people. Are you kidding me?" I got within ten feet of the elevator and a hand grabbed the back collar of my shirt and pulled me back. It was Shari, who else! She *told* me (not *asked* me) I was staying for the class.

All the class participants sat in a row of chairs, with Shari sitting in the middle seat of the row. The accompanist sat off to the left side of the room. Each person stood up in the center of the room, facing Shari, and did some prep work with Shari individually, and then each of these "singers" performed their song. Each one of them sang like professionals, and with each song, I became more and more anxious and took more quick glances at the door out to the elevator. Shari must have thought that I might bolt, so she reserved the chair next to her for me. Finally, it was my turn, the last to have a turn with Shari. It was stressful walking to the center of the room with all these "singers" watching me. As I turned to face Shari and before she could say a word, I confessed to the whole room, "I don't know why I am here, I cannot sing." Shari smiled that smile that got me to fall apart the first time I met her. I absolutely believed that I could not sing. Without commenting, she had me sing "Happy Birthday" a

David The Beloved

cappella. I did and it was no big deal. Who in the room would care? My God, it was only "Happy Birthday." When I finished, Shari said only one sentence to me and then dismissed the class. She said, "That will be the *last* time you ever say in this room that you can't sing."

Shari worked differently from most singing or acting teachers. She supported her students to move through the mental and emotional blocks that kept them from being in the moment and connected to their heart and soul while acting and singing. She taught us to treat the entire mind, body, and soul as the instrument. This was my experience from acting class, and now I needed to import this process to the singing class.

After attending the singing class each week for a few months, I discovered that the belief that I could not sing was created when I was five years old. My father, who worked as a proofreader at a legal printing house near Wall Street, was a very good singer and performed at a hotel on the weekends during the summer about twenty-five miles north of New York City. My mother and I would get to stay at the hotel for the whole summer in exchange for his performing. One time my father taught me two songs to sing for a Saturday afternoon show before a small crowd: "I'm a Yankee Doodle Dandy" and "Harrigan." He found straw hats for us to wear so we really looked like a father and son team. I was so excited to do this with my father since I never got to do anything with him. As we were singing, I missed some words because I was enjoying watching the audience enjoying us. It was so much fun – and I got to do this with my father! Afterwards many of the women from the audience came up to me, and either pinched my cheeks or deposited some yukky lipstick on them, all the while I was beaming. This five-year-old stole

From The Fire A Star Is Born

the show and my father seemed disappointed that I got all the adulation. Singing was his way to share his heart with people and feel that people liked him, really liked him. Unfortunately, in no other aspect of his life, at work or in his home life with my mother, did he get recognition or appreciation - only grief. After the performance I would ask him if we could do it again, but he always shook his head, no. That is when I decided I couldn't sing, as I believed the reason he wouldn't let me sing with him again was because I was not very good.

That belief stayed with me for forty-five years, until I started singing in Shari's class. The first song that I sang in class was one that always touched me deeply when I heard it: "Greatest Love of All," sung by Whitney Houston. The lyrics by Linda Creed are at the end of this chapter. It reminds my heart and soul of the truth that *I am a beloved*. Read the words slowly and see if it resonates with you, touches you, as it has always touched me.

Five years after I started singing class with Shari and doing countless practicing sessions with an accompanist, something happened that I had never even dreamed possible and that touches me as I write these words. I was practicing a song and tears started running down my cheeks - It was joy! Pure Joy! *I loved how I sang, how I heard me!* I proved the belief that I could not sing to be untrue. I had just needed to commit to practicing and allow for a melting of the belief. For me it was never about singing every note perfectly, it was about singing from the truth of where I was, touching my own heart, and hopefully, touching others.

In 1994 my parents celebrated their fiftieth anniversary at a banquet room in New Jersey. I decided that I would make a toast to them and then sing a song. In the toast I said what a perfect match

David The Beloved

they were; my father was hard of hearing and my mother was always talking very loudly (I wanted to say yelling, but it was their anniversary party). After the toast they got up and danced, the only couple on the dance floor. They only time I saw them happy together was on the dance floor, where they seemed free and connected.

When they sat down, I sang my song, telling everyone that it was dedicated to my grandmother Yetta, who had died about thirty years prior. The song was "The Wind Beneath My Wings" that Bette Midler made famous. I was hesitant to sing in front of my father, as a year before I had sung for him a cappella and he went on to tell me all the notes I had missed. I wanted him to be proud of me, proud that I loved singing as much as he did; but instead, I felt his disapproval. I was proud of one thing: his disapproval didn't send me all the way back to the five-year-old kid who believed he could not sing. Not in the least. I was in front of the hundred people attending the celebration and the most important person listening to me was my father. With the accompaniment of a three-piece band, I sang my heart out to my grandmother, to the one person in my life who loved me unconditionally. I am sure, because I sang from my heart, and had not rehearsed with these musicians, that I missed some notes. When I sat down at the table with my parents after the song, my father whispered in my ear that he had never sung with the depth of feeling that he felt in my singing. He was proud of me! If it weren't for all the people sitting at our table and feeling a bit of shocked by his words, which is not what I had expected, I would have lost it, gotten up and hugged him with all of me. To this day I remember his

From The Fire A Star Is Born

words: "I am proud of you, my son." It meant a lot to me. It reminds me to tell my son and my grandkids that I am proud of them just for being who they are.

After almost eighteen years with Shari, in weekly acting and singing classes, about fifteen to twenty theatre productions, almost two hundred performances, my acting and singing days would come to an end without warning. One day while singing in class, I could not hit some of the high and low notes that I had sung previously without an issue. Over the next eighteen months I would slowly lose the joy in my life from singing and acting. In Chapter Twenty I will share the full story of this loss.

"Greatest Love of All"

Music by Michael Masser, Lyrics by Linda Creed

> I believe the children are our future
> Teach them well and let them lead the way
> Show them all the beauty they possess inside
> Give them a sense of pride to make it easier
>
> Let the children's laughter remind us how we used to be
> Everybody searching for a hero
> People need someone to look up to
> I never found anyone who fulfilled my needs
>
> A lonely place to be
> So I learned to depend on me

David The Beloved

I decided long ago, never to walk in anyone's shadows
If I fail, if I succeed
At least I'll live as I believe
No matter what they take from me
They can't take away my dignity

Because the greatest love of all
Is happening to me
I found the greatest love of all
Inside of me

The greatest love of all
Is easy to achieve
Learning to love yourself
It is the greatest love of all

The Connection

My train was zipping along, and there was even Disney music playing: "Zip-a-dee-doo-dah, zip-a-dee-ay, My, oh, my, what a wonderful day..." Not that every day was great; there were days that felt lonely. But I had a good place to live, with another set of sweet owners next door, a good job with good pay, and much joy from my singing and theatre roles. The music stopped as we pulled into the next station, and I hoped that was not a portent of things to come. I was perplexed, more than perplexed, when I read the sign at the station: "From Russia with Love." WHAT? Okaaaaaay!

David The Beloved

Six years after the fire, I was still performing on stage, acting and singing my heart out. Even though acting and singing brought me joy, I often felt lonely, as I was living alone and isolated from friends. I didn't have a community of people like those I had met as a disciple of the Master in the eighties. In early spring of 1997, I heard about a San Francisco dating service and decided to sign up and give it a shot. What did I have to lose, I thought – and who knows? Maybe magic would happen. I went through the process of writing up something about myself in glowing detail and then proceeded to eight coffee meets with different women. Seven of the meets were awkward and uncomfortable, and I realized that the women and I were auditioning for each other. It was only my loneliness that kept me going ahead to the eighth date. The women would come in and the chit-chat would start, and most of the time I knew from the get-go that this was not the one for me – and I couldn't wait for an opening to end it. I now realize that I was looking for my grandmother's qualities in these women: the great warmth, nurturing, and unconditional love she gave me whenever I was in her presence. It was an unreasonable expectation to ask of these women. There was one woman, the eighth of these meets, in whom I felt some of those qualities, but as it turned out, she wasn't interested in me. What to do? This process felt hopeless and exhausting, so I stopped my search and put all my energy back into the theatre and kept myself busy to avoid feeling the loneliness.

Six months later, I received a magazine in the mail to which I had not subscribed. Since this magazine came unsolicited, I am sure they got my name from the dating service's mailing list. The magazine contained pictures and brief write-ups about women from

From Russia with Love

Eastern Europe or Asia looking for Western husbands. There were hundreds of gallery-type pictures and a one-paragraph write-up for each woman. I thought, how do you get to know someone just from a picture and a few words? I had entered romantic relationships based upon the feelings of my heart without waiting to see if we were compatible. But enter a relationship based on only a picture and a few words? Not even I would do that. Or would I?

The magazine had aroused my curiosity and sparked a reminder of the loneliness that lurked beneath my everyday life. I started peering through the pictures and reading a few profiles and found that most of these women were religious, which would never work for me, as I was no longer affiliated with any religion. There was one picture that stopped me in my tracks. Really stopped me in my tracks! I just stared at her picture as if I was time traveling to where she lived in a country I had never heard of called "Estonia." The woman was of Russian ancestry and her write-up said she loved the theatre. She had a son who would come with her and a daughter that would stay in Estonia. I kept my finger in the page as I continued looking through the magazine and found a Polish woman who was a doctor who also had a son. The Polish woman was interesting, but the Russian woman was, as they say in the Bronx, "something else." Such an angelic, innocent look, with one elbow on a table and her face in the palm of her hand, and her face so clear of any emotion. I did realize that to meet this woman and her family in Estonia, I would have to travel thousands of miles without knowing anything about Estonia, her family, or who she was. Yet there was a feeling, an intuitiveness. I had left IBM and my life in Texas not knowing where I was going; I had left for India not knowing what I would find. There I was again, feeling a force pulling me to do something – and all my worst fears of traveling, rejection, and heartbreak could not stop this force.

I wrote letters to the women in Poland and Estonia, but not in the style the magazine suggested; instead, I told them about myself, my life, my finances, admittedly in very positive light. It didn't occur to me that I was leaving out personal information; that I had a limited comfort zone, needed to have control, and could be intolerant. I had not been in a relationship of any consequence since V and that was about thirteen years earlier. I found some courage to "get back on the horse," though it took me a couple of days to go to the post office and mail the letters. Weeks went by and I heard nothing from the women. I figured nothing was going to happen, and I let go of all my anxiety and anticipation, and stopped constantly looking for the daily mail delivery. Then one day, two months later, after truly letting go of the whole deal, I received a letter from the Russian woman.

The First Letter from Tatiana

I was in a bit of shock, and like a high school senior getting a letter from their first-choice college, I was hesitant to open it. I waited a day. I thought: What am I scared of, being rejected? What's the big deal? I don't even know her. Just as I had met the Master in India from 8,000 miles away, I may have felt Tatiana in the same way – in my heart. When I read her letter, I was surprised to learn that she had not put her picture or write-up in this magazine; her friend had done it without Tatiana's permission. Her friend's behavior was strange, but I was glad the friend had done it. The serendipity of

From Russia with Love

this connection was profound. First of all, I had not requested the magazine and had to find her picture out of hundreds; and then Tatiana had not put her picture in the magazine, but her friend had jumped through hoops to get it in the magazine. Now there in front of me was a letter from a total stranger thousands of miles away in a country I had never even heard of, and all I knew about her was from a few words and a picture, yet what a picture!

Tatiana went on to share in the letter that she had received many letters (how could she not? The picture showed her angelic beauty and unique innocence). She explained that her letter was late in coming because she had been away on holiday and had just returned. She *seemed* to say that all the men in the letters (me included) were not a match for her. In that moment, I felt a bit disappointed, but I continued reading, finding her English okay, though some of the sentences were not clear and a bit confusing. When I had finished reading the entire letter, I found her phone number below her signature. That did not make sense; if I was not a match for her, why give me her phone number? I was confused and decided to let it go another day, then re-read the letter to see I had missed anything and what I would do.

Over the next twenty-four hours, every time I looked at her picture, I knew I wanted to meet this woman. There was an energy brewing in me, and it would not be contained unless I called the number and talked to her. After figuring out how to call Estonia, I dialed her number with anxiety thinking maybe she had put her phone number on the letter by mistake. When she got on the phone, she said something in Russian, and I said, "Hello, it's David - I wrote you a letter and you wrote me back." She then shifted to English and her voice was truly the voice of an angel. I am not exaggerating - it *was* the voice of an angel! I wanted to race through the phone cables to her house. We talked about ourselves, about our lives, about our families, and asked each other questions. I did not want to hang up; my heart was pounding, and I was already hooked. (Did I mention my heart falls in love easily?) There were a few more letters, a few more calls, and then I needed to decide when to go and visit her. It was not a question of *if* I would visit her, only *when*. In three weeks, I would start rehearsing a new show and the show would run until Christmas. It was either go now or wait three months, and there was no way I could wait three months - no way, Mr. King. The next day I went to the local travel agent and booked a two-week trip to Estonia. As Jackie Gleason used to say on his '60s TV show *The Honeymooners*, "And awaaay we go!"

Trip to Visit the Angel

In my last therapy session before leaving, my therapist asked me what I would do if it didn't work out with Tatiana. What was my backup plan? I decided, since this was my first trip to Europe (at age 52) I would get a Eurail Pass and see some other parts of Europe. He agreed it was a good plan, and with that, off I went. San Francisco to Seattle, then on to Copenhagen, with the last leg on Estonian Airlines. I had fears about Estonian Airlines, as it sounded like I might sit next to a descendant of Genghis Khan, the way you see in Indiana Jones movies on airplanes flying to countries like Nepal or Tibet. Okay, maybe a bit over the top, but I was afraid their planes were 100 years old. The plane was old but fine, and by the time I

From Russia with Love

reached Tallinn, the capital of Estonia, I was exhausted after twenty-four hours of flights and airport waits since leaving my house. I did find out by talking with a passenger on this last leg that Estonia had been annexed to the Soviet Union during the beginning of World War II and that Joseph Stalin had forcibly moved Russian citizens from their homes in Russia to Estonia, Latvia, and Lithuania. This is how Tatiana's family came to be in Estonia after being uprooted from where they lived in Russia.

After going through Customs, I recognized Tatiana and slowly went to greet her - and I naturally gave her a hug, at which she looked shocked. I discovered that people in Estonia don't do a lot of hugging. Tatiana was wearing a black leather jacket and looked a little like a motorcycle babe; the angelic image I had of her went poof! But I was too exhausted to feel disappointed.

I walked with her, without saying anything, to where her brother was parked. He would drive us to the hotel where they had reserved a room for me. I opened the door for Tatiana and as she got in, I got a full look at the back of the black leather jacket she was wearing and started to have thoughts that maybe coming to meet her was not a good idea after all. I sat down in the car seat next to her and was about to close the car door when her brother took off like a bat out of hell. I looked at Tatiana in disbelief at how her brother was driving and disbelief that we were both sitting in the back seat of a car in Estonia. Did I mention she was wearing this black leather jacket? Just when I was about to say something to Tatiana, her brother floored the gas pedal and passed a red light. Not yellow, it was red two seconds before we got there. Help! my inner voice was saying.

David The Beloved

Her brother drove worse than any New York City cab driver I had ever been in a taxi with.

This pattern continued with me trying to look and speak to Tatiana, but getting interrupted by survival fears generated by her brother's not stopping at stop signs and cutting off other cars. I didn't think to check my life insurance policy before I had left to see whether death by an insane driver was covered. My head was on swivel looking at Tatiana and the road, fearing her brother thought this was "bumper cars" at the amusement park. Tatiana looked unfazed by her brother's driving – obviously she had been on death-defying rides with him before. Each time I looked at her, the first thing I saw was the leather jacket and found it hard to integrate that with the angelic being I had talked to on the phone. I would soon learn, though, that people in Estonia wear dark clothing. During my two weeks there, walking around in my greenish-blue REI Gore-Tex raincoat, I stood out like a tourist. Not much was said in the car, between her brother's driving and the black leather jacket, until we got to the hotel.

When Tatiana and I got out of the car I felt like I needed to thank some god, but I wasn't sure which one. I looked at her brother, who didn't speak much English, and just shook my head and rolled my eyes. Tatiana got me checked in and came into the hotel room with me and promptly sat down on the bed. The room was big with high ceilings, and big windows covered with drapes that could have been older than me, with a couch and a desk. All the furniture was old but still had some character to it. I sat down on the couch and piled all my luggage next to me in case this was not going to last more than a few minutes – then I could pick up and go. (Go where? I had no idea!) I turned to look at Tatiana sitting on the bed with

From Russia with Love

her back up against the headboard and her feet up on the bed with her boots still on. The last poof of the angelic beauty I had held on the long journey went poof as well. Double poof is never a good thing! We were still looking at each other with disbelief that we were there together. I was wondering, who is she really? We were still total strangers, and because I was so exhausted from the long trip, there was no audition mode happening. I was vulnerable, sweet, unattached to anything happening.

The first thing I said to her was devised in my therapy session before leaving, "Tatiana, if it doesn't work out between us, I will get a Eurail Pass and go see Europe." I was not expecting any particular response from her, and what happened would not have even made it on the list if I had a list of possible responses. Almost before the last word left my mouth, Tatiana jumped off the bed into my lap. Yes, literally into my lap, in less than two seconds. Hello Houston, we have lift-off. She had felt my being in the moment, my open heart, my love from such innocence. We kissed passionately on the couch and then just as passionately started taking off our clothes. What a relief when I saw her without that jacket just before she was naked. We twirled and jumped into the bed and made sweet love. *Not too shabby a start, Mr. King!*

Meeting Misha and Mamachka

After the lovemaking, we chit-chatted a bit and Tatiana left for a while and I settled in to the hotel room. When she came back in an hour, she was no longer wearing that black leather jacket, thank you, Buddha. We took a taxi (gratefully, not her brother's car) to where she lived. It was a cement apartment building, Soviet style, dull,

David The Beloved

like one big cinder block with windows – to say not very appealing would be an understatement. Her apartment had one bedroom, a large living room, a small kitchen, and a small bathroom. Tatiana's son Misha was in the apartment as well as her mother; Tatiana's daughter was traveling with her boyfriend. Tatiana first introduced me to her mother, who had the same physical attributes as my grandmother, who was from the Ukraine. To this day, over twenty years later, I still call her mother "Mamachka," an endearing term for mother in Russian because she has been so loving to me. Meeting Mamachka gave me hope that I had found another family to plug into and another mother to be my mother. Even now that she is over ninety, her mother and I still have such a loving connection. Next, Tatiana introduced me to her son Misha. Misha, who was twelve, was a gorgeous kid with big beautiful eyes, very shy with me at first. I gave him a gift I had brought for him from the U.S., a sports watch with all sorts of dials and moving parts. That seemed to warm him and bring him out of his shyness. I told him it was waterproof and shockproof, and without hesitation, he set out to experiment to see if what I had said was really true. He tested to see if it was waterproof by filling the bathroom sink with water and submerging the watch and indeed it was still ticking. Next, he ran to the living room and dropped the watch from the third-story window to see if it was really shockproof. Sadly, that poor watch did not survive. I had given so much thought to getting him the perfect gift, and now it was shattered on a cement sidewalk. He had taken me literally and proved me wrong. I had failed to say that it was shockproof if it dropped off your wrist. Even if I said that it may have not made a difference, as everything I said had to get translated by Tatiana into Russian and it may have gotten lost in translation. Tatiana spoke very good English and even spoke some Estonian, but Misha and Tatiana's mother did not speak English. I was first in shock when I witnessed the watch go flying out the window but also impressed by Misha's curiosity and innocent experiment, so I bought him another watch, which I am happy to report had a longer life span.

After our introductions, I took everyone out for a nice dinner and we started to get to know each other, though it was a little awkward when all that was being said had to go through Tatiana. Tatiana barely got to eat anything, she was so busy talking for three other people. It was overwhelming, since I still was jet-lagged and most of the conversation was in Russian. But there was also a quality of sweetness in it, even though these people were strangers. I had the first glimpse of being part of their family and already felt more relaxed, hoping I was about to fulfill my childhood wish to find a new family. To this day, Tatiana and I are still like family and I have such a loving relationship with her Mamachka, Misha, and Tatiana's daughter. Many times, I thought I had gotten on the wrong train at the Begin Lives Train Yard. I felt that I should have been born into Tatiana's family. I have come to realize that I had to go through the family I was born into to get where I am today. And where I am today, as they say in the Bronx, is "not too shabby."

The Engagement

In the ensuing days, Tatiana and I talked a lot about what my life was like in California, about my job and family, my son Jason, my parents. And she shared more about her family and her work. There were

David The Beloved

no red flags for either of us when hearing each other's backgrounds. She took me on a tour of Tallinn, especially the old city, which had well-preserved medieval architecture and a huge city square with hotels, stores, and offices along the perimeter, and a big, open cobblestone space in the middle. I was very impressed. It felt as if we had taken a tour into history.

After a week in Tallinn, I took the whole family to Helsinki, Finland's capital, for the weekend, where we stayed in a little castle converted to a hotel in the downtown area. Almost everything I did had the flavor of a "first," and Finland was no exception. I was like a kid in a big outdoor toy store, and I felt relaxed with Tatiana and her family. I cannot remember everything else we did during those first ten days. But by then, I wanted nothing more than to be with Tatiana and to marry her, and I *thought* she felt the same way. Not so fast, Mr. King! The day after we got back from Finland, with my assumption firmly placed in my mind, we went to a jewelry store. At first, Tatiana didn't understand why we went into the jewelry store or why I asked her which ring she liked. She kept looking at me with a puzzled expression, and was hesitant to try on the rings, but she left the store with the ring on her wedding finger, somehow getting what had just happened. That was probably the most unromantic proposal I could have come up with, but I did the best I could, considering I was in Estonia, a country I had never heard of just a couple of months ago, with a Russian woman whom I had just met ten days ago and made love to two minutes after we got together in the hotel room. *Da!* (That's Russian for Yes!)

Next stop after the ring was to walk to the photographer's studio to get pictures of Tatiana and Misha for immigration paperwork to

From Russia with Love

the U.S., and that's when she had the *Aha* moment. Tatiana realized that with the ring, I was asking her to marry me. I realized that I had not yet fallen in love with her, but I knew in my soul I was meant to be with her and I still feel today that we were meant to walk the same path for the time we did.

I had spent some time getting to know Misha in the apartment, and a few places out and about with Tatiana, but something happened after we left the photographer's studio that I couldn't have imagined. We were walking along, Tatiana and I holding hands, with Misha off to my left side looking sad and dejected, looking at the ground with his hands in his pants pockets. My heart, in that moment, went out to him - and spontaneously I put my arm around him and brought him to my side. In that moment I fell in love with Misha. I fell totally in love with him even before I fell in love with Tatiana. He was such a sweet, dear kid, and totally honest about how he felt. I believe he reminded me of how I was at that age. Loving Misha was unexpected. However, what was to come between us would be one of the most difficult times of my life.

Before leaving to go back to the U.S., I took the whole family out to a wonderful restaurant for dinner. There were Tatiana, Mamachka, Misha, and Tatiana's daredevil brother with his wife and daughter. When I saw her brother enter the room, I thought it was a miracle he was still alive the way he drives. The dinner was very festive with much chatter, and once again, the burden of the translation fell on Tatiana, who barely had time to eat any of her meal. There was much laughter, a bit of vodka, of which I did not partake - and I even danced with Tatiana's brother's young daughter. She was shy and wouldn't dance with me; yet there we were on the dance floor, dancing separately and

David The Beloved

looking at each other, having fun with no translation needed. Before leaving, I bought her a tree for her room, which she loved. To thank me, this sweet five-year-old later drew a picture of the tree and sent to me. Twenty-four years later, I still have this picture.

The goodbyes were lovely. I hugged everyone, even though I was aware of their non-hugging ways, as I would not see anyone except Tatiana again before I left for the airport. First, I had a separate goodbye with Misha, no words, just a big hug and a kiss on the top of his head; and then with Mamachka, who kissed me on both cheeks and I did the same to her. I even hugged Tatiana's brother, whose sweetness I observed at the dinner. I had made a judgment about her brother's "construction" ("someone's inner and outer way of being" translates from Russian) based on how he drove, but he showed his open heart with the whole family, and in particular with his daughter. And he was especially sweet to his mother. I tweaked my judgment about his heart – but not about his driving.

Tatiana and I took a taxi to the hotel to get my belongings, and then we both went to the airport. Her brother had offered to drive us to the airport, to which I smiled politely and declined with a wave of my hand and a facial expression that said, "no need," all the while thinking I would rather have a root canal and a proctology exam at the same time. Before leaving, I gave Tatiana money for English lessons for Misha and money for her so she would have a cushion if she needed it until we would see each other again. It was hard saying goodbye to Tatiana, as I felt so at ease when I was with her. Before leaving, we decided to meet in a couple of months in London for the Christmas and New Year's holidays after my theatre production ended. I would rent an apartment in London for us, fly her and Misha there, and the three of us would spend the holidays together. I had wonderful fantasies about how the holidays together would be, and after many years alone, I would be with family for the holidays. This was going to be wonderful and fun. Once again, not so fast, Mr. King.

Holiday in London – Glimpse of What Would Come

In a safe and upscale section of London, I rented a well-furnished one-bedroom apartment with a tiny kitchen, and a large living room with a fireplace and couch, where Misha would sleep. We got there the day before Christmas, and after settling in, we went out for some lunch. Misha wanted to go McDonald's, which was not what I had in mind, but I felt it important to flow with his wishes so he would feel comfortable. We were still getting to know each other and all the things we did together were firsts, though some firsts to come I could have done without. Everything I observed on the walk was "so English," just like in the movies whose locale was London. What did you expect, Mr. King? It *is* London.

The day passed and we all went home to bed. Misha was anxious to open his Christmas present, but Tatiana and I convinced him to wait until the morning when we were all together. Tatiana and I went into the bedroom and got into bed, kissed good night, and held hands until we fell asleep, which happened quickly.

In the morning, Misha had his gift in his hand, unopened, raring to go – and the second we walked into the room, the wrapping flew off and he found the electric remote-controlled car that I had bought for him for Christmas. You may be wondering what I bought for Tatiana, but I don't remember; only the car is etched in my mind. He was excited and I was too. Unfortunately, this kid from the Bronx had forgotten to buy a converter. It was Christmas day and the stores were closed, so I told Misha to wait till tomorrow before using it after we got the converter. He didn't listen to me – lost in translation again? Or was it just that this little devil was doing what he wanted to do, even though he was told not to? I didn't know, and it would have been a good question to ask Tatiana, but I didn't. While Tatiana and I were in the bedroom, beloved Misha, curious Misha, who had thrown the watch out the third-floor window back in Estonia, now plugged the California remote car into the London outlet – exactly what he was *not* supposed to do. The outlet, the apartment fuse box, maybe even the London electrical grid, was not happy – it blew all the power in the apartment – Merry Christmas! No heat, no electric stove, no restaurants open; the only heat was the steam coming out of my ears.

    I was very upset and lost it and raised my voice to Misha, as I felt things were getting out of control. It brought up the trauma of losing my home in the fire six years earlier, as well as the trauma of my own mess-ups as a kid and getting hit for it. I was unaware of all this at the time, yet the connections to these traumas set off my panic, which set off my wanting to control Misha so I would not have to go into panic mode. This is how my mother and father had treated me when I was a child, but I could not see that connection to my behavior at that time. When I cooled down and saw the pain I had caused Misha and Tatiana, I felt remorse, but that did not change my behavior going forward. Tatiana wanted to call it off and go back to Estonia; not just the

From Russia with Love

trip, the engagement. Luckily, I found an electrician who was willing to come on Christmas day for a hundred pounds and my first born.

While I was trying to find an electrician, Tatiana was in the bedroom putting her things into her suitcase. When I went into the bedroom, the suitcase was half-filled, and my spontaneous reaction was to start removing her things from the suitcase. It was like a scene out of a romantic comedy; she kept putting things into the suitcase and I kept taking them out, until I made the motion of "timeout" with my hands. Thank God that translated in both languages. I said, "Let me call my therapist and let's talk to him." She took a breath and reluctantly agreed. I called my therapist back in California and when he returned my call two hours later, I explained what had happened and that Tatiana wanted to call things off. He said to both of us to not to make any decisions in a moment of crisis, which was a good idea, because after the electrician had restored power we both calmed down.

Tatiana cooked Christmas dinner for us, and all was good. We got through this one, but it was a sign of things to come, as having control of an adolescent is like trying to control the weather. My naiveté about being a stepfather was evident, and when mixed with my wants or needs to be a good father and not disappoint my stepson, it set me up for great disappointment in my own behavior. I had no idea what Misha was going through with the suddenness of our relationship, and I never asked. It never occurred to me to look at this whole situation from his perspective, the perspective of a twelve-year-old, who was getting a new stepfather, learning a new language, and in a short time, leaving the only home he had ever known to move to a new country and home. That is a lot for anyone,

David The Beloved

and he was only twelve. And Tatiana was dealing with her own processing of all the newness and was also caught up in Misha's and my relationship problem; she knew that what had happened in London was a portent of what was to come. I had missed seeing all that, and missed seeing what a big deal it would be for me to become a stepfather and husband to people I had known for such a short time. Yet I was blinded by my desire to have a family and a wife, and that suppressed any knowing I had that the three of us being together as a family would be combustible.

After a week in London, we put Misha on a plane back to Estonia so Tatiana and I could have some alone time together to bond. I feared sending the child back alone, knowing his uncle would pick him up at the airport and drive him home. It was much easier to spend time with Tatiana with just the two of us together. There were no upsets as we toured the London museums, rode the Underground, ate at niche restaurants, brunched at English cafes, walked at night, and sat by the fireplace and smooched. Our week alone quickly came to an end, and at the end of the holiday, we agreed to continue with our plans for her and Misha to come to California, and for us to get married, despite my meltdown on Christmas morning. As far as the immigration lawyer was concerned, I had set a record; in five and a half months, I had managed to get their permanent residency approved, and they came straight to the U.S. And one month later, Tatiana and I were married. My new reality was about to start presenting itself, and once more, I would ask myself, "What the hell did you get me into this time, David?"

From Russia with Love

Tatiana and Misha to America

A few months before I received the magazine and wrote the first letter to Tatiana, I was sitting in singing class feeling sad and lonely. My singing teacher, Shari, said to me very clearly and with no empathy or sympathy, "What do you want?" From the depths of sadness, I said to her, "I want to be married, with a family and house in the mountains." As the saying goes, be careful what you wish for – you just may get it. Shortly after declaring my want list to Shari, I found a foundation, but no house yet, built on a piece of property just below Echo Summit on the way to Lake Tahoe. Echo Lake was a very magical place for me, as I could sit by the lake and feel so fine, at home with myself, no problems. It was very grounding there, and the lake and surrounding nature were beautiful to take in visually. The air, filled with the scent of pine trees, brought joy to my senses. My dear friend Amitabh had a cabin on the lake. He had introduced me to the lake one winter, when he invited me and another man to help him close up the cabin. The property I found bordered the National Forest, and during the winter, cross-country skiers would go by just beyond the back of the property. The house to be built was 2,400 square feet: a spacious home with an open floor plan for the living room, dining room, and kitchen; plus three bedrooms, an office, two and half bathrooms, a sauna, and a river-rock-faced fireplace, with panoramic window views of the mountains. Before meeting Tatiana and Misha, I had settled on these house plans with the builder. Once they arrived, we made many visits to the property to pick out doors, cabinets, floors, counters, appliances, fireplace rocks – and the whole kitchen sink, so to speak.

David The Beloved

Our first year in the new mountain home was difficult on every level. I get stressed just thinking about those times as I write about them. The weather during the winter produced thirty feet of snow, as we were just below Echo Summit, at an elevation of about 7,400 feet, and the wind would blow snow off the mountain peaks onto the homes in our neighborhood. Now I was living with two people who could take me out of my comfort zone very easily; especially Misha, just by being a child and doing things children do. Sound familiar? This is just as I described my own experience as a child with my parents. I was just doing what children do and was getting punished for it. Unfortunately, my way of handling it, my strategy, which I learned from my mother, was to yell and scream in the hope that the person would not do it again. With Misha this strategy did not work – good for him, and I mean that! My behavior at times was cruel, abusive, and heartless. It came from a place of fear about what would happen to me if I didn't have control, and the belief that if I yelled, people would comply with my needs. I was totally unaware of what was driving this behavior. There was another part of me that could see how badly I treated Tatiana and Misha at times, a part that was remorseful and heartbroken. It was not until I became a student of the Diamond Heart teachings (which I'll discuss later) that I would truly understand where my behavior had its roots. I still had much love for Misha, just as I felt at that moment when I put my arm around him. Now I feel such love for him. As for Tatiana, she would become one of my best friends, knowing we can share anything with each other. They both will always have a space in my heart.

From Russia with Love

The Divorce – Again

After one year in Tahoe through the harsh winter, we moved back to the San Francisco Bay Area and rented a house in the city of Lafayette. I worked from home most of the time, and Tatiana was a typical housewife. Misha was able to ride the bike we bought for him to middle school, where he was in an English as a second language class as well as the regular middle school classes.

What had happened in London with my eruption would happen frequently during our years together. Misha being Misha, being an adolescent, took me out of my comfort zone, with me yelling at him and Tatiana in the middle of it. It was difficult, very difficult. Though I did take care of them in every way possible, giving them a nice place to live with a beautiful yard, the best schools for Misha, the best doctors. And I was not always a raving lunatic. There were good times, when I felt safe and openhearted, when I was available to treat them lovingly.

We were married for about six years, until Misha finished high school. Once we were empty nesters, though, Tatiana realized she only wanted to be married two days a week. This was not a surprise to me, as we had started spending more and more time apart, both physically and emotionally. She wanted to go off during the day on her own, do her own thing, and she spent hours in her room by herself. She needed to live like this to stay true to herself, to be the authentic person she was. I wanted more. I wanted to be with someone who wanted to do everything in the world together, to walk the path together literally. We both understood our differences and our incompatibility, and there was no blame, no making the other person wrong. We wanted what we wanted out of the relationship and we were just not compatible.

David The Beloved

One night at the dinner table, the words flew out of my mouth: "I'm tired of getting just the crumbs – I want a divorce." It was a poor choice of words on my part. I explained what I meant by that and told her I still loved her, that that had not changed. (That has never changed, in fact; we still consider each other family.) After the divorce we parted ways, with some contact every now and then that could be challenging and painful; it hurt me to look back and see my behavior. But mostly it was about healing and forgiveness. After years of being apart, we have said to each other all that needed to be said, needed to be felt so that we could remain dear friends. Misha and I also took years to work through the feelings around the abuse that I had inflicted on him. It took me longer with Misha to really hear him, feel his feelings, and be able to say from my heart how sorry I was for yelling at him for just doing his thing, being a kid, and learning about life by experimenting. The watch out the window, the car plugged into the London outlet, were innocent examples of a boy learning about how the world works. I was not aware at the time how my behavior was mirroring the behavior of my parents in response to my learning to be myself in the world. My father showing me, much later, how authentically the heart feels remorse allowed me to express my remorse to Tatiana and Misha. With them both I now feel complete, and I love them both dearly. In 2018 Tatiana's daughter asked me to be the grandfather to her newborn daughter. I was honored and said "absolutely," and I traveled to Latvia where they were living and met Tatiana's daughter and her baby for the first time. They were both beautiful beings – how could they not be, as they were from the same tree as Mamachka, Misha, and Tatiana. I had to get married, then divorced, and then travel to

From Russia with Love

Latvia to feel complete in my search for another family. They all will be a part of me, and me a part of them, for the rest of our lives.

It was too painful to live in the same rented apartment that Tatiana and I shared, so I moved to the city of Moraga nearby. Then at the end of 2007, two years after my divorce was final, the rest of my life seemingly was falling apart. My job at the university became tenuous, I had to leave the townhouse where I was living as the owners were selling it, and I was still grieving the end of my marriage. It was hard for me to find a place to live that felt safe and comfortable, so I was living out of my car and a storage area, sleeping on couches at friends' houses, or at hotels or B&Bs. The circumstances of my life were creating so much stress and tightness in my belly that there were moments when I was ready to get off the train. I did not want to live like that anymore. My immune system became so compromised that it could no longer hold off a disease that threatened to take me off the train unwillingly.

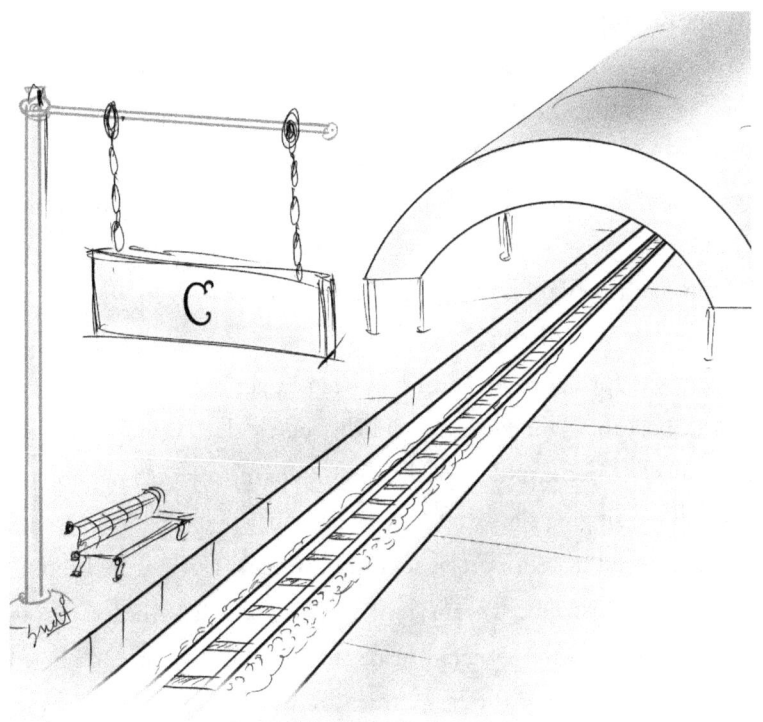

Finding Out

The train ride from my last divorce was difficult, but at least I had my acting and singing to bring me joy. There I was, singing and dancing in my train car when the next station came into view. Just before reaching the station, the train slowed down to a crawl - and I wondered why. Then something weird started happening with my voice. When I sang there were gaps, and words as well as notes would be missing. The lights in the train started flickering. What was going on? The train was still moving at a slow pace, and the car doors were opening and closing crazily. I was bewildered by all of this. As the

David The Beloved

train finally pulled into the station, I saw men and women walking around in white coats, some of them with stethoscopes – doctors and nurses for sure. Why me? When the doors opened there was a woman in a white coat waiting for me with a wheelchair; she looked at me and motioned for me to get in the chair. I shook my head "no" and kept on shaking it. But it seemed I had no choice, so in the chair I went, and they took me for a ride I will never forget. The station sign had only one letter – a capital "C."

It was spring, 2009, and I had been in acting and singing class with Shari for eighteen years. On this particular evening, I was in singing class in the middle of the room, starting my turn with Shari. To call it a singing class was only part of what this "class" was about. I experienced her support to identify the blocks that were keeping my singing instrument – my lungs, vocal cords, and heart – from singing freely in the moment in response to how the music moved me. Singing through the heart this way was healing and touching, and it brought me loving acceptance of myself just as I am. I brought what I learned from Shari's class to the stage as a theatre actor and singer, performing before audiences of strangers. They didn't know me, yet I knew they were all rooting for me to do well so they could be relieved from any stress in their day and relax with open hearts for those moments. And me? I was just doing what brought me joy, though getting their adoration via their laughter and their applause was a goodie gumbo. How lucky of me to have found this path. Had it not been for the fire that destroyed my home and all my possessions, and left my heart and soul in the ashes, I may never have found my way to singing and acting. As the Buddhist saying goes, "In everything there is both a positive and negative aspect." At the height of

C

my creative performing, earning my union card to Actor's Equity, Buddha's presence could easily have said, "See, I told you so." But you must watch out for Buddha, he seems to have a lifetime incarnated in the Bronx, maybe as a gambler with sleight of hand, since the wave I was riding on was about to crash down.

I was standing in front of the class and Shari, and while singing a song I realized that I had lost some of my range. I couldn't hit some of the higher notes. I was very surprised and confused, since I had been singing within this range for over ten years. I gave it a week and rested my voice hoping that would fix it, but it wasn't that my voice was strained. I didn't know what to do. I realized that the timing coincided with stopping my allergy shots, so I went to an ENT (ear, nose, and throat) doctor. I asked him if losing my range could have been caused by stopping my allergy shots. Without even looking down my throat he said yes, and for the next four to six months I got back to the top dose of my allergy shots. But not only did my singing range not go back to normal, it continued to get even more narrow. I cannot tell you what I wanted to do to this doctor, because it may be against the law to write it, but I guess you can imagine. If it weren't for his advice, this disease would have been caught at an early stage and I would probably still have my speaking and singing voice, though I don't know for sure. And I might not have learned the lesson this disease came to teach me and I'm not sure I would have started writing this book in earnest.

After realizing the allergy shots had nothing to do with my loss of range - and that now I also had a loss of volume just in speaking - I was scared. During my next singing class, I expressed this fear to Shari. I told her that I did not know what was going on, but I was going to get a second opinion. Thankfully I had very good medical insurance through UC Berkeley. Shari then said something about my medical insurance that startled me: "You will really need it." It seems her intuition envisioned the events that were about to unfold.

A few weeks later I went to a different ENT doctor who looked down my throat. He said he had an idea what was going on, but that he would need to bring someone in with special equipment to take a look. I asked him what he thought it was and he said "Let's wait until we can take a better look." This is not a good answer to hear from a doctor. I am a worrier from way back, and this took worry to a whole new level. It would be several weeks before this other doctor with the special equipment was available, and during that time, I tried to keep busy, but it was difficult not to languish in fear. Only once before had a doctor had this sort of look on their face and that was when my friend Cindy (from when I lived in Texas), had a bump on her neck and my MD said they needed to do a biopsy and found it was a form of cancer.

When I finally went to see the specialist, he put a micro camera down my throat, and he and the ENT doctor both looked worried when they saw the pictures. The ENT doctor said it might be vocal cord cancer, and the other doctor concurred. When I asked him what percent chance that it "may be" cancer, the ENT doctor said 50-50. I didn't believe him, as my mind has always tended to believe that the worst possible outcome will occur. (Imagine Woody Allen.) The next step was a biopsy, but unfortunately that would have to wait another month because of the holidays and the doctor's vacation.

I was very stressed while waiting out the month to find out whether I had cancer growing in my body; fearing at each moment

C

that something in my body was slowly killing me. This was my mindset during that month, and it was awful and terrifying! The possibility of having cancer blew out the stoppers, the resistance to feeling my feelings; I was now feeling terror at times every day.

When the day finally arrived for the biopsy, my son Jason, who had flown out to the West Coast from Houston, went with me. I cannot imagine going through that alone or with anyone else, as I totally trusted his love and caring for me. After the ENT doctor performed the biopsy, he came out to the waiting room and told my son and me that it would be one to two weeks before we would get the results. I cried in front of the doctor when I heard I would have to wait that long to know whether I had cancer. The doctor must have understood the depth of my despair. That very evening, while Jason and I were eating dinner, he called and told us he had rushed the biopsy results through. He said I had vocal cord cancer in my left vocal cord. This was the reason my singing range had narrowed, and why my voice had gaps in it.

As I approached the station, one of my vocal cords was not fluttering. At that moment my train station sign with the "C" flipped over, and the new sign said "Journey With Cancer." My son and I sat at the dining room table, digesting the biopsy results and the doctor's recommended treatment of radiation sessions. I was in shock. Jason immediately got on the Internet and started researching vocal cord cancer. He found that there were now lasers being used to treat this form of cancer, and at that time, there were only two places in the U.S. that had them. One of them was the University of California at San Francisco (UCSF) Medical School. We found the department and the director of that department (Voice and Swallowing Center), sent him an email asking about the laser treatment, and included my phone number.

That very night, Dr. Mark Courey, the director, called. I lost my composure and wept as I talked with him, as this doctor was compassionate and caring at a very dark moment in my life. Even though it was late in the evening, Dr. Courey was being there for me on the phone, as if I already were his patient. I did my best to regain my composure and speak to him with a clear mind, though I was in panic and shock. This was the same state I had found myself in when I was not able to get home after the fire, in panic and shock but needing to think clearly. He said, yes, they had the lasers, but then he said something that made me sure he was the surgeon for me. He said, "Nothing is more effective than instruments in the hands of a skilled surgeon." I knew this was the doctor, the person, into whose hands I would literally put my life.

Cancer - Treatments Begin

A few weeks before my first surgery in February, 2010, I sent out emails to family, friends from my acting and singing classes, and friends from my spiritual communities. I made a list of all the people who I knew would be rooting for me, praying for me, and sending their love to me. I was so touched that I wept, realizing that there were almost a hundred people on that list, that so many people cared and had loving feelings for me. I folded up the paper with the list, hid it in my hand in the surgery prep area, and took it with me into surgery. Driving to the surgery at six in the morning, I was calm

Journey With Cancer

and present, supported by my son Jason being there and by the love that many people were sending me. The surgery was scheduled for 9:00 a.m., but there was a delay, as the patient ahead of me in the operating room had complications. Once that surgery was completed, my surgeon had a meeting, so my surgery was rescheduled for 3:00 p.m. Though I had to wait six hours longer for the surgery, I remained calm and patient, which was out of character for me. I attributed it to the loving energy being sent to me by the cast of a hundred. Thank you to everyone reading this who sent me their caring and love that day - your support was greatly appreciated.

When Dr. Courey came in before the surgery, I begged him over and over to take it all out. I wanted the cancer totally out of my body that very day. I did not want to live with the terror that something was in my body slowly killing me. At that point, cancer only infected the left vocal cord and its associated vocal fold. He would not fulfill my request, as he knew I was a singer and how much I would mourn the loss of my singing voice. He also knew that radiation was 90%-95% successful with vocal cord cancer. He took narrow margins during the surgery, which meant he only went a small distance from the edge where the biopsy showed no cancer cells, hoping to preserve as much of my singing voice as possible.

Awaking from the surgery, I was hesitant to say anything to my son, afraid of what I might sound like. To my surprise and delight, I sounded normal - just like before my vocal cord stopped fluttering, and in a few weeks, even my singing voice range would return to near normal. For the first few months I could talk normally, and sing almost to my prior range. Gratefulness became a daily experience every time I opened my mouth and anything came out. Yet there was always a cloud hanging over my head, as Dr. Courey had warned me that if they missed even one cancer cell, the cancer could repopulate. And that is exactly what happened. After just three months, the symptoms of a loss in singing range and speaking voice volume reappeared. The cancer had come back. And I was beside myself, knowing that once again there was something in my body slowly killing me.

In late spring of 2010, another biopsy confirmed that. Dr. Courey had made the original decision to give narrow margins a chance, knowing that radiation, which he called "The Big Gun," was still a possibility, and for vocal cord cancer it was almost always successful. The cancer coming back forced me to have twenty-eight sessions of radiation over a six-week period that summer. I did not want the radiation as I was afraid what the "big gun" would do to me. I was strapped to a table from head to toe, unable to move for fifteen minutes, probably more stressed than I was aware of during the sessions, each time in shock, not knowing what was bombarding me. The stress was magnified by the conflict between wanting to move and being constrained physically.

The last few weeks of these treatments caused the side effects that included a sore and inflamed throat, dry mouth, and trouble swallowing. Especially during the last one to two weeks, I had horrific pain when any food went down my throat. I finally had to restrict my diet to liquids, soups, or liquefied foods from the blender. Towards the end I would have to take pain meds an hour before drinking my food just to be able to tolerate the pain of the liquids going down. There would be times the pain was so great that I would cry in pain. After the radiation sessions ended and my body

Journey With Cancer

had recovered from the radiation, my speaking and singing voice returned once again. Once I had passed three months after the last radiation session and there was no sign of the cancer, I felt hopeful. I took each day with the ability to speak and sing normally as a precious gift. But five and a half months after the last radiation session had been completed, my voice started to lose volume, and my singing voice started to lose range once again. The third biopsy confirmed that the cancer had come back. I was depressed, terrified, brokenhearted, and at the same time, in shock.

Dr. Courey now shifted from saving my singing voice mode into saving my life mode. In January 2011, I had my next surgery, and this time Dr. Courey took wide margins. By this time both vocal cords and parts of their attached vocal folds were affected, but thankfully, the cancer had not metastasized. Operating with his skilled surgeon's hands, Dr. Courey removed both vocal cords and parts of the vocal folds. When I awoke from the anesthesia, I was scared to say anything, and this time I knew I would not sound good. My ex-wife Tatiana was there with me and held a space for me to speak when I was ready. After a few moments, while holding Tatiana's hand, I said to her, "Tatiana, this is how I will sound for the rest of my life." I was whispering – and then the tears started rolling down my cheeks as I felt my own words deeply in my heart. My worst fears were realized: I had become a whisperer for life. I looked at Tatiana and said through my tears, "Tatiana, I will never sing again, I will never sing again." Even writing these words ten years later, I am weeping. I was in shock once again – an ongoing theme for the experience with cancer.

In a few days I had a moment where I heard from the Bronx Buddha, who reminded me once again, "It's just another wave, David. Right now, you are at the bottom of it; wait for the gifts from the ride back up. They are coming - this is the truth." The Bronx Buddha might have been right. Yet to this day I weep when I hear songs that I sang before cancer, songs that brought me so much joy and openheartedness when I sang them. Songs like "Beauty and the Beast," "My Way," "The Greatest Love of All." There are many songs I miss singing, and often over the past ten years, these words fly out of my mouth: "I want to sing again," "I want my voice back," "I want to sing again," and every time, I weep deeply. Thankfully, my ex-wife Tatiana had come to be with me for the surgery and during the weeks ahead. She asked Doctor Courey a question in our post-surgery visit that would change the course of my life once again.

The Defining Moment with Cancer

One week after surgery, with Tatiana's support and presence, I went to Dr. Courey's office for my post-op appointment. Dr. Courey, after a look-see at the area where he had performed the surgery, said that all looked good, but he needed me to know that if the cancer came back a third time, there was only one more surgery he could do for me, which was to take out my entire voice box. That would leave me with no easy way to talk with people, not even with the loud whisper I had now. That would also mean I would have a hole in my throat that I would breathe through; the air no longer going through my nose and throat. That shocked me, but I was glad he had said it. I asked him whether I would die if he took out my voice box and the cancer came back afterward. He said yes. Before I could feel anything or process his answer, Tatiana asked him the question that launched a thousand ships for me: "If he does not heal whatever caused the cancer, will it come back?" And Dr. Courey, once again, said yes. I was lost, in shock, overwhelmed as my mind jumped from the word "death," to "hole in my throat," and "not being able to talk." All this information was causing my head to spin. I wanted to live - at least I *thought* I did, and I wanted to keep my whisper. I did not want a hole in my throat - *what do I do?* I had no idea at that moment. *How do I make sure the cancer does not come back?* The moment I asked that question, my train left the "Cancer" station. I was sure there was going to be a repeat of the dive downward into the darkened tunnel walls. But just the opposite happened. My train continued to go upward - and in the far distance, I could see a pinhole of light in the middle of the darkness. Were the gods playing with me, trying to give me hope? As it turned out, it would be far more than hope.

Finding My Way to Stay Alive

My days and nights were now filled with my mind trying to figure out where to find the answer to the question: How can I make sure the cancer does not come back? My first action was to ask Dr. Courey the question: "What causes vocal cord cancer?" He said vocal cord cancer is caused by acid reflux, smoking, doing drugs, or drinking alcohol. None of these fit me, and to make sure about the acid reflux, I had an endoscopy, which showed no sign of it. If none of these, then what? At least I knew what *hadn't* caused my cancer, but I was still left with the question as to what *had*.

David The Beloved

If I were looking to buy a car and doing research on the Internet, I would get overwhelmed in minutes. Now I needed to figure out how to save my voice box and my life - and this took overwhelm to a whole new level. I didn't know where to turn or who to talk to for guidance. Initially I was thwarted by my resistance to doing the research. But by its very nature, cancer made me what's known as a "motivated changer," and at times allowed me to bust through the frozen state I found my body and mind to be in. In moments when I allowed myself to feel the fear or the terror, a doorway opened to the discovery of what I needed to do next. And who were these resistance busters, these door openers? They were qualities that I was born with: The intention to live, inner strength, perseverance, and will. They were taking turns kicking in on a daily, sometimes hourly, basis, when the resistance would arise. It was challenging and difficult, yet I felt I had to keep going, as my mind kept reminding me I was one surgery away from having no voice box, no way to communicate with people - and staring death in the face. Whatever I was doing, I was doing alone. My old belief from childhood, that I needed to take care of myself, that there was no one else that would do it for me, was driving the car. This belief came from the time when I was eight to ten years old, and in my mind, I had disowned my parents because of their yelling and hitting. There I was in a ballpark where I didn't know how to play the game and believed there was no one that wanted to help me.

The post-operation biopsy that Dr. Courey did a few months after the surgery showed that the surrounding area from which the vocal cords and parts of my vocal folds were removed was all cancer free. I was still in fear that the cancer would come back, as it had twice before. And I still didn't know what had caused the cancer in the first place. I had to find the answer – *had to!!!*

A year before the symptoms of cancer arose, my life was in chaos, as I was still feeling the loneliness of being divorced, my job at UC Berkeley was not secure, and the lovely place I was living in was being sold by the owners and I had to move. The perfect storm of stress generators: divorce, loss of job, and moving. It has always been hard for me to find a safe and comfortable place to live with no odors. For four months I lived out of a storage area, with clothes hung in my car and office, laundry in the back seat of my car, shuttling from friends' couches to B&Bs or hotels. Some days I didn't know until late in the day where I was going to sleep that night, nor what I would do for work in a few months. Every day I found myself more depressed, forlorn, hopeless, and helpless.

After months of this state of mind, I had thoughts that I couldn't do this anymore, that my life wasn't worth living. I no longer valued any part of my life and I wanted to get off the train. It didn't occur to me in 2009 – a time when my job was secure and I was able to move back into the same townhouse in Moraga (as the owners could not sell their property), and my heart had healed from the divorce – that the events of the previous year had anything to do with my cancer. Dr. Courey told me that vocal cord cancer grows very slowly, and I was sure that it had started growing at least a year before I noticed it in singing class in 2009.

The stress associated with those life-changing events, and the thought of getting off the train, had caused an incalculable amount of damage to my immune system. It had left the door open and put the welcome mat out for cancer. But why the vocal cords? I was

David The Beloved

certain it was because all the singing I was doing and the impact of all the yelling I had done most of my life had left my vocal cords vulnerable to cancer. It is my belief that cancer will look for the most vulnerable part of the body to set up shop. When I presented my thesis to Dr. Courey, he smiled, looked down my throat with his video camera, and said "All looks beautiful; keep doing what you're doing," and never gave me a grade on my "thesis." I wanted him to agree with me, *needed* his agreement so I would know the cause, and could now concentrate on the healing. All I received was the smile and encouraging words as to the current state of my vocal cord area. My friend Amitabh had a great saying, "I may not be right, yet I am absolutely certain." This was exactly how I felt about my thesis; I was certain that stress had caused my cancer and I had to reduce the stress in my life significantly. I will provide some support for my thesis later in this chapter.

While in the waiting room for one of my monthly post-op look-sees with Dr. Courey, I saw a patient leaving the office who was actually happy. I thought I would love to talk to her, and find out what she had done to get her to her happy place. And then it hit me - I needed someone to talk to who had gone through what I was going through. With Dr. Courey and my thesis in my tool belt, I realized the next step was to find a mentor. When I was learning how to be a computer programmer in my twenties I had a mentor. When I was learning to become an actor, I had multiple mentors, and to become a singer I had Shari and my accompanist Dan as my mentors. To make sure I stayed cancer free, I now knew I needed a mentor. And that meant letting go of the belief that I had to do all of this myself. I needed support, a lot of support, and now I was going to allow

Journey With Cancer

that support into my life even when the resistance to accepting that support showed up.

To find a mentor, I started by making a list of friends and acquaintances who I knew had survived cancer to ask them what they had done. One friend, who had gone through tongue cancer, told me she was very clear that her cancer was not coming back. I liked the sound of that, and even though I did not yet have the same mindset, that's where I wanted my tracks to go. I asked her if she would become my mentor until my own inner guidance system took over, and she agreed. She gave me her "recipe" for healing, which included different alternative healers. I started following that recipe, though I decided that I would keep my wonderful Dr. Courey as my surgeon and do anything he recommended. And never once did I entertain any idea, during the entire time before all the surgeries or after, to stop with Dr. Courey and only use her recipe's alternative healing methods. His advice always plays in my head: "Keep doing what you're doing." Yet I would add some alternative healing methods to what I was already doing for insurance.

The first step of my mentor's recipe was to book sessions with one of the people who wrote the book on hypnotherapy. I wanted to make sure I no longer had any hint of wanting to get off the train. The hypnotherapist was a gentle, sweet man in his seventies, who immediately put me at ease. He explained to me that the hypnosis he would do with me was nothing like what you see on TV or in the movies, where they cause a person to bark like a dog. Instead, he would support my going into a relaxed state where he could ask me questions from the thoughts hidden in my mind. And that is exactly how I experienced the sessions, being relaxed with a channel

David The Beloved

opened to my hidden beliefs, issues, and ideas as they made themselves known to me and the therapist. I had four sessions, each with the same experience, a state of ease. The conclusion was that I did *not* have a death wish. *I now wanted to stay on the train.*

Next on the recipe list was Reiki sessions, and so I did these with a practitioner who was a mutual friend of my mentor and me. Reiki is a Japanese form of alternative medicine called energy healing. Reiki practitioners use a technique called palm healing or hands-on healing, through which a "universal energy" is said to be transferred through the palms of the practitioner to the patient to encourage emotional and/or physical healing. That sounded good to me, even though I had no idea what that meant. I trusted my mentor's recommendation and my Reiki practitioner friend to do her thing, as I knew she loved me. I had a session each week; though mine were not hands-on, they were via the phone, yet they were still a valuable healing method to add to my tool kit.

Another friend who had gone through cancer recommended bodywork massage, as she had found it helpful to reduce her stress and quiet the constant radio playing in her mind about cancer. The minute she said "reduces stress," I was all in. I read that stress cripples the immune system from doing its thing. Two months after starting weekly Reiki sessions, I started weekly bodywork sessions with another good friend. It was not a pleasure when she was working on the places in my body where I stored the tensions of the stress. It was painful, but when the session was over I felt like a different person, more grounded and more present.

Four months after starting my quest to make sure cancer would not come back, with weekly Reiki and massage, my own guidance

Journey With Cancer

system kicked in. I was ready to up the ante and bring even more healing energies into my life, as much I could afford financially. I didn't really know which ones would work for me, so the more the merrier. As W.C. Fields used to say, "Just trying to cover every angle." My mind wanted "more now," this immediacy driven by the lurking fear that the cancer would come back. Yet my mind, the source of those fear-provoking thoughts, would create resistance to making a "now" timeline possible. I needed enough time to assimilate each new healing so it wouldn't be overwhelming, which would cause me to stop doing it. The amount of time I needed for this assimilation was not days or weeks, but months.

My next step was to start meditating every day; most of the time, twice a day for twenty minutes each session. It took me several weeks to get into the habit of fulfilling this twice-a-day regimen, yet I had a sense it was serving me, and I did feel less stressed after the meditations. One initial hurdle was that I kept looking at the clock to see how much time was left, and I had to build my capacity to sit, doing nothing, for twenty minutes. It had been many years since my days connected to Osho when I had a meditation practice. I was a rookie again.

After getting into the pattern of meditating every day, I turned to my singing teacher and asked about seeing her for a healing session that didn't include singing. She suggested that I see her healer instead, a man I knew who'd had a near-death experience. She called him a shaman. I called him Philmore, as we knew each other from singing class before his near-death experience. Philmore was a big black man who played some mean drums, and we once did an improv duet together in singing class that was a one and only.

David The Beloved

I really liked Philmore. I experienced him as authentic, light, and joyful. I did not hesitate to reach out to him and start weekly one-hour phone sessions with him right away. Even after ten years I still can't tell you for sure what happens in these sessions. I would lie down on the couch, and at times I'd feel as if something was moving in me – but I wasn't doing anything to make it happen. Sometimes I felt an energy circling around me. In all the sessions there was a cycle where my mind kicked in with this and that until I became aware of it, and then I shifted back to being present with what is. After most sessions, I felt more present with myself and more grounded. Dr. Courey kept telling me to "keep doing what you're doing" and that's what I was doing.

Six months after hearing the two "Yeses" from Dr. Courey, I now had daily sessions of meditation and weekly sessions of Reiki, bodywork, and Philmore the Shaman. I have never thought that I performed a healing on myself. I had associated any healing benefits from the alternative healers I have had sessions with as something they did. *They* were healing *me*. It is said by many "healers" that if I would get out of the way, my body would heal itself, my immune system would perform at the top of its game, and the best possible healing would occur. Despite my mind responding sarcastically, with a "thank you very much," a light bulb went off. I had the realization that I was a part of my own healing equation, and my part was to make my immune system my best friend and take care of it the way I would take care of my son Jason when he was a child. As I had this realization, the pinhole of light I observed down the tracks was getting bigger and closer. This would be the new pattern: as I took in more and more information and my next steps showed themselves, the pinhole of light continued to get brighter and larger. I had no idea what this light was or if it was good or bad. I would find out in the coming years.

Sitting in Dr. Courey's office six months earlier, hearing the reality of my prognosis if the cancer came back again, I could not have imagined that I would be in weekly Reiki, bodywork, and sessions with a shaman. There were other alternative healing methods I tried – some really out there, like the "gazing healer" – that I'll present in the Afterword chapter, "Healing My Cancer." It seems the only two options I did not try during my exploration into alternative healing were a medicine man and a voodoo priest. I still had some doubt about my thesis – that stress had caused my cancer – but then, by accident, I found a book that supported my belief that what had created the cancer was indeed stress. I had experienced stress all my life, but the episode that broke the camel's back was my time being marriage-less, home-less, and potentially job-less.

Einstein's Quantum Physics and Love

The book I found was titled *The Healing Code* by Dr. Alexander Loyd. Dr. Loyd, while trying to cure his wife of her long-term depression, discovered a process to activate a bodily function that heals 95% of all illness and disease. Dr. Loyd captured my attention when he explained in the first twenty-nine pages that almost all diseases are caused by *stress*. Paraphrasing Dr. Loyd as well as my trauma therapist, traumatic events when we are young leave an impression in the memory of our body's cells and nervous system. This is so powerful that even when an event happens in adulthood that is similar in

David The Beloved

some way to the traumatic event in childhood, the cells' memories will reactivate the original trauma and provoke stress. I resonated with Dr. Loyd's and my trauma therapist's conclusions. My birth experience, having the cord tied around my neck and almost dying; the loss of my grandmother as I had known her before her stroke; my parents' yelling and the beatings – all of these were traumatic for me. As an adult, that stress reoccurs if circumstances trigger a memory of a childhood trauma. For example, when someone yells at me or at someone near me, I will get stressed, because it reminds my body's cellular and nervous system of the yelling in childhood.

Dr. Jed Diamond (PhD) offers the following credence for Dr. Loyd's conclusions:

"When we are stressed our cells literally close up; nothing is going in or out. Our cells don't receive nutrition, oxygen, minerals, etc., nor do they get rid of waste products and toxins while under stress. Under normal conditions the stress comes and goes quickly, and shutting things down for a short period of time does not cause damage. But increasingly we are under chronic stress and our bodies, minds, and spirits cannot repair themselves." I agree with both Dr. Loyd and Dr. Diamond. It is my experience and intuition that stress has caused the ailments that I have had: cancer, TMJ, trouble falling asleep, tendonitis, and neck spasms. All of these I trace to the major stress in my life from events like my divorces, the fire, leaving an entire life behind, looking for and moving to new living places, and looking for work.

After reading *The Healing Code* I had a realization between stress and my diseases. If I broke the word disease into two parts, I got *dis-* and *ease*. What is dis-ease? Stress!!! When I am at ease and relaxed, my cells and my immune system can function at the top of their game. This had to become my way of life. One of my new sayings to myself when I messed up became: "Nobody died." If you only read the first twenty-nine pages of this book it would be worth the cost. Based on quantum physics and measurements made by Dr. Loyd, he concluded that there is an energy vibration that neutralizes the vibration of our dis-ease energy. And that energy vibration is called "Love." Yes, I resonate with this as well. When love is present there is no dis-ease, only ease. And I have experienced times when love is present within and surrounding me – and there is no stress in those moments.

Loving My Cancer

Not long after reading *The Healing Code*, I had the epiphany that I could not *fight* the cancer. I knew this went against the Western world's idea that if we had cancer we must combat it. After reading *The Healing Code* and resonating with the fact that stress is the worst state of being for healing and that it also compromises the immune system, I could not go along with this "fighting" technique. This led me to the realization that fighting cancer would cause stress and be self-defeating in my healing. I would be creating a dis-ease by *fighting*. It made no sense to me to fight cancer, as the cancer was inside my body, part of me. Was I supposed to fight myself with myself? I knew that my immune system was set up to fight harmful invaders, and it felt that my cancer was something that I had created, not something that had invaded me (more on this soon). I was not trying to demote my

David The Beloved

immune system from doing what it was designed to do organically. Not at all! The right course was to *"love"* the cancer, and the love would melt away the dis-ease (resonating with Dr. Loyd's conclusions that love balances out dis-ease). I did not give up Dr. Courey, or anything he told me to do, and I continued his course of treatments in addition to loving the cancer as long as it was in my body. I have shared this realization that you cannot "fight" cancer, with others or their loved ones going through cancer, and they all "got it" and appreciated hearing that. There was a mother of a co-worker who felt relieved by this, and that supported her through the days and weeks before she passed away. The most important message that I would give to people with cancer, which I have drawn from my own experience, is: *Do everything in Western and Eastern medicine available that you feel supports healing your cancer, and don't fight it – LOVE it.*

I wish I had the funds to put up a series of billboards. As you were driving down the road you would see them in this order, in very big letters:

"I had cancer, and I found a way to love my cancer"
  "If I fight cancer, I have one part of me fighting another part of me"
    "This causes dis-ease in my body"
      "Loving my cancer brings ease and supports healing by my immune system"
        "Healing my immune system will heal my body"
          "Healing my body will heal my soul"
            "Healing my body and soul will heal my heart"
              "Healing my heart will bring me more joy and love at a time when I need them the most"

My Mantra

I met a woman, during my early years of being cancer free, who played a tape of a healing method that involved releasing tensions and emotions. There was a mantra on the tape to support the releasing, which I adapted for use in conjunction with the concept from *The Healing Code* that love neutralizes stress. This in turn allows the immune system to work at the top of its game. When I knew cancer was inside my body, I would say the following mantra out loud; first for cancer, several times a day, and then for the terror I felt in the morning that made me too paralyzed to get out of bed:

> "I welcome you my *cancer*,
> and I send you my love,
> as you are a part of me in this moment,
> and all parts of me deserve to be loved."

> Then I adapted it for the terror:
> "I welcome you my *terror*,
> and I send you my love,
> as you are a part of me in this moment,
> and all parts of me deserve to be loved."

After many weeks of saying the mantra for terror, one morning, the following words came out of my mouth after reciting the mantra. "Okay, terror, give me your best shot." I thought it was the kid from the Bronx speaking, and maybe it was, but it was the last morning I would wake up in terror. In that moment, I was accepting the terror inside of me and willing to experience it totally. In that moment, I had found

David The Beloved

a way to *love* my terror. I am not sure if I ever totally loved my cancer, but I feel I totally accepted it and found I accepted more of what was in my life day by day. Here is how that acceptance presented itself to me:

During my journey with cancer, I had a moment where I envisioned my unique personness as an infinite harmonica. And I thought and felt, in each moment, that existence was blowing through a certain set of harmonica slots to create a note. And all these notes together made up my life symphony.

Then I imagined that when my mind's judgments, reactions, beliefs, and strategies were active that they would block these slots, and existence could not create notes. It was then I realized that these blocked notes were notes as well, and that they were also part of my life's symphony.

When I looked at my life that way, everything that happens each moment – whether I am being present in the moment or my mind is disturbingly active – is part of my life, part of my symphony, and it needs and wants to be embraced and loved.

It has been over ten years since my vocal cords were removed, and *I am still cancer free*. My work every day is to stay vigilant and to make choices to stay out of stress. The question of which relationships to end or keep included family, friends, support people and groups, and even the places I shopped. Activities to continue doing, or discontinue, included my work, exercise, what TV or movies to watch. I had to look at every facet of my day-to-day life. I found I had to be totally truthful – asking for what I wanted, instead of scheming to get it. To stay simple and truthful would aid me in being at ease and keeping my heart open, allowing love to heal any stress present in those moments. I did all of this because the number-one priority in my life was and is to stay cancer free; everything else was priority two or lower. In the Afterword chapter, "Healing My Cancer," I will explain in more detail what I did to heal my cancer.

The Gift of Cancer – What it Came to Teach Me

After about two years of being cancer free, I went out on second date with a woman I met on an online dating site. She was what I would call a spiritual person, versed in meditation and other Eastern ideas. During our chat she said something that surprised me, maybe even shocked me a bit: "So you gave yourself cancer to free up your throat chakra." I was taken aback by her statement and I felt confused, not really knowing very much about chakras. I was hung up on the words "You gave yourself cancer." I didn't ask her what she meant, and I also didn't see her again. Yet her words stayed with me for a while; I often asked myself, sometimes out loud, "Did I *really* give myself cancer?" What I realized was that everything I had done in my life, leading up to having cancer, constituted the tracks of my life. And yes, everything that I had done up to having cancer led me to cancer. She was right about that. Though I have no idea about giving cancer to myself to open my throat chakra. Okay, I get it, I gave myself cancer. But for what possible reason did my tracks take me to this station? I was obsessed with knowing the answer.

One day, after the cancer had come back the second time, while reciting the first two lines of the mantra, I stopped; the light bulb went on. "I welcome you my cancer, and I send you my love." Poof! There I was at this moment, welcoming the cancer inside of me, the darkest possible part of me, the part that was killing me – and I was

David The Beloved

accepting its presence and sending my love to it. I was loving and accepting "my" cancer, and if cancer was love-able, then so must I be. If my cancer was deserving of love, so must I be. I realized that cancer had come to teach me that I did not love myself. It was telling me how *un*love-able and undeserving of love I held myself to be in my beliefs. These old beliefs from childhood, created by my parents' emotional and physical abuse, were buried in a place where, for my whole life, I could not see them. Cancer opened the door to show me what was hidden deep in the recesses of my mind. Cancer shone a light down into these recesses, and if I did not want cancer to come back, I needed to muster the courage, will, and strength to go down to the darkest places in my mind, and to welcome and love these false beliefs about how love-able I am - to bring them into the light so they could be healed and the truth be restored, that I was love-able and deserving of love. And that there was nothing wrong with me. The moment when I understood what cancer had come to teach me, my train pulled out of the Cancer Station and my train car became a healing sanctuary. I had just left the "3" on the circular journey of my train tracks; going counterclockwise, I was now heading towards the last set of stations.

I Arrive at My Mother's Bedside

On July 26, 2015, four years after I had lost my vocal cords and four years being cancer free, my train car was still a healing sanctuary. As they say, it takes five years to "kiss the wall" (meaning that your cancer wasn't likely to come back), and I had one more year to go. Because of this, I was surprised there was a station coming up. As the train slowed down, I could see that this was the longest station platform to date, seemingly going on for a mile. On the walls were pictures of me and my mother, some with us photographed together, starting out when I was a baby and continuing through the years.

David The Beloved

How odd, I thought, as I didn't feel I needed a history lesson of our time together in this lifetime. When the train stopped, at the very end of the station platform, and the doors opened, there was one picture of my mother with a black wreath around it. I knew what this meant, and I knew that day would be coming. I would have thought this station sign would say, "Your Mother Died." I was close: it read, "My Mother's Passing – Four Fleeting Days."

Four days later, on July 29th, my mother passed away at the age of almost ninety-nine. Sitting here years later, I am still moved as I recall the days and moments of the final days we spent together before she died. After I moved out of my parents' house at age twenty-two, within an hour of my arrival at every visit back, she would get on my nerves, telling me what I needed to do or what I shouldn't be feeling or that I didn't call her or visit her enough. Hearing her telling me, as an adult, what I should and should not do, just as she would do during my childhood, would send me into a rage and I would start yelling at her.

A few years earlier, my son and his mom, T, and I had flown to New Jersey to say goodbye to my mother, as we all thought she was going to die. The three of us were sitting around the dining room table eating Chinese food and enjoying conversation when my mother walked into the room. My mother saw the nice connection between my first wife T and me and said to us: "I can call the rabbi and you can get married again." She was serious and would not let go of this thread. Finally, without another moment's hesitation, I jumped up, took a cup of water from the table and threw it in her face. I used to tell her that the verbal cruelty and insensitivity that she would exhibit towards people, especially me, would leave her to

My Mother's Passing – Four Fleeting Days

die alone. I was wrong – she didn't die alone – I was there for her last four days, despite the past.

I was supposed to fly to New Jersey over the July 4th weekend when my son and grandkids would be visiting from Houston. The trip was also to take care of some business. I had to sign short-term loan papers to pay for my mother's 24/7 care over the coming months before we sold her house, and I had to check in with her caregivers. Some angel must have been watching, as the loan papers got delayed and delayed until I finally arrived in the early evening on Sunday, July 26th with the signing scheduled for the next day. I arrived without ever thinking that she would soon die, although three days before I arrived, the main caregiver called to tell me she had fallen and broken her nose. My mother was upset, all riled up, because a dear friend of hers, who loved my mother, had inappropriately called her and told her the house was going to be sold and she would need to go into a nursing facility. My son had innocently mentioned this fact to my mother's friend. My mother did not want to leave her house. She wanted to die in her house and was terrified of losing control of her life in a nursing facility. When my mother had fallen, the caregiver called 911 and they came out, but my mother refused to go to the hospital. I could not have forced her even if I had been there at that moment, since New Jersey law, astonishingly, would still have considered my mother competent. Once again, this situation brought conflict to me as my mind and heart knew it was right for her to go to the hospital. I got why she feared going – and why she had not been to a hospital as a patient in over seventy years – because we both had almost died when I was born. Her fear would turn out to be prophetic!

David The Beloved

The evening I arrived, nothing and nobody could have prepared me for what I was about to see. For the heartache I would feel, for the tears I would suppress, suddenly feeling the need to act strong. There was my mother in her bed in almost a fetal position, black and blue all over the skin not covered by clothing. A bandage was covering her nose, which was still draining blood, and she could barely move on her own. She had a food container with four sections, each with a different kind of food. She would move her hand ever so slowly and deliberately, her fingers shaking, to one of the compartments and remove a small bit of food with a couple of fingers and slowly put it into her mouth. I would not let myself feel the sadness and heartbreak of watching her. The thought, *What did I let her do to herself?* kept playing in my head, over and over. I just could not believe what had happened to this poor soul.

Even more problematic was the fact that her hemoglobin counts were quite low and she had no energy. When the caregiver sat her up to feed her, my mother could not stay sitting on the edge of the bed without falling, as her body was now dead weight. Despite seeing and experiencing all of this, I still felt conflicted about taking her to the hospital. I waited for her to finish her dinner and then left the room to make the first of many phone calls to my son Jason to share my experiences, bouncing reasons off him for taking her to the hospital or not. Finally, my heart gave me a clear picture, and I called 911. Thankfully, the paramedics came within minutes of my call. She kept telling them she was all right, but she was not - she was in pain, and she was suffering!

From the moment we arrived at the hospital, she started telling everyone she saw: "I'm all right. I know what's wrong with me. I'm anemic." She was so sweet while doing this, and hearing this from this ninety-eight-year-old woman brought smiles to the hospital staff. She was put in a room where people came in to take her vitals and start an IV. Everyone who came in received the same greeting: "I'm all right. I know what's wrong with me. I'm anemic." Once they put fluids in her, she perked up. I typed on my iPad, in big letters, to play with her, as it had been over seventy years since she was last in a hospital, as a patient. "Wow, you are in the hospital and you are still alive! So far so good!" She read it and she looked at me and said as clearly as possible, as in the moment as possible, as if she truly *were* all right: "I hate you." The caregiver who had accompanied me to the hospital joined me in laughing hysterically. My mother was truly authentic in that moment. My mother! When had I ever used the words "sweet" and "authentic" to describe my mother? The answer was "Never." Here, near the end of her life, she was rewriting the way I had known her.

Second Day

They decided to keep her overnight at the hospital so they could give her the needed blood the next morning. During the night they aspirated her (drew fluid from her lungs). Her blood pressure had wild swings; the hospital team did not think she would last the night. Yet, with medication, the staff was able to stabilize her. The doctor, who was very compassionate, told me in the morning that she did not have six months to live, and suggested that after they gave her blood, I should take her home under hospice. In that moment, I let go of the idea of putting her in a nursing home or selling the house before her death, and I told the doctor that's what I would do.

They gave her blood that evening instead, and her speech became clear again. I wrote again on the iPad, in big letters, to tell her that tomorrow she was going home. She said in such a sweet young way, "To my house?" She couldn't hear me say "Yes!" because of my lack of vocal cords and her not having her hearing aids, so I gave her a thumbs up. She asked again, as if she couldn't believe my answer. *"To my house?"* Again, a thumbs up, and I nodded my head many times. She seemed to relax and feel happy that she was going home. My mother was so very sweet; in fact, the sweetest a person could be when facing what was unthinkable only days ago. I went over and kissed her many times on her forehead and sat there for as long as I could, just holding her hand. Most of the time while at her bedside, all I did was hold her hand. I wanted her to know she was not alone. In my entire life, those were the most connected, most loving, sweetest moments I had ever shared with my mother. The nurses came in to give her the blood. She gave them no resistance and I left for the night.

Third Day

On the third night she was again having trouble breathing, and so the staff aspirated her. Her blood pressure was still very high. They were able to stabilize her with medication, but very early in the morning I received a call from the hospital to get right over there. When I arrived, the doctor said they needed to put her in hospice at the hospital, immediately, and I needed to sign the papers. I am glad I did not witness those two nights of the suffering she must have gone through, as it would have broken my heart completely. Now

My Mother's Passing – Four Fleeting Days

they started giving her morphine, and whenever she showed signs of struggling or discomfort, they would up the dosage.

On her last full day alive I spent as much time as possible at her bedside, just holding her hand. Some of her friends from the neighborhood and some folks from the Jewish temple she once belonged to came to say hi. By then, she was out of it and even though she opened her eyes every now and then, there was no recognition of these folks. There was one moment when we were alone, where she mumbled a few times to say something that sounded like "I'm sorry." Whatever it was, she repeated it numerous times. Was she really saying to me before she died: "I'm sorry for all the times I yelled at you." "I'm sorry for all those times I triggered your father to hit or beat you." "I'm sorry for making you do all those things that were not in your nature." "I'm sorry for not honoring your feelings." Now I have no way of knowing if the mumblings expressed her sorrow for doing those things and that she was apologizing to me. I don't know whether that's what she was feeling sorry about. I didn't know – nor did it matter! I choose to believe that this sweet, loving woman was sharing with her son her deepest sorrow for those times she treated him cruelly and unlovingly. It was her choice to name me David, and in some way I knew she considered me a beloved, but the circumstances and events of our lives had made it impossible for her to honor my belovedness.

The Last Day

I arrived at the hospital for my mother's last morning alive, not knowing it would be her final hours. I sat with her for a while, unaware of the sadness and heartbreak that lived just below the surface. The

David The Beloved

hospice folks came by and we talked in the hallway. I didn't realize that the same old tune was still playing in my head. "Look what I let her do to herself." I shared that with these folks, and I started falling apart in the hospital hallway with these two strangers. They reminded me that she had wanted it to be the way she wanted it, and that I could not have forced her to go to the hospital. I heard what they said, and while that was true, I kept thinking that because I was not willing to fly across the country frequently, I had let her keep hurting herself. I did the best I could with a very difficult person to care for, yet I could not find peace at this time, or believe that none of her suffering was my fault. I asked the hospice folks how long they thought it would be before she passed; they thought she would only have a few more hours.

I went out for an hour to run a few errands and when I returned, just as I pulled into the hospital garage, I got a call to get to her room fast, as her passing was imminent. I missed the moment by three minutes. I went over and kissed her on the forehead, and without thinking, I walked to the middle of her room, put my arms out to the heavens and said out loud: "You're free - and so am I." And then I fell apart in the room. Now I truly understood the meaning of the station sign.

As I sat in a visitor's area, not far from my mother's body, I remember something that had happened a few years earlier. When I was healing from cancer, I had sessions with many different alternative healing techniques. There was one Reiki healer who, during an in-person session, told me that my grandmother was in the room with me during our session. She said that my grandmother had a message she wanted me to give to my mother: "Tell your mother not to be afraid of death. That she (my grandmother) would be there waiting for her (my mother) to take her to the other side." I wrote my mother a letter and shared the message from my grandmother. Her reaction? She called my son Jason and asked him if there was something wrong with me. But because of that message I knew my mother was in good hands. It is my intention to remember that message when it is my time to leave this lifetime. I am sure there will be someone waiting for me as well, and I know it will be my Grandmother Yetta. I know it with every fiber of my being and my heart!!!

My mother told me many times how she felt I had loved my grandmother more than I loved her. After her death I read in my mother's unpublished book the following words: "The love and devotion that Mom (my grandmother Yetta) and David had for each other was the most wonderful thing to watch. I didn't seem to exist when his grandma was around. It was that way until she died. I was happy that they had this relationship. Mom had so few pleasures. If this brought a warm smile to her face, then it was worth sacrificing my share of my son's love." My mother never shared these thoughts with me, and in a way, she was right. But the part my mother had missed was that my grandmother was much more *open* to my love than she herself was. Yet how could I not love the woman who gave me life, and almost died in the act of giving this gift?

Saying Goodbye with All My Love

Ten months after my mother died, a friend of mine suggested holding a ritual for her, to say goodbye to her spirit. I thought about it for a while, and then I remembered the only time I had ever experienced my mother at ease was either on the dance floor with my father, at family celebrations, or lighting the Sabbath candles on Friday night.

David The Beloved

I decided to find someone who would light the candles, and I would say a few words. After making inquiries, I found a woman who gave me the gift of doing this, and we arranged, one Friday night, to meet her at the temple where she attended services.

The night of our meeting, with the words I had prepared, I walked into the temple and observed several women rehearsing the music for the Friday night service. When they finished playing the piece, one woman arose and walked to the back of the big sanctuary room to where I was standing. She came over and introduced herself and told me to sit in the back, as they had just a few more minutes to rehearse. While I sat there, huge goose pimples suddenly began popping up all over my body, and then energy started flowing up my legs and through my entire body. I don't know how I knew, but I knew my mother's spirit was there with me then, and I knew I was doing the right ritual to connect with her and say goodbye. When the woman was ready, she took me into a side room from the sanctuary, where she had prepared the candles. After she lit the candles and said the prayers in Hebrew, I said my final words to my mother's spirit. As I said them, both the woman and I were touched, and tears streamed down my cheeks. Even today I feel such hurt in my heart for all the cruelty my mother and I inflicted on each other - and at this moment, as I am writing this, my tears are healing more of that hurt. The words I said to my mother were these:

Beloved Mother,

> *I don't really know if my releasing you from me will make any difference to your freedom of spirit, your meeting with your mother, and your journey to come. I must say to your spirit - and to my own*

My Mother's Passing – Four Fleeting Days

mind, body, and soul – how sorry I am for all the times I was cruel to you in my adult life, for all the times I missed accepting your love in your moments of dropping into lovingness, for all the times in your last months when I said "I'm done," and had to make decisions for your care based upon that – and mostly for allowing you to hurt yourself those times by giving you your way and not making the paramedics take you to the hospital. I am forgiving myself in this moment, and I know you have already forgiven me. Conscious journey, journey of freedom to you, my beloved mother, and to me as well.

Your loving son,
David

It was a slow ride with lots of tears leaving the "You're Free" station – tears of loss, healing, and forgiveness for my behavior towards my mother. I needed this slow ride to truly assimilate not only the loss of my mother, but also of my father and my ten aunts and uncles who were gone, too. I was now the oldest of all my first cousins from my mother's side of the family. I pictured myself standing on a conveyor belt moving ever so slowly toward the end, where I would eventually fall off. Behind me I could see my son in the middle, and behind him, my grandchildren near the beginning. I realized that I would probably (and hopefully) be the next one to leave this lifetime. It was a sobering thought, which I did not let myself hang out with very long. I

David The Beloved

reminded myself that my grandmother would be there waiting for me in the afterlife. Seeing this mental picture gave me a sense of urgency – for what reason, I wondered? My train was still a healing sanctuary, and the number-one priority in my life was still to stay cancer free. As I pulled into the next station, there was nothing on the platform; only the walls painted red gave any contrast to the empty nothingness of the station. As the doors opened and I stepped out onto the platform, I heard a drum beating; thump-thump, then a slight pause; then another thump-thump, and then another slight pause; with this rhythmic pattern continuing. Unexpectedly, I felt a sensation in my heart – not a hurt or pain, just a calling for my attention. I looked up to read the station sign: "Your Heart Is Here Waiting For You."

In earlier chapters, I have written about all the traumas of my childhood that started to close the door to my heart, feelings, innocence, and belovedness. The beating, followed by the two vows I made the next morning, slammed the door shut on everything that would allow me to feel like a human being. Those two vows cemented in my mind the belief that I was not love-able, was undeserving of love, that there was something wrong with me – and if I felt my feelings I would die. And I found one strategy that would take care of everything: if a feeling was about to arise, I would contract in my throat and belly.

My mind was actually very smart. It figured out that by contracting, I would not feel the pain in my heart from the beating, and I also would not let the rage come out to give me the energy to get the knife and kill my parents. If I had ever tried to kill my father, he probably would have killed me; so, this strategy probably saved my life. But, as I have mentioned, the loss was enormous – all the jewels of human beingness, feeling loved and loving, and the feeling of belovedness that goes along with that. I was cut off from all feelings – even hurt and fear – and cut off from breathing, allowing just enough for life to barely exist in my chest. From age thirteen on, my mind, with its beliefs and strategies, was steering my train down the tracks it felt safe going down, and I had no awareness that I was *being* steered.

My awareness of all of this came very slowly at first; it would start to arise a few years after I first joined a self-awareness group with my ex-wife Tatiana, and then re-joined, at the suggestions of Mradu and Amitabh, two years before being diagnosed with cancer. The self-awareness process is called the "Diamond Approach to Self-Realization," founded by A. Hameed Ali, and the groups I attended and still attend were (and are) called "Diamond Heart." Through Hameed's teachings and recommended practices, I was able to discover how the traumas of my childhood affected me, how the beliefs in my mind were created, and what strategies my mind came up with to avoid my feelings and protect my heart at all costs. The Diamond Heart groups, in which I have been a student for twenty years, were the very tracks that my train car traveled on as a healing sanctuary, and they gave me the support and grounding to go from one station to the next. The teachers and other students of these groups provided loving support and reminded me that I was love-able, deserving of love – and that nothing was wrong with me. To say it simply, they reflected the truth in me – in contrast to my parents, who reflected the lies. The Diamond Heart practices, which I continue to do daily and weekly, are an important aspect of my life. In the Afterword, I give more information about the "Diamond Approach to Self-Realization," A. Hameed Ali, "Diamond Heart" Groups, and the Ridhwan School. The Afterword also has information about one of the main practices

David The Beloved

of the Diamond Heart Group called "Inquiry," a practice of opening a channel to the unconscious using our natural curiosity (done mostly with one or two partners), which I still do every week.

For my first few years attending the Diamond Heart Groups, I found the teachings difficult to sit through because I did not understand most of what was being spoken. My mind would be merciless in its resistance towards hearing what was being taught, and its unwillingness to look at "who I was taking myself to be." It reminded me of when I was in Bud's class and he asked us during our first session how well we knew ourselves, and of course, Mr. Bigshot wrote down a BIG 10, meaning that I knew myself perfectly. At the end of Bud's class, I wrote down a zero - and there I was, once again, resisting the "zero." In those early years I found the Inquiry practice foreign; it seemed as if I were being asked to open my soul to strangers, and I did not have the foggiest idea how to go about it. I wanted to run, but I didn't. Before my cancer diagnosis I had not started "the work": the introspection into myself. I still believed that my thoughts were to be trusted and obeyed, and did not question who I was. Finally, after two and a half years I left the group, shortly after my father's death. It was a relief, as I would not miss the constant chatter in my mind during the teachings. I was done, relieved - and overall, I felt no regrets. Yet, after three years away, I would come back to Diamond Heart. I was now open to letting the teaching transmissions in and earnestly doing the exercises. This was two years before being diagnosed with cancer.

With the motivation to heal cancer, I started allowing the teachings to land in me. While exploring with Inquiry, I discovered how I had become the David of my childhood, and how I had acted from that place most of my life until cancer. At one group we were asked to draw a picture of how we saw our inner selves. I am no artist, as you can see from this drawing, yet the features are unmistakable. This is a picture of a person with such fear on his face, with a contraction around his belly and an arrow pointing to the contraction as if to say, "Hey, don't miss me – I'm here, I'm contracted," but also with a big heart radiating love. When people viewed this drawing, their first impression was: Yes, David, this is you, such a big heart. It was hard to let that in at the time, but it must have planted seeds that would be watered with more introspection, and more feedback about my heartfulness. And it brought into the light the recognition that I had a heart, a big heart, and it was a loving heart – words I would *never* use to describe myself for most of my life. These seeds would grow into the "big reveal" in the coming years.

David – as drawn in a Diamond Heart exercise

The Big Reveal

In mathematics, 2+2=4, of course. However, when I brought forth the courage, strength, and willingness to continue to explore who I *really* am - if not the conditioned patterns, beliefs, judgments, and strategies of my marriage to my mind (orchestrated by my parents) - I entered the world of "magic math." When I started directing my train from a place of freedom, 2+2 added up to a big number - any number possible, in fact. I call it the magic of "reality mathematics."

This is what occurred during a self-exploration exercise at a Diamond Heart group meeting in 2017. While doing this exercise with two partners, I said to them: "I don't feel my heart, and I haven't felt my heart for sixty years." It was not that I had never felt touched or had feelings. I did have moments of feeling ever since the night my father shared his remorse and I fell apart. But I still was not aware of feeling any sensation in my *physical* heart. This statement was a revelation; and it stunned me to hear those words come out of my mouth and acknowledge this truth to myself and others. It was a secret I had kept for all those years to avoid going where all the hurts and the wounds were hidden. I was afraid to feel all of it because of my belief that if I felt all that pain and hurt, I would die. This belief was not true, but simply a strategy of my mind to never allow anyone to break my heart again so totally as my father had on that fateful night when I was almost thirteen - the night I lost my connection to my heart, my innocence, my feelings, and my belovedness. By saying the words out loud to those two people, I could no longer hide it from myself. I would go on to share this truth with a group of a dozen people, and then a bigger group of seventy-five

Your Heart Is Here Waiting For You

people. I had to acknowledge this truth again and again, out loud to others, so that the door would not shut and hide the truth again. It's like when someone with an addiction takes the first step to sobriety by admitting they have an addiction. I had taken my first step to reclaiming my heart, innocence, feelings, and belovedness. It had taken many years of inner exploration and learning to access some of the qualities I was born with: the perseverance, strength, and courage, which I would need continuously, to keep going down the tracks to this moment of truth.

Now, four years after admitting this simple truth, I find that, little by little, I have more awareness and more feeling in my heart area. I often feel touched during meditation or Inquiry sessions, when there is a recognition of my empathy or compassion for others – and for the young David who had to endure abuse in childhood and live with contractions for most of his adult life. I am touched when reading a story or watching a movie where I can relate to the characters' pain and heartbreak, or when someone is vulnerable and shares their feelings with me. For all these moments when I am in touch with my heart, I am grateful. There is a knowing from my experience with V that there is still more unfolding to happen, and I want it *all*. I want to reclaim all that I lost that terrifying night when I was not yet thirteen – and especially my belovedness. I don't know how much of the "all" I have or don't have at this moment. I am still a work in progress. In the next station, though, I will get a glimpse.

Seeking A Japanese Wife

It was a two-year ride from the station where I had the revelation that I didn't feel my heart. My train car had continued to be a healing sanctuary ever since my cancer was first diagnosed. Throughout those years, my train car had traveled solo, uncoupled with any other train car, and I was very often lonely on that long ride. Many years went by and finally, thankfully, the next station came into view. As we slowed down and stopped I could see Japanese paper and bamboo lanterns lighting up the station. The colorful lanterns, hanging from the ceiling at different heights and in different sizes, created a wave effect as I

David The Beloved

looked out the train window. I had a good feeling that I was coming to a station that would provide a sense of well-being. The train came to a stop and when the doors opened, I saw Japanese tatami (mats) on the ground, and a woman in a kimono in front of me, with her face painted like a geisha, bowed to me. I did my best to return the bow, though I'd had no practice in the art of bowing. Even a kid from the Bronx knows that all of this represents Japanese style, and yet my train was not in Japan; it was in California. So, what's up with that? I looked up at the station sign and saw that the words were written in Japanese, with the English letters forming the word *Kon'nichiwa* (Welcome).

It had been fourteen years since my last divorce. During those years I had one short relationship which I got into very quickly. The woman and I shared open hearts, but it turned out that we were not compatible in how much time we wanted to spend with each other. Simply put, we had different models of relationship. I wanted to be with her most of the time, but this was not her cup of tea. From that experience, I still had not learned the importance of going slowly into a relationship and finding out whether we would be compatible in day-to-day life. My heart was longing for a beloved, to be in relationship, and to not be alone on holidays, birthdays, Valentine's Day, etc. I did learn something from my marriages and my time with V. In my first marriage to T, I was just a kid, and had started dating young. I was naive and did not take T into account or think about her feelings. Most of the time in that marriage I was coming from the patterns, beliefs, strategies, and programming lodged in my mind since childhood.

My relationship with V was a mix of the mind's thoughts *du jour* and moments of being my authentic self. The scale was tilted

こんにちは - KON'NICHIWA

toward the mind, but there were many loving, exquisite moments, moments of joy and happiness. Unfortunately, most of the time I was living life cut off from my feelings. Yet - and this is a big "yet," I was now aware that I was contracted, something I was not in touch with when married to T.

In my marriage to Tatiana, and as a stepfather to Misha, I had many moments of intolerance and was still tilted towards the mind; but there was a new feature - remorse. For the first time, I truly observed and felt on the inside how my intolerance and abuse affected others. Feeling deeply remorseful, and in tears, I would ask for forgiveness. At times during that marriage, I was afraid of myself and my behavior, as I now realized I was breaking my own heart.

With my marriage to cancer came a new level of awareness about my behavior and a new depth to my experience. All my marriages remind me of the line Stan Laurel would say to Ollie, his sidekick in their comedy routine: "Well, here's *another* nice mess you got me into!" Yet even messes can have their beauty and lessons. And there I was, once again seeking a woman to say "I do" with, but from a place of wanting to support each other to see our belovedness. There was one surprise waiting for me, a gift from the introspection after the big reveal.

I have always been attracted to Asian people. My son would marry a woman whose family came from Vietnam, and with this union, they would create my two beautiful grandchildren. When my son was still an infant, after my separation and divorce from T, I would leave him in the care of a Vietnamese woman who lived across the hall from us when I went to work. She and her husband, an engineer, also had an infant son. Sometimes I watched her sing in Vietnamese to both of our children. She truly sang from her heart, and she put these babies

David The Beloved

at ease with the love she gave them in those moments. I was not at all surprised that my son married a Vietnamese woman.

I also remember sitting with V in a Chinese restaurant in Berkeley in the 1980s. Nearby there was a Chinese family, with three generations sitting at a round table. One seat at their table was vacant, and it was all I could do to restrain myself from going over to sit with this family. It was a profound experience, as I honestly felt that I belonged at the table with them. It was not just my heart and soul talking to me, but also the seven-year-old David who believed he had lost his family after his grandmother's stroke and the abuse he suffered from his parents. The young David had yearned for the safety of being part of another family.

At this station, all the parts of me were in agreement, and speaking in unison, so loudly that I could not miss the message. Somewhere out there was a woman from an Asian culture that I wanted to be with, to marry. But who was it? And from which culture? I signed up with a Chinese matchmaker who set up a few dates for me with Chinese women, but their wants did not match mine and they lived a long car ride away. Then I asked a psychic about my future mate and she said there would be two Japanese women and one Filipina woman. I had contact with a Filipina woman, but religion was an issue, since she was Christian and I was spiritual, not following any organized religion. Next, I signed up with a Japanese matchmaker, who was very professional, and we had a thorough two-hour interview that I thought would help her find someone for me. About six weeks later, she matched me with a Japanese woman who lived only ten minutes from my house. When I saw J's profile, I could not believe she was sixty-three; she looked to be in her thirties. Her

こんにちは - KON'NICHIWA

religion was listed as Buddhist, which I valued, and I immediately told the matchmaker to arrange the match.

Meeting J - Wow!!!

When I was about to leave to meet J, I looked at the picture of my grandmother and said to her spirit: "Grandma, please let her feel my love as I felt yours." And with that, I left to meet J. When we met, we hugged as a greeting. She was even more beautiful than her pictures had shown her to be. She was stunning! I sat down with her and we talked for about fifteen minutes, and then I said something about my grandmother. She was so touched that tears welled up in her eyes. I asked her if I could sit closer to her and hold her hand, and she said yes. Then it was my turn to feel touched, and my eyes filled up with tears too. It was a beautiful moment. Our hearts met, and the love flowed freely and gracefully between us, surrounding us in a way that felt almost as if I was being lifted out of my chair.

We decided to go for a walk out in nature. While walking to her car, we held each other closely around the waist, wanting to be as close as possible to each other. We were already in love, with such joy and happiness. J dropped off her car and changed into clothes for walking. I changed into clothes I had in the car and off we went - not just for a walk, but for a new life together. That is how it felt.

On the path of the walking trail, it was obvious we wanted to be with each other. We laughed and said, in a matter-of-fact way, that we were going to get married. We had only known each other for less than two hours, and yet so much love was flowing between us. I did not "get" in that profound moment that I was now capable of having an overflowing exchange of love with a woman. *Not only was it possible, it was happening!* I felt my heart - really FELT it. I was being shown how far I had come since the big reveal.

We decided to see each other the next day for dinner at my house so she could see where I lived. We had dinner, laughed, played, danced, and talked about our lives to get to know each other better. Throughout the evening, there were many passionate embraces - as if we had finally reached the oasis where a loving person was waiting for us. It felt like our passion could burn down the house. I had not experienced that much passion and love since V. I assumed that this would be the norm for our lives together, and that thought excited me. I could not get the thought of making love to J out of my mind.

The very next day, the third day of our knowing each other, J started to move into my home, and within the week she was totally moved in. We talked about getting married on August 10th, 2019, when my son and his family could come. We made reservations for a honeymoon at a luxury hotel on the island of Maui in Hawaii for the end of August, and wrote our vows using the Buddhist wedding vows as a starting point. I was so in love, so in my heart, so excited. And then J gave me the first of a series of surprises by sharing some important information. Surprises that would take me out of the in-love space and bring fear, hurt, and disappointment into my experience.

Married Again - Really?

During that first week we talked about each of our medical conditions, and she told me that her health care provider "wanted to cut

こんにちは - KON'NICHIWA

her open" and do a biopsy. "Cut her open" is how it got translated from the doctor's English into Japanese. I will not get more specific out of respect for J's privacy. We requested and received a copy of her medical records from her health care provider and found that because of a high count in some blood test she might have a serious illness. Her health care provider asked Stanford Medical for a second opinion, and they said it could either be inflammation or something more serious. I did not trust her health care provider, as I had heard from dear friends about their bad experiences. And I knew from my own experiences that the earlier you start treatment for a serious illness, the better your chance of healing it.

I was scared, in a panic - freaked out. I had finally found "the one," the love of my life, and I was terrified of losing her. I could not let that happen and would do anything to prevent it. And I did. I proposed to J that we get married right away, which would allow her to be on my work health plan, and we could go to see a top doctor in San Francisco. And that's what we did.

Five days after we met, we had bought each other rings, and nine days after meeting, we were married at the Marin County court in California. It was a beautiful and rare moment in my life, as I felt relaxed, content, and bathed in a field of love. I had only ever experienced this as a child, with my grandmother's love, and later with Osho's grace and love. In our wedding picture, it's clear that she shared similar feelings. If you could see the picture of us from that moment you would see two people totally in love, totally trusting each other, and each feeling they had found "the one." The suddenness of the marriage came as a shock to both of our families and our friends. Initially, August 10th was going to be the day. In hindsight, it would have been better to pay out of pocket for a top doctor and ultrasounds. As it turned out, J's blood tests were heading back to normal and the San Francisco doctor felt it was most likely an inflammation. Yet we were married, wearing wedding rings, and living together. Then day-to-day life set in.

Day-to-Day Life

J had three jobs, which took a lot of time, as two of them involved teaching small children and preparing for the class meetings. There was a plan to let go of two of the jobs by mid-June (six weeks after we were married). Then the last job became full-time for two weeks. Even though I knew there was a light at the end of the tunnel, it was very hard for me to go from such a loving connection with J to being second to her work. There was a lot going on inside of me, and it was hard to share it with J, as she was not totally fluent in English. She didn't understand that I was not blaming her for anything. The situation became very difficult and uncomfortable for both of us. I will not go into detail about all the issues we had. Both of us had made assumptions about what we would get from the other, and in some important ways, it turned out to be the opposite of what we had hoped.

After six weeks of marriage, my mind was blasting thoughts of divorce, and am sure I was not the only one. J said that her friends were telling her to leave me because I wanted her to quit all her jobs. This was very selfish of me, as I knew how J loved her work with the kids, and I apologized for saying it. I took it back immediately, as I knew I had crossed a line. But the words hung in the air with no wind in sight. My apology was not going to be enough. That would

こんにちは - KON'NICHIWA

be a defining moment in our relationship that could not be reversed. I was afraid I would always be number two - even if, someday, I needed her to take care of me because I could not take care of myself.

The word divorce was in both our thoughts but unspoken; neither of us wanted to say it, hoping the other would say it first. This went on for many weeks - and the hugs and kisses became less frequent, the space and time between us became more prevalent, and the disconnection between us became obvious. The final straw was in the dentist's waiting room. I won't go into detail as to what was said, but this was the proverbial straw that broke the camel's back. The truth is that our marriage was not viable - we both knew it - and that could not be denied any longer. The hurt from J's words at the dentist's office made my pain greater than my fear of saying the word "divorce," knowing I would be living alone once again. It was a *"That's it"* moment.

I did not grasp all the implications at that moment, nor did I see or feel J's hurt, pain, anger or whatever else she was going through. My upset was because I had done so much to try to make J happy, and yet I still felt starved to have a Beloved in my life. It was not until our drive home from the dentist that I would let go of the anger and really see her with my heart once again. I was in shock from having uttered the "D" word, as we had only been together for three months. I felt lost, and yet when I tried to share a feeling with her, she got angry with me and let out her rage. I understood that it had nothing to do with me. I felt she trusted me enough in that moment to show me her real feelings. Once the anger and rage came out on the drive home from the dentist, we both acknowledged with sorrow that divorce was the right thing to do. We were both relieved in that moment, and the connection and love between us re-emerged for a day or two - until the reality hit J that she had to move again, and the reality hit me that I would be living alone again.

Divorce Again? Yes, Really!

J moved out and we filed the divorce papers in the coming weeks. I had loved J more than any other woman in my adult life. Not that I did not love my mother, grandmother, V and previous wives. Just that I was aware of how much capacity I now had for allowing myself to love and be loved by a woman. It was profound to see how far I had come in my lifetime.

Did I Learn This Time?

The Buddhist saying, which I mentioned in a previous chapter, is pertinent once again: "There is both a positive and negative aspect to everything." Separation and divorce have brought up very painful, confusing, and lost feelings for me, and having to do the paperwork and deal with the courts was not a pleasure (the negative aspects). But I finally realized what the positive aspects were in my relationship with J, and in our divorce. To have a beloved in my life, there must be compatibility as far as what we want from the relationship and in our day-to-day life. J and I assumed that we were each "The One" for each other, and maybe we will be some day, but not at this moment in time. We were not because we did not have that compatibility in important areas of the relationship. I had seen this before when following my heart into previous relationships. This time the

こんにちは - KON'NICHIWA

pain in my heart was acting as the teacher, and this time the student was willing to learn.

When I was not getting my needs or wants met with J, I explained to her what I felt was not happening by using a metaphor: each of us was a circle, and our lives, day-to-day, filled the space inside the circumference of our two circles. Before we knew each other, our circles were totally separate. When we met, our circles starting merging and overlapping, and we each needed to decide how much space we were willing to make inside our circle for the other. And with the space and time that overlapped, did we enjoy the same activities? I was looking for most of our circles to overlap and merge, a marriage where we moved in the world together, spent most of our time together. To be in a loving relationship, I was willing to accommodate, to narrow the area of overlap yet I couldn't go all the way to where J was willing to go. J, because of her work and other needs, could not make the amount of space in her circle, in her life, as I felt at the time I needed or wanted. These circles, for the first time, allowed me to see clearly our incompatibility. I had not taken the time to see whether I was compatible with her when getting to know J (or any woman), because my heart had opened so quickly and our love brought me such ease and trust with a woman as I had never experienced before.

I know there will always be a space in my heart for J, just as there is for my other loves I have written about in this book. I believe that is the way my heart works. Once I love someone to the depth that I love them, I will always carry that love, that connection, in my heart. I still truly care about and love J. I want her to have the life that brings her joy and happiness, and I want the same thing for myself. As with

David The Beloved

my grandmother, my love with J was pure and innocent and unconditional when we met and I know that will always be possible with us.. I will not forget the learning about compatibility with a woman for a day-to-day life to work. For love and trust to build a foundation, we need to be able to like each other, play with each other, and find activities that bring us happiness and joy together. I hope to keep this learning and the two circles of compatibility at hand when I meet another woman my heart goes out to. We will see!

As my train slowly pulls into the next station, I look out the train window and see an image just ahead, as if someone has merged with a white cloud. I am not dreaming; it's in the form of a person made with white clouds. I look closer and sense that this form is a woman. I have a trusting feeling about this form, and when I look at it, I feel a softening and a warm sensation in my heart. The train stops, and the train doors open directly in front of this form. Her arms are outstretched and beckoning me to come to her. Even the form's fingers are slowly and gently motioning me to come into her arms. I cannot see her face distinctly, yet I have a sense that she has loving feelings for me, and this gives me the confidence to move

David The Beloved

towards her. I am about to take a step out of the train car towards her, when I suddenly feel someone holding my right hand. I look to my right and there is David at age seven, on the day when his grandmother didn't recognize him because of her coma. He is holding my hand tightly, as I can see on his face that he is very scared. Then I sense someone at my left, and I turn to see myself at almost thirteen, after my father's beating. He is standing a bit away from me looking dejected, insecure, and very heartbroken. I reach out and pull him to my side and wrap my arm around him, holding him tightly to me. I bend over and kiss the top of both their heads, and tears start rolling down my cheeks. Without waiting to compose myself, the three of us get off the train together, without hesitation, and walk into the arms of the cloud form who is waiting for us lovingly. With our eyes closed, we are embraced, engulfed, by the love of this angelic form. We feel safe, trusting, loved - ready to surrender to her love, care, and compassion. When I open my eyes, still feeling enveloped by love, I see that the form has disappeared, as have both my seven- and thirteen-year-old selves. I now understand that the form - an angel, guide, or spirit - has come to show me the essence of who I am - *Love*. I look up and see the station sign. It says, "David The Beloved." I feel the truth of the words in this moment, and I weep.

I had much resistance to writing this chapter. I sat down numerous times to write it, but I just did not feel the truth of the words I was writing. I realized that I was scared, even terrified, to acknowledge the truth that "I am David, the Beloved." I felt I would be misunderstood, as if I were trying to proclaim that "I am *THE* David the Beloved," which I am not. Nor am I intimating that I have achieved

David The Beloved

a higher state of love, filling or flowing from my heart, than other people. That's not true from my experience. The truth is very simple but profound. I am declaring that the belovedness I was born with, and was my birthright, still exists. I am reclaiming the truth that I am love-able and deserving of love.

I have shared my entire journey to date - all the stations and tracks in between. Even though my birth experience was rough, as I almost died at that station, I was provided with unconditional love for my first seven years by my grandmother Yetta. Even with this birth trauma, I still had a wide-open heart, with qualities of innocence and vulnerability - and I trusted that at each moment I would be cared for, as there were no thoughts or feelings to tell me otherwise. I had no thoughts, and therefore no judgments, no wondering *if*. I didn't act in a heartless, cruel, or abusive way, since I didn't yet know what that was. Early in life I was a precious miracle that soaked up love like a cherished pet in the lap of its owner. I was a perfectly imperfect newborn human being, trusting that I would be loved and cared for. Trust is one of the qualities of my true nature, a gift from existence or God or whatever name for spirit you resonate with. Regardless of all the difficult things that have happened to me in my life, the truth is that I am still a beloved. Everything I would need to stay alive and blossom is being provided in abundance. Air, water, warmth, food, shelter, care, and love in various amounts - all these are provided, and I am not doing *anything* for that to happen. They are just being given to me because I am a miracle and a beloved.

Then in a few years I got married to my mind, which was part of my imprinting, programmed by my environment - mostly my

David The Beloved

parents – with good intentions to support my survival. At our marriage, my mind and I were given wedding presents in the form of judgments, beliefs, and strategies; like computer programs, these were meant to run all aspects of my life. Yet I was also given the experience of being unconditionally loved by my grandmother, and I kept this in my back pocket my whole life and pulled it out at the worst possible moments. Everything in my environment was telling me in many ways and instances who I should be, what I was supposed to be feeling – that what I wanted or desired was not good, not right – or that I needed to be something else, or I needed to do something else or act differently than my authentic self. As if my authentic self was not good enough. The problem was that I believed this story, and it led me to the inevitable conclusion that there was indeed something wrong with me – and that I was not love-able, deserving of love, or valued for who I really was. And to make sure no one would know about these beliefs, I hid them deep in my mind. *But this is just the way it had to happen; it was not bad. It was caused by my imprinting and my environment!*

Then one day, serendipitously, I was in a class with a guy named Bud, listening to a tape of an enlightened master, and then finding myself on the front steps of the university with my arms and legs forming an X. Bud had thrown the switch on the train tracks, and my life would never be the same. In the years that followed, I would be reintroduced to the gifts that I was born with – love, joy, compassion, empathy, creativity, curiosity, innocence, and belovedness – through the teachings of the Enlightened Master Osho; by Shari (my acting and singing teacher); by the Diamond Heart Groups; and by the many people

David The Beloved

I shared these experiences with. Cancer showed me a big billboard that said: "David, you don't love or value yourself?" And I would start down the path of healing, forgiveness, and melting away old beliefs. One of the Diamond Heart group meetings, where the words came out of my mouth "I don't feel my heart," led me to this station. My next stop of the journey would be to reclaim my heart, and all else that had been lost.

As I look back at the story I have shared in this memoir, I am struck by how remarkable, how filled with adventures my life has been, even though there was much suffering. Yet, all in all, from where I sit today, I would quote my buddy Amitabh and say "not too shabby." I must remind myself that the journey, the adventure, is not yet over - oh no, not by any means, Mr. King!

In *Love Unveiled* by A. H. Almaas, the pen name of A. Hameed Ali, founder of the Diamond Approach to Self-Realization, he writes: "Close Relationships are called love relationships, intimate relationships because they are about intimacy and closeness and, ultimately, about union. All desire, all yearning for nearness and union in any relationship, in any situation, reflects the original yearning of the deepest heart's desire - union with the Beloved" (page 140). Now I am clear that I am on the path to this union with my own belovedness, having moments of this experience of being so grateful for being me, being David. I am also clear about my longing to form a union with a woman with whom we can mirror our belovedness to each other. This union will support the final journey to the final union with the beloved in myself. I feel that I will stay at this station until I meet a beloved - and both we and our trains have coupled.

David The Beloved

When the pandemic hit in March 2020, I heard a voice instructing me to get back on my train. I hurriedly stepped into the train car, and the doors closed, but the train didn't move. Once in the train car, I heard a voice that I thought I recognized from long ago: "David, it's me, the Train Yard Master. Thought I forgot about you? Not a chance, kiddo." When he said "kiddo," I knew who it was. "You will need to stay here until the pandemic is over, and then you can leave the train and start seeking a beloved woman to share love with. While you are waiting, I want to show you something

David The Beloved

that may inspire you. Look out the front window of the train car and you'll see the bright light at the end of the tunnel. When you and your beloved return to the station, your train cars will be coupled, and you will be going toward that bright light. I don't know how long that ride will take, but I am sure it will be a beautiful, a joyful, and a loving ride. You're probably wondering what that bright light is. I don't know exactly; it's a bit of a mystery even for me, yet you will find in this bright light all that you journey to reclaim. One last thing, David, from here to the end of the line there will be no more worries: all will be taken care of for you, just like when you were born. Remember, I was there with you guiding you from the start. And at the very end of the line, I will see you again, in the Afterlife Train Yard, guiding you and your beloved, when it's each your time. I take care of the start, the end, and some stops in between. And by the way, David, I am still rooting for you, kiddo, and your beloved."

I have come to really like this guy!

David The Beloved

I'll leave you with my everlasting truth:

> When I was born, I was a beloved, deserving of love and being loved. This is my truth.
> Nothing I have ever done, or will ever do, changes that truth.
> Nothing I have said, or will ever say, changes that truth.
> Nothing I have ever thought, or felt, or will ever think or feel, changes that truth.
> I have been, and always will be, David the Beloved.
>
> With love,
> David

Feel free to contact me via the website: DavidtheBeloved.com
Or email me at: David@DavidtheBeloved.com.

Afterword

Healing My Cancer

People who knew I had survived cancer, who had loved ones going through cancer, asked me for suggestions how could they support their loved ones in their healing. I told them I didn't feel comfortable making suggestions, as each person's path to healing cancer felt different to me - yet I would summarize for them what *I* did. This would be the same information I would give if someone asked me to be their mentor. Here are the most significant steps I took:

1. The first and most important step I took was finding a mentor, that one person I could talk to who has gone through the process and has survived. It kick-started my healing process, as it set my intention for healing and allowed me to push through my resistance toward asking for help. My mentor offered me her methods to start with until my own inner guidance system took over. I had an independent person that I could bounce ideas off whenever I got stuck, and someone who would remind me that what I was feeling and experiencing was par for the course - as she had gone through those same feelings

and experiences herself. Just knowing I was not alone, that there was someone willing to be there for me - without trying to be strong in front of me or take my mind off the process - was invaluable to me in finding my path to heal cancer.

2. I had to ask myself this *not*-simple question: "Do I want to live?" Throughout my life there were times I wanted to get off the train - was cancer another way to get off the train? After four sessions with a hypnotherapy therapist, he told me that I had no death wish inside me. With his support, I was now sure I wanted to live.

3. I started to look at all aspects of my life, asking myself the question: does this part of my life bring dis-ease (stress) into my life, or does it bring ease into my life? Everything in my daily life had to be examined, evaluated - does doing this support my healing or not? If not, it must go or be changed. Some things, or ways of being, or people in my life took longer to let go of or transform. My work, family, friends, TV programs, food, exercise, where I lived, every aspect of my life had to be examined to see which column it fit into, dis-ease or ease. I kept reminding myself that *all the tracks, all the doing in my life before cancer, led up to my having cancer.* I created the dis-ease in my body, mind, and emotions, which diminished the effectiveness of my immune system and allowed cancer to take hold. And I had to see this *without judgment* of myself, and realize that this was a whole new ballgame. This process would not be easy, as resistance to change kept coming up. The thoughts of the alternative to healing (dying or losing my voice box) kept me motivated, kept kicking me in the tush to keep going.

Afterword

There is an ancient parable that says "Life forces are ready to take ten steps towards you to support you and you only have to take one step towards the life forces to get these ten for free. But the "catch" is that you must take the first step and truly let go. The moment I truly let go of something that was not serving me, life forces started to bring towards me what *did* serve me. My letting go sometimes came from an "Enough is enough" experience – or other times from exhaustion, when I would say "I just can't do this anymore," or through meditation. In all of these, I experienced an organic "letting go."

4. I created a good support system for myself with people who I knew loved me, accepted me as I was, were empathetic with me, and were willing to give me their time to talk, hang out, or drive me to an appointment. If someone was *telling* me to do something like "Why don't you do this or that," they were not being there for me and I would not include them in my support community. I only wanted people who would offer their suggestions if I *asked* for it. I found healers with healing techniques that I was open to experiencing, even if it meant stretching my comfort zone. All the healers I chose were friends, or people I knew, who were trained in their healing techniques. I chose the people, not their techniques, because I knew that they were loving and caring people. I chose all my doctors carefully and made sure they were really caring of me. If a doctor was not empathetic, not caring, or not totally wholehearted in supporting my healing, I changed doctors. I deserved the best possible medical care! I also stayed open to people who were not friends or people I knew, yet had heard about in a very positive way. I will mention a couple of them.

David The Beloved

Many of the changes in my life that I've described in this chapter were supported by or based upon the learnings and realizations from the teachings, exercises, teachers, and fellow students of the Diamond Heart Groups I attended. I cannot put into words how truly supportive this group was to me when I needed support the most.

I also started bringing alternative healers into my life. Michael Broffman was one such person who only works with people who have cancer. I wanted to see him because a few friends I knew who had cancer went to him and they were all still alive. Michael suggested, based upon evaluating my medical history past and present, a regimen of supplements that would support my overall health and support the strengthening of my immune system, which would help support the natural healing of my cancer or other dis-ease in my body. I still take the supplements Michael suggested, even after ten years of being cancer free. As Dr. Courey said to me each time he looked down my throat and observed that all was well, "Keep doing what you're doing." And I am! Most importantly, I treated my immune system as my best lifelong friend and started taking care of it as if it were a living organism and my life depended on it – both of which were and are true.

Another healer I spent a few moments with was named Braco, a young man from Croatia. He was also known as "The Gazer," as he used his gaze to heal people. A month after my vocal cords had been removed I went to a large group session he was holding in San Francisco, accompanied by my ex-wife Tatiana. I had little expectation and a lot of skepticism, as it sounded "out there" to be healed by a person's gaze. When Tatiana and I checked in, because I'd had cancer surgery

Afterword

recently, we were given seats in one of the front rows. We sat in a large banquet room of a hotel which was filled with a few hundred people - all there to be healed by Braco's gaze. After we had waited in this crowded room for twenty minutes, a woman came out and addressed all the participants with instructions, and explained the types of experiences one might have when his gaze moves over you. She said some people may see colors, some feel energy, and some may hear voices and a few more which I cannot list - as I stopped listening, since I was now more dubious. Braco was a handsome man with long blond hair, and when he entered the room, in front of the large audience, he had this calm, innocent, and clear look on his face. Not an emotion or a smile could I detect from him. He stepped up on this high platform facing the audience, which set his feet at the level of everyone's heads. Then as he started from his left, tilting his head a bit down, I could see him casting his gaze first to the people on the left in the front rows, and then tilting his head back up a bit, casting his gaze to those from the front to the back of the room. This continued by sections of people from his left to right, until he finally arrived where Tatiana and I were sitting on the other side of the room. I perceived that his gaze was stronger the closer you were to him, which explained why we were seated near the front. I was getting anxious waiting for him to get to us, trying to imagine what I would experience. When his gaze came into our area I heard a voice I had never heard before. This deep male voice said "You are already healed." The voice repeated itself again: "You are already healed." Wow, I was blown away, as I had never heard this voice before. Could I believe this voice? Was it really true? I reminded myself that my cancer had come back twice – after only three and a half months after the first surgery, and then five and a half months after radiation – and I was only six months removed from the last surgery. Five years after my last surgery, when my vocal cords were removed, I was still cancer free, and I remembered the words of the voice I heard when being gazed at by Braco. Those words turned out to be true then and now, as my cancer has never come back again. Tatiana felt his energy strongly in her body and said to me he was the "real deal." That did not stop me from continuing all the healing techniques that I have brought into my life. I am still doing many of them today, even though I am ten years cancer free, as the one voice that has never left me is Dr. Courey's, saying "Keep doing what you're doing."

5. As I wrote in the chapter "The Journey with Cancer," I started loving my cancer, and I use the following mantra each morning. This was an important step for me to learn the lessons that cancer had come to teach me.

I welcome you my cancer,
And I send you my love,
As you are part of me in this moment,
And all parts of me deserve love.

The big mistake, in my opinion, which I have stated previously, is this idea to "fight cancer." I read these words from many different organizations, and for me it was 100% the wrong approach. I wish I had the funds to put up a series of billboards. As you were driving down the road you would see them in this order in very big letters:

Afterword

"I had cancer and I found a way to love my cancer"
 "If I fight cancer, I have one part of me fighting another part of me"
  "This causes dis-ease in my body"
   "Loving my cancer brings ease and supports healing by my immune system"
    "Healing my immune system will heal my body"
     "Healing my body will heal my soul"
      "Healing my body and soul will heal my heart"
       "Healing my heart will bring me more joy and love at a time when I need it the most"

6. I needed to get selfish with my energy with people in my life that previously I would have freely been there for. I now needed to keep all that energy for my own healing.
7. I needed to look at my diet, and I started reading articles on what foods strengthened my immune system and what foods weakened it. Wherever possible, I started eating only organic fruits, vegetables, eggs, butter, chicken. I would buy my meat and fish from a meat department that had quality products. I removed sugar pretty much from my diet. I was not perfect with this. Every now and then I would give myself slack and have some dark chocolate or ice cream. Okay, I confess it was not every now and then; more like every day or so. I read that we release endorphins when we are happy, and I hung my hat on that, because dark chocolate and ice cream made me happy – and still do!.
8. I started to exercise more and went to the gym one to three times a week and did thirty to forty minutes of exercise. For

me, this one was a struggle, though realizing it was not an option at times. I have relaxed this one after ten years, though before the pandemic, I still went to our community gym once or twice a week.

9. My mentor recommended that I only watch comedies. Any movies that have violence or cruelty, create fear, or invoke old traumas, I've stayed away from. Even watching sports has been stressful at times, yet I had to give myself some slack, as I wanted to watch the UC Berkeley and San Francisco 49ers football games, as well as Golden State Warriors basketball games (remember the endorphins). In all courses of action to heal cancer, I feel that I kept needing to find ways to give myself slack, and not strive for perfection that would bring on stress. I understood what was at stake - yet for me to heal the cancer, I needed to be able to accept the times when I failed to stick with the program I'd set up for myself.

Please remember that these steps were *my* ways. I want to be sure to state clearly that if you are going through cancer, or a loved one is going through cancer, the person who has the dis-ease must find their own way to heal it. Anything your mentor did, or anything I have written here, is just what *we* did to stay alive and heal from cancer. It was unique to us, and I have no doubt your path will be unique to you. I truly hope this chapter, in particular, is supportive to anyone who has been diagnosed with cancer or has a loved one going through cancer.

Afterword

"Diamond Approach to Self-Realization"

The "Diamond Approach to Self-Realization" was founded by A. Hameed Ali (whose pen name is A. H. Almaas). Those in the Ridhwan School refer to him as Hameed. It is offered by the Ridhwan School, based in Berkeley, California, and it has students from all over the world. Hameed comes across as very down-to-earth person, with the inspiring traits of a trustworthy presence and an immense curiosity, like an anthropologist of reality – endlessly investigating the human relationship to that reality. I have spent twenty years experiencing and learning from the teachings of the Diamond Heart groups, and I have found this indispensable in the ongoing process of my growth, and my return to being with my birthright – my belovedness. I am still in a Diamond Heart Group.

These groups I attended had either nine weekends or two nine-day retreats each year. Each day there were two sessions, with each session lasting three hours, and composed of four components in this order: a meditation, a teaching *du jour*, an Inquiry, and then a Q&C (Questions and Comments). The meditation and Inquiry practices I use almost every day still. The meditation practice I do consists of sitting still in a chair, with good posture, and being present with whatever arises, including thoughts and body sensations. The Inquiry practice, which I currently do three times per week with a partner, uses my natural curiosity and my willingness and desire to know the truth about myself. To know more about the Diamond Approach, A Hameed Ali, Diamond Heart Groups, or the Ridhwan School, visit the Diamondapproach.org website.

Inquiry

In the most frequent Inquiry practice that I do, I work with one or two other people. Each person gets a turn while the other person(s) holds a space in silence, yet brings their presence to support the person who is doing the Inquiry. The Inquiry is an exploration on a certain topic, or an open-ended questioning on what is present with each of us in the moment. Two qualities are important for me to bring to the Inquiry process: my natural curiosity and my wanting to know the truth of what I am inquiring about. As with any other practice, it took me a while to get into the process, and to bring my curiosity and my desire to know the truth, to enable me to feel trusting and comfortable while doing this in front of other people in the groups. The practice can open a pathway into feelings, beliefs, strategies, judgments, and patterns that I have hidden from myself – allowing me to take one step closer to being free from their control over me. Yet it also opens a pathway to experiences of reality that arise from an emptiness that sometimes is prevalent. It is a practice I have the intention of doing for the rest of my life, as after I complete a session I almost always feel freer, more present, and more at home with myself.

Here is how A. H. Almaas, Robert Brumet, and two other students in my Diamond Heart Group describe the Inquiry process:

"According to A. H. Almaas, founder of the Diamond Approach, real transformation comes from equal parts experience *and* understanding: you won't get the key to the treasure inside you with either one by itself. In the Diamond Approach, the practice of Inquiry taps into your own feelings and intuitions, honoring

Afterword

your experience, so that you recognize the truth *as it lives in you* - in your own precious depths. Without this process of deeply recognizing and understanding what's true for you - at each step of your path - you may find that once-potent practices only lead to plateaus; that despite the many workshops you've taken, real transformation remains elusive; that at the end of the day, you just don't feel like a different person." From the Diamond Approach Online Website with information on Online Inquiry Groups: https://online.diamondapproach.org/online-inquiry-groups-spring-2021/

And from Robert Brumet:

"An inquiry is the process of discovering something hitherto unknown to conscious awareness. The purpose of inquiry as a spiritual practice is to gain deeper insight and understanding into your own essential nature. The inquiry process always begins with your present moment experience. It can begin with a question or simply be an open inquiry of your present experience.

If the inquiry is prompted by a question then hold the question in mind as you begin the process. Regardless of the question, always explore your present moment experience. The purpose of inquiry is not to get an 'answer' in the usual sense but to simply use the question (or your present experience) as a starting point for your exploration. Let the question be open-ended; don't become focused on getting a specific answer. Let the question be lived in the present moment." From Robert Brumet's website, The History of Inquiry Web Page: https://www.robertbrumet.com/blog/the-practice-of-inquiry.

"Inquiry is digging through all the thoughts, ideas, experiences, and connections mapped in your head about a certain topic, and even opening yourself to the subconscious material, noticing tensions and feelings in your body that arises in relation to certain expressed statements. It's about really seeing what's there under the default first layer of what you normally would express to others, and even to yourself." - Courtesy of Jason Miller

"Learning Inquiry has been discovering the 'water' I've been swimming in - what the hell is this I've been calling 'my experience' - what are experiences made up of? This has led to realizing how much my past history has limited, conditioned, and predicted how I experience the present. But, all is not lost, because sticking with Inquiry there is a way to be with one's experiences that are not stunted and stifled by the past." - Courtesy of Chae Mcclure

Acknowledgements

There are many people who supported me, in different ways, with the train ride of my life – and many more who supported me in completing the writing and publishing of the journey presented in this memoir.

First and foremost, I am deeply grateful to Chae McClure for the six months she spent working with me as my beta-reader, friend, and teacher of writing with her inspiration, joy, and presence. She presented her feedback to me in creative, spontaneous, authentic ways and sometimes with lots of laughs. She grew to know how important it was to me to write this memoir and brought her caring and total energy in support of making this happen. For all that she gave to me, there is not enough sushi in the world to repay her.

I am grateful to cartoonist Sudi Narayanan (Swami Anand Teertha) for all the station signs and cartoons. Sudi and I were brought together by our common connection to the grace and love of the Enlightened Master Osho. Sudi offered his time graciously and effortlessly and brought forth his professional skills, which were beyond anything I could imagine. You can find more information and examples of Sudi's work on his website at http://spiritoons.com/.

David The Beloved

To Ruth Schwartz, I am grateful for her guidance, caring and vast years of knowledge in guiding me through the overwhelming self-publishing process. She truly is the "wonderlady" of self-publishing. To Kendra Langeteig, my appreciation and gratefulness in bringing her many years of experience, skill, and heart to developmental editing my memoir. And to Rosina Tinari Wilson, I am grateful for her copy editing that kept my voice at hand and my story in her loving hands. To all the folks at AtriTeX Technologies, my thanks for their patience and skill in creating the interior format of the memoir.

To my friend Mani Feniger, my gratefulness for sitting with me for hours and graciously sharing her experience of publishing her own books. To Victoria and Sikha for giving of their time to allow me to bounce ideas off them when I was confused or insecure. And to my dear friend Jett, much gratitude, for finding space during her moving to come to the support of an old friend and create the book cover I had long envisioned. To Paul and Molly, my gratefulness for your support in creating the website to bring David The Beloved to the world.

To all those who attended the Mechanics' Institute Library Thursday Writing Group, I am grateful for all your inspiration, encouragement, and knowledge, which you so generously shared with me during our weekly sessions. I am grateful to Dr. Loyd for writing The Healing Code, which inspired me to understand what caused my cancer. And am grateful as well to Dr. Jed Diamond for allowing me to use his words that added credence for me to Dr. Loyd's conclusions.

Acknowledgements

To my son Jason and my grandmother Yetta, for the love we share / shared, without which there would be no story and no David. To my beloved mother, Fannie, who fought to stay alive during childbirth so I could live this life. To my father, Howard, I am grateful that you taught me about forgiveness and remorse. To you both, please know from the afterlife that I know you had caring and love for me even at times when you couldn't show it. To all my aunts, uncles, and cousins, who loved me and felt my heart, even when I didn't. To my grand-kiddos, who continue to bring such joy into my life, just by being who you are. And to Tatiana, Misha, Mamachka, Maria, and Ornella for allowing me, to this day, lovingly, to be part of your family.

To Osho, for beaming his love and grace to Houston and Santa Fe so I could be touched, and for introducing me to the world of love, reality, and my beloved Amitabh. To Amitabh, for your loving and caring of me for so many years, and for your guidance whenever I was at the bottom of the well. The buddyhood we shared will always touch me, deep in my heart. And to Hameed and Karen for your many years of caring of those of us on the path, with your teachings of the "Diamond Approach to Self-Realization."

To Dr. Dinardo (Bud) Vasudeva, you were the train operator, who flipped the train switch so my train would go down the tracks toward my belovedness. I am so sorry I waited so long to reach out to you and missed hearing your laugh and your voice one more time. To Shari, for eighteen years of supporting me with our acting and singing classes together, my gratefulness for our friendship, and most importantly your love and caring of me. And for reminding me so

David The Beloved

often to live in the moment - and for bringing singing into my life and my heart.

I am grateful to my oldest, dearest friends: Satyam, Sikha, Anupama, V, Dharma, Jett, Prabhata, and Chitta for our loving friendship of forty years and still counting. For being there when I was a friend in need. To my beloved friends Nura and Priti, who have left their bodies, you are both missed. And grateful to the healers who supported me on my journey through Cancer: Sangeet, Irv, Anupama, Dr. Courey, Philmore, Sevanti, and Michael Broffman.

I am grateful to all the teachers in the Diamond Heart groups I have attended (DH6, DHR4 and DH9) who supported my growth and shared their caring of me. Much gratefulness especially to Jeanne, who kept reminding me to be with the tightness in my belly and not try to get rid of it, and for leading our group so selflessly. To Victoria for her caring, who always asked me how I was doing while dealing with cancer. To Evelyn for being Evelyn, and loving me and bringing Amitabh back into my heart when she and I are brought together. To Milia and Patricia for their continued guidance on my journey to belovedness. And special gratitude to David S, whom I came to love, and for becoming, like Amitabh, not just a teacher, but my buddy from the Bronx as well. To all the students of the same Diamond Heart groups, I am grateful for your sharing your presence and your hearts with me. I'm especially grateful to my buddies in DHR4, Lauren and Roxanne, for our time hanging out together, and for our many laughs. To my small groups, my gratitude for the love we shared.

Jenny Lake
Publishing

Dear Reader,

I am grateful to you for reading my memoir. I hope that my personal journey impacted you in some way - and perhaps gave you some perspective or realizations into your own life's "train stations." Most of all, I wish that even for a few moments, you experienced or realized that you yourself are a Beloved - "love-able" and deserving of being loved.

If you felt touched in any way by this memoir, I would, very humbly, like to ask you to write a review on the Amazon web page where the book is displayed. You will have to scroll down to find the box "Write a customer review."

Please also know that I am open to speaking to groups, via Zoom or in person (if health protocols permit), about my experiences, as described in *David The Beloved*. This would consist of a short reading from the book, a short talk, plenty of time for questions, and a book signing if the event is in person.

If you have any questions or comments, or if you would like to create an event, please email me at david@davidthebeloved.com. You can also visit my website at davidthebeloved.com.

I would love to hear from you!

With love,
David

www.ingramcontent.com/pod-product-compliance
Lightning Source LLC
Chambersburg PA
CBHW072143100526
44589CB00015B/2070